DATE DUE

12-30-95			
MY 27 '99			

DEMCO 38-296

Other Books in the Jossey-Bass Public Administration Series:

Collaborative Leadership, *David D. Chrislip and Carl E. Larson*

Communicating for Results in Government, *James L. Garnett*

The Enduring Challenges in Public Management, *Arie Halachmi and Geert Bouckaert, Editors*

The Ethics Challenge in Public Service, *Carol W. Lewis*

Facilitative Leadership in Local Government, *James H. Svara and Associates*

Facing the Bureaucracy, *Gerald Garvey*

Handbook of Practical Program Evaluation, *Joseph S. Wholey, Harry P. Hatry, and Kathryn E. Newcomer, Editors*

Handbook of Public Administration, *James L. Perry, Editor*

Handbook of Training and Development for the Public Sector, *Montgomery Van Wart, N. Joseph Cayer, and Steve Cook*

Improving Government Performance, *Joseph S. Wholey, Kathryn E. Newcomer, and Associates*

Making Government Work, *Martin A. Levin and Mary Bryna Sanger*

Managing Chaos and Complexity in Government, *L. Douglas Kiel*

The New Effective Public Manager, *Steven Cohen and William Eimicke*

New Paradigms for Government, *Patricia W. Ingraham and Barbara S. Romzek, Editors*

Reinventing the Pentagon, *Fred Thompson and L. R. Jones*

Revitalizing State and Local Public Service, *Frank J. Thompson, Editor*

Seamless Government, *Russell M. Linden*

Strategic Management of Public and Third Sector Organizations, *Paul C. Nutt and Robert W. Backoff*

Strategic Planning for Public and Nonprofit Organizations, *John M. Bryson*

Supervision for Success in Government, *Dalton S. Lee and N. Joseph Cayer*

Total Quality Management in Government, *Steven Cohen and Ronald Brand*

Trustworthy Government, *David G. Carnevale*

Understanding and Managing Public Organizations, *Hal G. Rainey*

How Do Public Managers Manage?

Carolyn Ban

How Do Public Managers Manage?

Bureaucratic Constraints, Organizational Culture, and the Potential for Reform

Jossey-Bass Publishers • San Francisco

Substantial discounts on bulk quantities of Jossey-Bass books are available to corporations, professional associations, and other organizations. For details and discount information, contact the special sales department at Jossey-Bass Inc., Publishers. (415) 433-1740; Fax (800) 605-2665.

For sales outside the United States, please contact your local Paramount Publishing International Office.

TCF Manufactured in the United States of America on Lyons Falls Pathfinder Tradebook. This paper is acid-free and 100 percent totally chlorine-free.

Library of Congress Cataloging-in-Publication Data

Ban, Carolyn.
    How do public managers manage? : bureaucratic constraints, organizational culture, and the potential for reform/Carolyn Ban.
        p.   cm. — (The Jossey-Bass public administration series)
    Includes bibliographical references and index.
    ISBN 0-7879-0098-2
    1. Public administration—United States.   2. Civil service—United States.   3. Government executives—United States.   4. Civil service positions—United States—Classification.   I. Title.   II. Series.
JF1351.B26   1995
353.07—dc20   94-47405
                                                                            CIP

HB Printing   10 9 8 7 6 5 4 3 2 1   FIRST EDITION

The Jossey-Bass

Public Administration Series

Consulting Editor
Public Management and Administration

James L. Perry
Indiana University

Contents

Tables and Figures   xi

Preface   xiii

The Author   xix

Introduction: Bureaucratic Constraints, Administrative
Coping Strategies, and the Potential for Reform   1

Part One: The World of the Public Manager

1. Varieties of Organization: Four Cases   21

2. The Different Roles of Public Managers   53

**Part Two: How Public Managers Cope
with the Civil Service System**

3. The Personnel Office: Friend or Foe?   89

4. The Labyrinth of the Hiring Process   123

5. Addressing Performance Problems   157

Part Three: The Budgetary Imperative

6. The Position Classification System: A Budgetary
Control System in Disguise   189

7. Coping with Ceilings, Freezes, and Reductions
in Force   227

x   Contents

Conclusion: Loosening Constraints and Changing
Culture: The Potential for Reform   263

Notes   281

References   285

Index   295

Tables and Figures

Figure 1.1. Competing Values Model of
Organizational Culture   25

Table 1.1. Employment in Subject Agencies, 1980–1991   27

Table 1.2. Budgets of Subject Agencies, 1980–1991   29

Figure 2.1. Competing Values Model of Managerial Roles   71

Figure 2.2. Coding of Managerial Responses   73

Table 2.1. Complexity of the Managerial Role   74

Figure 2.3. Managerial Role Definitions Using
the Competing Values Model   76

Figure 2.4. Managerial Role Definitions by
Supervisory Level   80

Figure 4.1. Agency Division of Labor in Recruitment   131

To my parents

Preface

It has become somewhat of a truism that government managers face a range of constraints that limit their ability to manage and that they are more constrained than are private managers (Allison, 1980). Managers themselves bemoan the fact that it is hard to hire and fire, and that they are given little discretion in how to manage their budgets. Academics decry the dysfunctional effects of rigid controls imposed on federal agencies by the Office of Management and Budget (OMB) and the Office of Personnel Management (OPM) (Wilson, 1989; DiIulio, Garvey, and Kettl, 1993), and some call for solutions such as contracting out the government's work (Savas, 1982). There have been increasingly broad calls for reform—for deregulation that would loosen the constraints managers labor under and for changing the culture of government that has grown up within this rigid system, a culture that is seen as overly cautious and risk-averse (DiIulio, 1994; National Performance Review, 1993a; Osborne and Gaebler, 1992).

Yet there have been few empirical studies of how bureaucratic constraints actually affect managers' behavior. To assess the desirability of deregulation and of reducing bureaucratic constraint, we need to have a much more nuanced understanding of the effects the current system actually has on how managers manage. In particular, we need to understand how official rules and regulations are interpreted and implemented in different organizational settings. And we need to look at the range of ways that managers find to operate within or to circumvent the formal systems of constraint. This work provides an empirical basis for advancing our understanding of the effects of bureaucratic constraints. Based on research in four federal agencies, it examines managers' reactions to constraints stemming from the civil service system and the budget process, focusing particularly on how coping strategies differ across agencies. It derives from this research some conclusions about the need for reform and the likelihood of reform, given the current political environment.

Audience

This book is designed for several audiences. Students of public management, particularly those concerned with civil service and budgetary systems, should find in this study a somewhat different picture of these systems from the one offered in the standard texts. The book may therefore be used to supplement texts in introductory courses in public administration, as well as in courses in human resources management and public management. The research reported here should also be of interest to scholars in the field of public management, and should, I hope, advance the scholarly debate about deregulation.

Practitioners, both in the federal government and at other levels of government, should find much that is useful to them. While this book is not designed to be a how-to manual, for reasons I explore in the conclusion, it may give managers a sense that they are not alone in struggling to find positive ways to deal with the highly restrictive web of constraints in which they feel enmeshed, and it may encourage them to push against these constraints more effectively.

Finally, the book is intended to contribute to the policy debate over deregulation in government. At the federal level, attempts to loosen the constraints discussed here are being made even as this book is being completed. Reform of the procurement system has been passed, in the form of the Federal Acquisition Improvement Act, signed by President Clinton on October 13, 1994. And the

National Performance Review (NPR) has proposed sweeping reforms of the civil service and budgetary systems discussed here. This research can add to the policy discussion about the need for such reforms; it can help us to understand what pitfalls will be encountered in implementing changes; and in the event that changes do take place, it can serve as a baseline of comparison for future research on the effects of reform.

Overview of the Contents

The introduction to the book explores the issue of bureaucratic constraints—the main types of constraint, where they came from, and what purpose they were designed to serve. It then examines some of the arguments in favor of deregulation and looks at current proposals for loosening bureaucratic constraints, particularly those contained in the National Performance Review. Finally, it describes the research approach used in conducting the study on which this book is based.

Part One provides a contextual framework for discussing how public managers manage. Since one of the central themes of the book is that managers are likely to cope differently with bureaucratic constraints depending on the organization in which they work, Chapter One begins with an introduction to the organizations in the study and a discussion of how they differ on such key variables as mission, size, structure, resources, and leadership. A central focus of this chapter is the organizational cultures of the four organizations studied and the ways these cultures differ on certain dimensions that are relevant to how managers cope with bureaucratic constraints.

In Chapter Two, the discussion moves down to the level of the individual manager. Here I look at how organizational differences affect managers themselves—the kinds of people selected to be managers, the career paths they are likely to follow, and the management training they receive. I then turn to an analysis of the managerial role. I look at the dilemmas faced by what I term "worker managers" at all levels, but particularly first-line supervisors, who have to combine the tasks of management with the daily technical work of their organization. Attention is also given to the even greater dilemmas of what I call "pseudo-supervisors"—people who are officially classed as supervisors but who actually perform very few supervisory functions. Chapter Two concludes with a discussion of how managers see their roles. Utilizing the "competing values" model of management roles, I show that managers in different organizations as well as at different organizational levels stress different parts of the management role.

Part Two explores the problems created for managers by the civil service system and the range of strategies managers use for coping with the system. In Chapter Three, I turn to the world of the personnel specialists. I look at the formal civil service system, focusing on the role conflicts it creates for the personnel staff charged with administering it. I then examine the different ways that the personnel staffs in the four agencies have dealt with this role conflict, and the implications of these different approaches for the personnel staff's relationship with managers. One approach to managing this relationship is the creation of "shadow" personnel offices within line organizations.

Chapter Four explores the labyrinth of the hiring process. I look at the range of ways both managers and personnelists define their roles in that process and at the strategies some managers use to find short-cuts through the maze.

Chapter Five treats the processes for disciplining or firing employees. It examines the factors that cause managers to avoid dealing with problems—both external factors, such as the complexity of the process, and internal factors, including managers' role definitions and lack of preparation for this aspect of management.

Part Three focuses on areas in which the civil service rules intersect with the budget process to constrain managers. Chapter Six focuses on the position classification system, used for setting pay in government. I argue that this system is really a budgetary control system masquerading as a personnel system. Chapter Seven examines how managers cope with personnel ceilings, hiring freezes, and reductions in force.

Finally, the conclusion discusses the implications of this research for managers and policy makers. It raises questions about what individual managers can do to work more effectively within the existing system and, perhaps more importantly, looks at the likelihood of success of current reform efforts designed to loosen the constraints managers face.

Acknowledgments

This work would not have been possible without the generous help of many people. My greatest debt is to the agencies that participated in this study and to all the managers and personnel specialists who agreed to be interviewed. Since I promised them confidentiality, I cannot thank them by name, but their generosity and openness were remarkable. I would also like to thank my liaisons at the agencies: Tom Wyvill at the U.S. Environmental Protection Agency, Carmen Queen-Hines at the Animal and Plant Health Inspection Service, Jill Quirin and Isidor Patapis at the Department of the Navy, and Peter Shepard and Roger Peterson at the Food and Consumer Service.

I was a guest scholar at the Brookings Institution for six months while I did the interviews at agency headquarters in the Washington, D.C., area. I thank the institution and the director of the government division, Thomas Mann. I also received extraordinary support from the Office of Planning and Evaluation of the U.S. Merit Systems Protection Board. My thanks to the director of that office, Van Swift; to the deputy director, John Palguta; and to the entire staff, who gave me much sage advice as I was planning this project and who commented on a draft of the book.

I also received thoughtful comments on all or part of the book from Frank Thompson, Norma Riccucci, Mitchel Abolafia, Harry Redd III, Sue Faerman, and Ralph Brower. Jim Perry, Alan Shrader, and two anonymous Jossey-Bass reviewers also gave me useful suggestions for revision. Able research and editorial assistance was provided by two doctoral students: Javier Pagan Irizarry and Aimee Franklin.

The qualitative data analysis and references were managed using Notebook II Plus software. I would like to thank Oberon Resources, and particularly Lynn Fauss and Matthew Dicks, for their assistance.

Albany, New York   Carolyn Ban
March 1995

The Author

Carolyn Ban is associate professor in the Department of Public Administration and Policy at the Rockefeller College of Public Affairs and Policy of the University at Albany, State University of New York, where she also directs the Masters in Public Administration program. She received her B.A. degree (1964) in government from Smith College, her M.A. degree (1966) in regional area studies of the Soviet Union from Harvard University, and her Ph.D. degree (1975) in political science from Stanford University. Prior to joining the faculty at SUNY, Albany, she directed a research unit at the U.S. Office of Personnel Management.

Her research has focused on human resources management, and particularly on civil service reform. She has coedited two books: *Legislating Bureaucratic Change: The Civil Service Reform Act of 1978* (1984, with P. W. Ingraham) and *Public Personnel Management: Current Concerns, Future Challenges* (1991, with N. M. Riccucci). In addition, she has published numerous articles on civil service and labor relations issues.

Ban has served as chair of the Section on Personnel and Labor Relations of the American Society for Public Administration and has provided consulting services to a number of federal and state agencies and to the World Bank.

Introduction

Bureaucratic Constraints, Administrative Coping Strategies, and the Potential for Reform

Public managers face a number of difficult tasks, and they often complain that their supervisory duties are made more difficult by the constraints they face, particularly those imposed by the civil service system. Let us begin by listening to the voices of two federal managers. The first one explains how he goes about hiring new employees: "I've spent from six months up to a year, depending on the position, interviewing people on the outside or the inside. Then once I sort out those people, I begin to talk to the personnel office and design a PD [position description] and get the paperwork in order and do a general advertisement, and I'll be honest, I prepare the paperwork and the advertisement in a way which fits the job I want and the person I've already interviewed out of many. And I usually get the person I want through the system."

Another describes how he chose to face the management challenge of dealing with a problem employee: "One person that I had when I happened to come to that job . . . I'd been told he was a performance problem, and I started off—we set up standards. We did a lot of things, and it was taking up an incredible amount of my time. And the thing is, he was good enough to do just the minimal amount of things so that I could never close the book on him. . . . And so I finally just said, 'Here are two or three things that you're going to do.' He at least did those. He did them slowly, he did them poorly, but he did them, and they weren't that important to the organization, and I just let him, until after four years, he finally retired."

Public managers share a common problem: how to work within

an environment of multiple and complex constraints. But as the two managers quoted here demonstrate, they cope with these constraints in different ways—some actively, finding creative ways around the system, and others more passively, sometimes even choosing to avoid dealing with a problem when the costs appear too high.

The primary constraint in these cases is the civil service system (both the formal rules and regulations and the way they are interpreted and used by the agency personnel office). But lurking in the background in many cases are constraints imposed by the budgetary system, which requires, for example, budgetary approval before hiring. Budget process constraints are, of course, greater when agencies face tight budgets. Thus, managers may face strong pressure to keep classifications—and, hence, payrolls—down.

The field of public administration is currently engaged in considerable debate over the merits of many formal control systems that constrain managers; both in academia and in government, there are calls for a loosening of the constraints—for deregulation and delegation of greater authority to line managers. But these proposals for reform are not always grounded in empirical research. Indeed, there have been few empirical studies of how bureaucratic constraints work in practice and how managers cope with them. (One notable exception is Kelman, 1990.) This study is designed to fill that gap; it can help us to test some of the assumptions implicit in the proposals for deregulation.

The primary focus of this study is on the federal civil service system, but early in the research it became evident that there is an interaction effect between the various constraints—that one cannot look at civil service constraints without also examining the role played by budgetary and even procurement constraints.

It is important in examining the effects of these constraints to understand where they came from and what purpose they were designed to serve.

The Genesis of Bureaucratic Constraints

The current calls for deregulation are based on the premise that managers need more discretion in order to be effective. But the genesis of the elaborate system of constraints that they labor within was the perceived need to limit managers' discretion because they could not be trusted. The intent was to place controls on the bureaucracy to ensure that it would act both honestly and efficiently.

The current civil service system reflects the values of a past generation of reformers, whose primary aim was to eliminate the abuses of the spoils system. On the one hand, they championed a movement toward a nonpartisan, professional civil service based on the value of neutral competence, that is, a cadre of technically competent civil servants who could ably serve any administration, arguing that this would improve government efficiency. On the other hand, the reformers also had a political agenda: they were attempting to break the power of the urban machines by removing the political leverage of the patronage system and to change the political balance of power by opening the civil service to a "better class" of people (Van Riper, 1958; Hoogenboom, 1961; Rosenbloom, 1982).

The goal of eliminating the spoils system, coupled with application of the scientific management theories current in the early twentieth century, led to the development of a system that placed control over critical management functions—such as hiring or classifying jobs for pay purposes—in the hands not of managers but of "experts" in the personnel office. Similarly, protections that made it difficult to fire civil servants were designed to prevent political abuses.

The main elements of the current budget process can be traced to reform efforts at roughly the same time. Budget reformers espoused similar values, particularly the idea of a dichotomy between politics and administration and a stress on neutral competence and scientific management—or, in the term of the time, "the science of budgetmaking" (Wildavsky, 1988, p. 55). Sound management principles, according to these reformers, required a national budget prepared by the chief executive. The passage of the Budget and Accounting Act of 1921 created the Bureau of the Budget (later the Office of Management and Budget, or OMB), once again taking power away from line managers, even agency heads, and placing it in the hands of "experts" in a staff agency.

The budgetary process is constraining to managers not just because of the central role of OMB; their fights are often with the budget offices within their own agencies. There are many aspects of budget planning and expenditure control that cause problems. They include the annual budget cycle, which makes long-term planning difficult, and the fact that funds are budgeted for very narrow purposes, so that moving money around to meet current needs (technically known as reprogramming or transferring funds) is difficult or impossible (Wildavsky, 1988; Levine, Peters, and Thompson, 1990).

The current budgetary environment has made these problems even more acute; in a time of scarcity, OMB, Congress, and the budget offices of individual agencies have an even greater tendency to micromanage the expenditure of funds, requiring ever-increasing levels of justification for proposed budget items and making it even more difficult to spend budgeted funds. For example, funds are generally apportioned so that they are available to an agency on a quarterly basis. This is designed to ensure that an agency does not overspend early in the year, which would force it to come back to Congress for additional money to cover the remainder of the fiscal year. While such micro controls make good sense for agencies trying to stay within an overall budget, they often require managers to go through multiple clearances to fill a vacant position or to buy needed equipment. The problems created by tight micro controls on spending are exacerbated, as we shall see in more detail later, when either OMB or an individual agency puts a freeze on a whole category of spending; for some period of time, all hiring may be frozen, or managers and their staff may be prohibited from spending any funds on items such as travel. In short, limits on the amount of money available combined with limits on how that money may be spent leave very little discretion for managers to use resources most effectively.

Limits on the ability to spend stem also from the complexities of the procurement system. As Kelman (1990) has pointed out: "The procurement system is highly regulated. Government agencies may not simply purchase what they want from whomever they wish. Voluminous rules govern both contract award and contract administration. The rules are embodied in statutes, in the 744-page Federal Acquisition Regulations (FAR), and in the thousands of pages of supplementary rules for specific agencies (of which the Defense supplement is the most important) and for specific kinds of acquisitions" (p. 3).

All of these systems—civil service, budgeting, and procurement—were designed to reduce the risk of abuses, ranging from wasteful spending to favoritism to outright corruption. Constraints are designed also to make sure that government agencies meet what Wilson (1989) terms "contextual goals," that is, secondary goals or "descriptions of desired states of affairs other than the one the agency was brought into being to create" (p. 129). Such constraints include freedom of information requirements, laws on open meetings and privacy, and ethics in government legislation. They may also include requirements for open announcement of job openings and minority set-asides in contracting.

The Effects of Bureaucratic Constraints

To assess the need for changes in this elaborate system of bureaucratic constraints, we need to have a clear sense of its current effects. On the one hand, how successful are these systems in meeting their goals—whether in reducing abuses of power by managers or in ensuring that contextual goals are met? On the other hand, what are the actual costs of these constraints? And would deregulation actually improve the management of government?

Has Regulation Prevented Abuse?

Most of the current literature on regulation stresses its costs. Yet, as we have seen, the reformers of an earlier era saw the development of these regulations as necessary to curb abuses by government officials. How well have they succeeded? Overall, the complex system of rules governing personnel and procurement has been at least moderately successful in reducing the level of abuse. Certainly, the major goal of civil service reform, to eliminate the worst excesses of the spoils system, has been achieved. The most systematic high-level abuse of the system occurred in the Nixon administration, which used a variety of stratagems (actually spelled out in a manual for political appointees by Fred Malek) to manipulate the civil service system so that ideologically acceptable people were hired into career positions and those who were not politically trustworthy were neutralized (Maranto and Schultz, 1991; White House Personnel Office, 1991). But most observers would agree that the current level of abuse is relatively low, although higher levels are found in those agencies that have been most politicized (Ban and Redd, 1990). Indeed, President Carter's Civil Service Reform Act, passed in 1978, was in large part a response to the feeling that the pendulum had swung too far in the direction of protecting civil servants from political pressure, making them unresponsive to legitimate political control (Ingraham and Ban, 1984; Gormley, 1989).

Procurement abuses have been more common—or at least more visible—than those involving the civil service; they range from wasteful spending (for example, the overpriced hammers and toilet seats made famous by the media) to occasional severe scandals involving outright corruption (for example, selling insider information or throwing contracts to cronies). Nonetheless, most observers would agree that, in most agencies, by far the majority of hiring and purchasing decisions are based on the merits of the options rather than on political ties or friendships.

No formal rules and regulations can protect against abuses by individual "rotten apples." But they can prevent widespread, systematic abuse, particularly if they are enforced effectively. Perhaps equally important is the symbolic role that such regulations serve. They articulate, both internally and for those outside the government, key values such as openness, fairness, merit, and due process—values that are essential for maintaining the legitimacy of the federal bureaucracy. Further, in an environment where managers' actions are scrutinized closely, both by internal watchdogs and by the press, and where the appearance of wrongdoing is as damning as real abuse, following the rules protects managers from charges of cronyism or malfeasance. In short, one could argue that abolishing the safeguards provided by the existing system could further diminish popular trust in the fairness and openness of government.

The Argument for Deregulation

Calls for loosening the tightly regulated civil service system are certainly not new. In fact, as early as 1949, the first Hoover Commission charged that "executive authority and discretion have been so weakened by rigid and detailed statutes and regulations that the effectiveness of these services has been impaired" (cited in Mosher, 1976). But in recent years, there has been increasing support for the view that the highly regulated environment created by past reformers in order to protect against abuse has succeeded mainly in reducing the efficiency of government.

Calls for reform have come both from inside government and from blue-ribbon commissions. The arguments in support of the Civil Service Reform Act (CSRA) in 1978 were based on the need to increase flexibility and management discretion in the area of personnel. Alan Campbell, who led the fight for CSRA and served as the first head of the Office of Personnel Management (OPM), summarized the argument for change: "Rules which originated as a defense against spoils and the ineffective government which widespread patronage provided have resulted in as much inefficiency as they were designed to prevent. The system is so encrusted that many managers feel it is almost impossible to manage effectively" (Campbell, 1980, p. 161).

Several reports by outside bodies in the 1980s and 1990s have advocated further reform. In the early 1980s, the National Academy of Public Administration (NAPA) helped set the terms of the debate in calling for broad deregulation in personnel, budgeting, procurement, and information resource management. NAPA defined the problem as a loss of management control caused by overregulation, leading to a "widely perceived decline in Federal management" (National Academy of Public Administration, 1983, p. 4). The report conveyed its message graphically, featuring on the cover a picture from *Gulliver's Travels* of Gulliver being tied down by hundreds of Lilliputians. NAPA called for a more flexible budgeting process and for deregulation and delegation in personnel management and procurement.

In the late 1980s, a second report came out, this one issued by a blue-ribbon panel, the National Commission on the Public Service (dubbed the Volcker Commission after its chairman, Paul Volcker, the former and highly respected chairman of the Federal Reserve Board). Many of its proposals came from the same intellectual roots as the NAPA report; the stress once again was on decentralization and deregulation. The report called for decentralization of governmental management as well as deregulation and delegation of hiring and pay-setting authority to agencies. The Volcker Commission also emphasized the need to increase the attractiveness of government service and to improve relations between political appointees and career employees.

Many of the same themes were echoed by the National Commission on the State and Local Public Service (known as the Winter Commission after its chairman, William Winter, former governor of Mississippi), which also called for reform of both budget and personnel systems, with a stress on decentralization and simplification (National Commission on the State and Local Public Service, 1993; Ban and Riccucci, 1993).

Academic Rationales for Reform

At the same time, the movement for deregulation gained critical support in the academic community. The arguments followed two strands—one focusing on efficiency, the other on culture.

Efficiency Arguments for Deregulation

Many academics have supported deregulation because they see the costs of overregulation as being far greater than the benefits. Steven Kelman (1994) makes this point cogently when calling for deregulation of the procurement process: "I take very seriously the goal of keeping corruption out of government. The current procurement system, however, exacts such an enormous toll on the quality of government performance that the nation must seek other ways of keeping corruption out" (p. 121).

In brief, the overregulated systems are seen as slow and cumbersome, adding high transaction costs for virtually any action. Further, critics charge that overregulation may lead to suboptimal decisions. For example, hiring a new employee under the "merit system" typically takes from three to six months, which means that, often, the stronger candidates are lost to other employers along the way. Procurement regulations that forbid consideration of contractors' past performance may also lead to suboptimal procurement choices (Kelman, 1990). Gruber (1987) says these "effectiveness costs" are caused by controls that "constrain a bureaucrat in ways that undermine the bureaucrat's ability to do his or her job" (p. 62).

Gruber also points out a problem caused by what she terms "enforcement costs." Since merely passing a law or issuing a regulation does not enforce compliance, governments are obliged to develop ways to hold managers accountable. These include increasingly elaborate structures for monitoring behavior, which add costs and slow down action.

Cultural Arguments for Deregulation

A further cost of overregulation is psychological; some maintain that it fosters development of a bureaucratic personality—rule-bound, turf-conscious, and risk-averse. James Q. Wilson (1989) sums up this argument clearly: "Managers learn by watching other managers. They will judge the significance of a constraint by observing what has happened in the agency to a person who violated it. The greater the costs of noncompliance, the more important the constraint. . . . They will become averse to any action that risks violating a significant constraint. The more such constraints there are, the more risk averse the managers will be" (pp. 128–129).

The danger here arises from what I would term a "culture of control." In other words, the problem is not just the formal rules, but the culture that engendered them—a culture within which managers have spent most of their working lives. Those who are used to managing in a highly regulated environment may complain about regulations but, at the same time, may like the security of having what they can and cannot do spelled out for them. Therefore, simply removing the regulations will not necessarily change how managers behave; what is needed, in addition, is a change in the organizational culture.

It is the recognition that formal deregulation by itself may not be sufficient to change how government actually works that drives the advocates of cultural reform. This approach, heavily influenced by studies of the private sector, such as that of Peters and Waterman (1982), and by private sector experiences with Total Quality

Management (TQM), calls for sweeping changes in the distribution of power and the culture of public sector organizations. TQM stresses delegation of authority down through the organization, the use of teams of employees to analyze and improve work processes, and a strong customer focus (See Cohen and Brand, 1993; Carr and Littman, 1990).

The National Performance Review

Both deregulation and cultural change were central themes in the only best-seller in recent memory on the subject of government reform: *Reinventing Government*. Osborne and Gaebler (1992) advocated a more open, decentralized approach to government, reducing the emphasis on rules and process and stressing instead results and customer service. They took on the standard approaches to both budgeting and personnel management, with such sweeping statements as, "The only thing more destructive than a line item budget system is a personnel system built around civil service" (p. 124). Their call for reinventing government was picked up by the Clinton administration and helped spur the efforts, led by Vice President Al Gore, of the National Performance Review (NPR).

The NPR report (National Performance Review, 1993a) was a broad-gauge call for government reform that included proposals for deregulation and decentralization of personnel, budgeting, and procurement. In personnel, the NPR recommended drastic deregulation, including abolition of the entire ten-thousand-page *Federal Personnel Manual*, which gave detailed interpretations of the law (Title Five of the U.S. Code) and the regulations (contained in the Code of Federal Regulations). At the same time, the NPR called for phasing out agency-specific regulations. The vision was of a much more flexible system, with authority delegated to "agencies' line managers at the lowest level practical in each agency," using much simpler guidance—provided by OPM—in the form of "manuals tailored to user needs, automated personnel processes, and electronic decision support systems" (National Performance Review, 1993a, p. 22). The NPR also called for significant reforms in budgeting, including a reduction in Congressional restrictions on expenditures—in such forms as line items and earmarks—and, probably most important, elimination of the use of personnel ceilings to keep costs down.

The National Performance Review (1993a) linked reduction of the regulatory burden to reduction in the number of staff needed to maintain complex regulatory systems. As the NPR report put it: "As we pare down the systems of overcontrol and micromanagement in government, we must also pare down the structures that go with them: the oversized headquarters, multiple layers of supervisors and auditors, and offices specializing in the arcane rules of budgeting, personnel, procurement, and finance" (p. 13).

But the NPR report, significantly, combines both of the approaches to reform identified above: it stresses not only formal deregulation and decentralization but also the need to change the culture throughout government, The report calls for an emphasis on customer service, for the empowerment of employees, and for the encouragement and rewarding of risk-taking. While the process of deregulation is not easy, changing deep-seated cultural values will probably be a more difficult and long-term effort.

Images of the Constrained Manager

The reform proposals discussed above share two key assumptions: first, that the current system is not working—that the costs it imposes are too high; second, that managers would welcome reform and that it would lead to improved managerial performance. But managers have developed a variety of styles in response to the current system and might respond differently to reform. Let us look at three management types that are implicit in the reform literature.

The Manager as Gulliver

As we saw, the proponents of deregulation often portray managers as Gulliver, a powerful giant bound hand and foot by rules and regulations. The implication is that managers' creativity, now frustrated, would burst forth as soon as the restraints of overregulation were cut.

The Demoralized Manager

Others argue that managers, far from being full of suppressed creativity, have been so socialized into the culture of control and so burned out by the stresses of working within the bureaucracy that they have either passively resigned themselves to the rigidity of the system or thrown up their hands in despair. This view is far more critical of managers, seeing them as mediocre in their management skills and as unimaginative paper pushers incapable of rising to the challenge presented by deregulation.

The Creative Coper

Still a third view portrays managers as having learned to cope creatively by working within the system. As Wilson (1989) puts it, "Talented, strongly motivated people usually will find ways of making even rule-ridden systems work" (p. 344). This perspective sees managers as actively involved, pushing the system and finding informal routes around the roadblocks it imposes.

Which of these images of managers is most accurate will have a direct bearing on the appropriateness or likelihood of success of current reform proposals. Deregulation will work best if the Gulliver image holds true. If demoralization is the norm, culture change may reenergize the burned-out, passive manager or encourage more entrepreneurial types to move into management. The likely reaction of the creative coper is harder to predict. Managers who have found their own routes around the system may hesitate to give up a competitive advantage. But even those who have learned to "work" the system effectively may welcome processes with lower transaction costs.

But these are ideal models. In order to test the assumptions about managers implicit in the reform strategies, we need to look carefully at the current system and how it works in practice from the perspective of managers. That is the purpose of this study.

Research Approach

The research reported here was designed to look specifically at the problems posed for managers by bureaucratic constraints and at the range of methods used to cope with these constraints, particularly in the area of the civil service. A few key assumptions governed the research. First, I assumed that there would be a range of responses— that I would find examples of each of the three types of manager. Second, I assumed that one of the variables that would powerfully affect managers' choice of coping strategies was the organizational context within which they managed and particularly the culture of the organization. If there is, in fact, a culture of control, it is likely to be more or less obvious in different parts of the government. These cultural differences, if they are significant, are likely to mean that systems such as the civil service, which are designed to be unitary (that is, to be applied consistently across government), are in fact applied or interpreted very differently from one organizational setting to another, and these variations will reflect both agency needs and cultural values.

A case-study approach was chosen in order to provide an understanding of how managers coped with the systems of formal constraints within specific organizational contexts. Case studies cannot provide a basis for generalizations about the population at large; thus, the study does not permit us to say that a certain percentage of federal managers are likely to use a specific strategy, although it does give us a sense of the range of likely behaviors. The strength of the case-study approach is that it helps us to understand the functioning of complex processes embedded within organizational environments (Yin, 1984; Kennedy, 1979).

This study is based on interviews with managers in four agencies. Since a primary focus of the research was an examination of the effects of organizational culture on management style, agencies were selected that varied in a number of respects presumed to affect both culture and management style; they included size, mission and function, organizational structure, and reputational quality of the personnel office. In each agency, the study included both all or part of headquarters as well as at least one field or regional site.

The Navy stood as an example of a large military agency that was facing major changes in missions. The Navy field office that was chosen, the Portsmouth Naval Shipyard, provided an example of an organization that had recently gone through a "reduction in force."

The Environmental Protection Agency (EPA), in contrast, is a relatively small, young regulatory agency with a very different culture from that of the Navy. The regional office chosen was in the forefront of implementing Total Quality Management.

The Department of Agriculture is one of the oldest domestic agencies. Looking at two component parts of the department, the Food and Consumer Service (FCS) and the Animal and Plant Health Inspection Service (APHIS), permitted a comparison of the different coping strategies that may be adopted (by both managers and personnel staff) within a single agency in which responsibility is decentralized. In these two agencies, the regional and field offices I visited were quite small, so I have chosen not to name them to ensure confidentiality for the managers I spoke to. Since my intent was not to pass judgment on the work of individual personnel offices, all of the agencies chosen had personnel staffs that had good to excellent reputations in the personnel community.

My plans for data collection were driven by my desire both to get a sense of the organizational culture and subcultures in each agency and to find out from managers how bureaucratic constraints affected their ability to manage. In studying organizational culture, I followed the recommendation of J. Steve Ott to use interviews of homogeneous groups, that is, groups of members of the same organization, as a basis for forming a picture of an organization's culture. As Ott points out, on the one hand, "organizational members tend to adjust their language when talking with outsiders, especially in individual interviews. . . . On the other hand, organization language often creeps into group interviews because the interviewees talk with each other as well as with the interviewer" (1989, p. 112).

Thus, at each agency (and at each site, where practicable), I began my research by conducting one or more group interviews with managers. At headquarters, where the management team was larger and had a wider grade range, I generally conducted three group interviews: one with first-line supervisors, one with midlevel managers, and one with members of the Senior Executive Service (SES).[1] At each of the regional and field offices, where the number of managers was generally lower and the organizations flatter, I conducted one group interview, which included both first-line supervisors and midlevel managers.[2] These were very useful in helping to identify differences between the headquarters culture and the organizational culture out in the field. A total of fifteen group interviews was conducted, most typically with about seven or eight people. A total of ninety-four people participated in these interviews.

The group interviews were followed at all sites by in-depth individual interviews with both line managers at all levels and with personnelists. The interviews with managers focused on their personal backgrounds and experiences. For example, I encouraged them to reconstruct a specific recent attempt to hire someone or to describe, step by step, how they had dealt with a problem employee on their staff. Interviews with personnelists covered their personal backgrounds, their definitions of their roles, and with as much specificity as possible, their relationships with line managers. A total of 117 managers, at all levels, and 45 personnel specialists were interviewed personally. For both the group interviews and the individual interviews, semistructured interview protocols were used. All those interviewed were promised confidentiality, and those who were interviewed individually were given the opportunity to review for accuracy any quotes used in the book.

Part One

The World of
the Public Manager

Chapter One

Varieties of Organization: Four Cases

A central theme of the research presented in this book is that managers respond to bureaucratic constraints such as personnel and budgetary systems differently from one organization to another. Managers' approaches to these constraints are affected directly by such aspects of the environment as the size, structure, and resource level of their organization. These factors, along with the history and mission of the organization, also help shape the underlying organizational culture. Embedded in the culture are norms defining the appropriate role for managers and values concerning bureaucratic constraints.

This chapter begins with a general discussion of the concept of organizational culture. It then presents a typology of such cultures, which provides a framework for examining the specific organizations featured in the study.

Organizational Cultures and Subcultures

Inherent in the assertion that agency cultures help determine the behavior of individual managers are assumptions about the nature of organizational culture in the federal government. The recent research on organizational culture has reflected three different approaches, frequently described as "integrated," "differentiated," and "fragmented." The integrated approach stresses the beliefs and values that are held consistently within an organization; the differentiated approach looks at consensus within subcultures but sees inconsistency and even conflict between subcultures; the fragmented approach emphasizes the ambiguity and lack of consensus within organizations (Trice and Beyer, 1993; Martin, 1992; Frost and others, 1991).

The research presented here supports a differentiated approach to organizational culture in the federal government. While there are a few common beliefs and values that federal managers tend to share, agencies have markedly different cultures, which arise from their distinctive missions and histories. Cultures are likely to differ in their strength and internal consistency; most organizations, particularly large organizations with multiple missions, have a variety of internal subcultures reflecting geographical proximity and function. For example, Navy shipyards usually have organizational cultures that are different from those of Navy labs.

Further, like most large organizations, federal agencies contain a number of occupational subcultures, which draw on common education or training, shared experiences, and close working relationships (Trice and Beyer, 1993). Indeed, a key question, which is addressed in detail in Chapter Three, is the extent to which the personnel staff in federal organizations forms a distinct occupational subculture, and the degree to which its values support or conflict with those of line managers.

Federal managers do share some basic values and assumptions. For example, they generally share the typical American belief in rational approaches to problem-solving that dominates most management literature (Trice and Beyer, 1993). Career federal managers also tend to hold a related belief in the efficacy of technical solutions. This is not surprising, since—as we shall see in Chapter Two—most enter government with technical backgrounds. The preference for technical rather than political solutions to problems sometimes puts career managers at odds with their political superiors.

It is questionable whether the basic values shared by federal managers constitute a "federal culture." Most managers identify with their individual agencies rather than with the federal government as a whole. And the differences between these working environments are so great that the federal government cannot even be viewed as a single entity; it is a loosely knit group of organizations that sometimes act in cooperation but generally perform quite separate functions. As a result, individual federal agencies have evolved differently and have developed distinct organizational cultures reflective of their particular working styles.

The Competing Values Approach to Organizational Culture

The popular view of federal agencies is undifferentiated; we tend to see them all as large bureaucracies—a term that carries both positive and negative connotations. In the descriptive or positive sense, bureaucracy is seen as the most efficient way of managing work in large organizations. But the very characteristics that caused Max Weber, as well as later scholars, to stress its efficiency—hierarchical structure, division of labor, reliance on formal rules and regulations—have caused recent critics to fault traditional bureaucracies as inefficient, inflexible, and unresponsive to customers (Osborne and Gaebler, 1992; Savas, 1982).

The traditional model of the bureaucracy does not, in fact, fit all government organizations equally well. While they all work within the same formal system of rules and regulations, their cultures differ significantly. Some, for example, are far more formal and impersonal, while others are smaller, more informal, and stress the importance of personal relationships. They differ, too, in the extent to which they stress use of formal regulations and other internal systems of control to guide managers' behavior. The "competing values" model (Quinn and Rohrbaugh, 1983; Quinn, 1988; Quinn, Faerman, Thompson, and McGrath, 1990) presents a useful framework for analysis both at the organizational level, the focus of this chapter, and at the level of individual managerial behavior, examined in Chapter Two.

Part One

The World of
the Public Manager

The model posits that organizations differ on two critical dimensions. One dimension ranges between the poles of control and flexibility. The other reflects the degree to which organizational focus is on internal or external functioning. Taken together, the two dimensions define four quadrants (see Figure 1.1), each representing an organizational culture. The cultures are termed *the hierarchy*, *the market*, *the clan*, and *the adhocracy* (Quinn, 1988; Hooijberg and Petrock, 1993; Cameron and Quinn, n.d.).

The Hierarchy

The hierarchy culture comes closest to the traditional model of bureaucracy, with a strong emphasis on controls and on formal rules and procedures. The values stressed in this culture are stability, predictability, and efficiency.

The Market

The market culture also has an emphasis on control, but the focus is on external competition. The organization values hard-driving competitiveness and achievement of measurable goals and targets. While this model is more typical of private sector organizations, reformers are increasingly calling for a market approach to management in the public sector; they believe that the introduction of market incentives would improve government efficiency (Osborne and Gaebler, 1992; National Performance Review, 1993a).

The Clan

In a clan culture, the organization is seen as a family—a friendly, supportive environment in which to work, where organizational members have a voice in decisions and where group cohesion, teamwork, and morale are highly valued. This culture reflects values from the human relations school of organizational theory and

Figure 1.1. Competing Values Model of Organizational Culture.

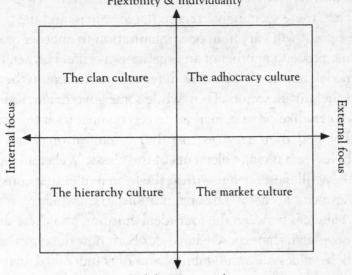

Flexibility & individuality

Internal focus

The clan culture   The adhocracy culture

External focus

The hierarchy culture   The market culture

Stability & control

Source: Hooijberg and Petrock, 1993, p. 33. © by John Wiley & Sons, Inc. Reprinted with permission.

from both the quality movement, with its reliance on group decision making, and the advocates of labor-management cooperation.

The Adhocracy

The adhocracy is an open culture, focusing on external relations and flexibility. The working environment it fosters is seen as a dynamic and entrepreneurial one, where creative problem-solving and risk-taking are rewarded. The adhocracy is able to adjust to rapidly changing external conditions and is committed to being on the cutting edge.

These are, of course, ideal models. No organization is purely one or the other. But the competing values model is extremely useful in forcing us to recognize that there are positive values that are competitive with one another. It is hard to imagine a culture that is simultaneously stable and dynamic, dependent on regular routine and permitting flexible approaches. Yet organizations regularly try to balance these seemingly irreconcilable values, and the proper balance point will vary from one organization to another or even from one phase to another of an organization's life. Further, these ideal models may have somewhat different applications in the public and the private sectors. Thus, while some government agencies may act very like private, market-driven companies if (for example) they sell their services to other organizations, they will nonetheless retain major elements of the classic Weberian model, since they still must operate within the formal rules that constrain all government agencies. The organizations in this study reflect different balances between the four ideal cultures, and these differences have significant consequences for both how the organization as a whole values rules and stability and how individual managers cope with formal bureaucratic constraints. Let us look at each of the organizations in turn, examining such "objective" characteristics as size, organizational history, and resource levels, and then relating these to the organization's culture (or cultures).

The Navy: From Hierarchy Culture to Market Culture?

The Navy is by far the largest agency in this study and certainly the oldest. The Department of Defense as a whole employs fully half of all *civilian* federal employees, and the Navy has a goodly share of them—over 329,000 in 1991, with roughly 10 percent in Washington and the remainder all around the world. Table 1.1 compares the workforces of all the organizations in this study.

The Navy also has a great diversity of organizational missions and structures. In addition to the fleets—staffed largely by uniformed staff and officers—there is a complex structure of commands (or SYSCOMS, in Navy lingo) that provides a broad range of planning and support functions. Some parts of the organization design

Table 1.1. Employment in Subject Agencies 1980–1991.

	Full-Time Equivalent Employees		
	1980	1986	1991
Navy	308,700	345,000	329,000
NAVSEA	102,000	104,400	112,300
SPAWAR	N.A.	N.A.	N.A.
Portsmouth	7,900	7,600	7,000
Agriculture	82,700	98,800	109,300
FCS	2,300	1,900	1,900
APHIS	5,600	5,000	5,900
EPA	10,900	13,100	16,800
Headquarters	8,600	7,500	8,600
Region Three	600	700	900

Note: Figures have been rounded to the nearest hundred.

Source: Data from *Budget of the United States, Fiscal Year 1992*. Washington, D.C.:
U.S. Government Printing Office, 1991; and internal agency reports.

weapons or ships; some maintain them; some provide intelligence,
legal, or other services. Of the thirteen SYSCOMS, I selected two
to look at: Naval Sea Systems Command (NAVSEA) and Space
and Naval Warfare Command (SPAWAR). NAVSEA is enormous,
comprising a third of the Navy workforce. SPAWAR is a relatively
new organization, formed primarily from the former Naval Elec-
tronics Systems Command, charged with coordinating high-tech
research. Together, the two have roughly 6,000 employees at their
headquarters in Crystal City, Virginia (just outside Washington,
D.C.). My field site for the Navy, the Portsmouth Naval Shipyard
in New Hampshire, had at the time of the study 7,000 employees,
but by 1994 that number had fallen to 4,000 as a result of reductions in force (see Chapter 7).

The Navy's history dates back to the Revolution, and the sym-
bols of its tradition, which began with John Paul Jones, are proudly
displayed in its offices. The mission of the Navy has remained

essentially unchanged since that time: to provide, along with the other branches of the military, for the defense of the United States. But the interpretation of that mission is changing now that the Cold War has ended, and managers are participating in a sweeping process of reevaluation. The changes underway are reflected in the resource base of the Navy. Table 1.2, comparing budget trends for the organizations in this study, shows both the rapid growth of the Navy budget under President Reagan and the more recent decline.

In a large organization with many separate subcomponents, shrinking budgets lead to increasing competition for resources. The natural rivalry that exists between various segments of the organization may be exacerbated by the budget cuts and by subsequent attempts to reorganize. In the case of the Navy, many managers saw that cuts were falling unequally on different parts of the organization. Particularly at headquarters, where cuts have been taken mainly through attrition, those subcomponents unlucky enough to lose several people were badly hurt, while others had fewer problems and felt that resources were only "medium tight" or "not very tight."

Some conflict over resources was in evidence both at headquarters and at Portsmouth. At headquarters, one person told me about resisting a "power play" to take over his functions. Another told me that it was hard to reallocate resources from one part of the organization to another because managers are, understandably, loath to give up resources, so no one will admit that he or she could get by with fewer staff.

Doing Things "The Navy Way"

The Navy's large size and military mission affect the organization in several ways. Navy managers are very aware of the size and diversity of the organization and are more likely to stress the differences between units of the Navy than the similarities. Indeed, the Navy is composed of distinct organizational structures, with their own cul-

Table 1.2. Budgets of Subject Agencies, 1980–1991.

	Appropriation Level (In Thousands)		
	1980	1986	1991
Navy	$46,948,000	$93,168,000	$100,379,000
NAVSEA	14,262,000	20,620,000	19,293,000
SPAWAR	N.A.	N.A.	N.A.
Portsmouth	240,000	344,000	412,000
Agriculture	21,612,933	38,232,764	46,434,067
FCS	10,708,433	17,887,955	22,871,215
APHIS	220,976	242,004	314,408
EPA	4,669,000	3,663,000	6,094,000
Headquarters	2,351,845	1,849,815	3,077,470
Region Three	368,851	289,377	480,662

Source: Data from *Budget of the United States*, *Fiscal Years 1980, 1986, 1991*. Washington, D.C.: U.S. Government Printing Office, 1979, 1985, 1990; and internal agency reports.

tures and career paths. Even at headquarters, the SYSCOMS are quite separate and manage their own resources. Nevertheless, certain common themes and common values emerged from the interviews. One was the formal, bureaucratic style of the Navy. Of course, older and larger organizations tend to be more "bureaucratized"; that is, they tend to be highly structured and to depend heavily on formal rules and "standard operating procedures" (SOPs). This tendency to bureaucratization is even stronger in a military environment.

In the Navy, people address or refer to their superiors by their last names, if not their rank. They dress quite formally. They are very conscious of issues of rank. For example, at the Portsmouth Naval Shipyard, both rank and organizational location are indicated by the colors and markings on the hard hats worn on the job.

Coupled with this formality is the impersonality of the bureaucracy. Weber was probably the first to use the analogy of the machine, describing the bureaucrat as "only a small cog in a ceaselessly moving mechanism" (Weber, 1978, p. 988). While many might see this as dehumanizing, at least some Navy managers perceive it as functional for the organization, as is evident from the following discussion among a group of Wage Grade (blue-collar) supervisors:

> *First supervisor:* "I think . . . if you look at the system and analyze it . . . you could drop an atom bomb right in the middle of that base out there, and this system would still roll. There's got to be something said for that. I don't think the government system is all wrong. The wheels still turn. Every day, no matter what happens. It amazes me. . . . I don't know, it just seems to work."
>
> *Second supervisor:* "I think part of the government philosophy is not to make any one individual so important that his absence would be missed."
>
> *First supervisor:* "It's true. It just absolutely amazes me, though, that the wheel just keeps right on turning. That might be ego-busting, but it's the right thing to do. It's the right way for it to be."

The Navy culture, like the hierarchical model, values stability and tradition. Navy managers talk about doing things "the Navy way." This is not an environment that welcomes a free spirit; there is considerable resistance to marked deviance or to dramatic change. As one manager described it, "[People] pretty much are set in their opinions, and there's not a lot of latitude for deviation. That's the bureaucratic organization that you're dealing with."

The Navy's management style is more "by the book" than that of EPA, for example. This is not to say that no one ever bends the rules, but the attitude of Navy managers is somewhat more accepting of working within the rules. In fact, while in the other agencies people complained, sometimes vociferously, about the excessive rules and red tape, in the Navy such complaints were more muted, and some people actually saw the written rules and guidance as useful, providing "fairly comprehensive instruction on how to handle most situations."

Civilian and Military: A Clash of Cultures?

The hierarchical, bureaucratic culture in the Navy certainly stems in large part from the fact that it is a defense agency. The people I interviewed were all civilian managers, but they worked within a prevailing culture that was military, and many reported directly to military officers. The military environment means that many of the top management positions are reserved for military officers. Further, officers frequently work beside career civilians, and consequently, at least some of the military culture rubs off—though much of it rubs civilians the wrong way.

Several managers I talked to complained about the problems created by military leadership. Anyone acquainted with the literature on political appointees in government will hear a familiar ring in these discussions. In general, the complaints are that military officers do not understand or care about civilians, they do not understand the civilian personnel system, and they come and go so fast that the organization is constantly disrupted.

Let us look at some examples of how civilian managers describe their interactions with military officers. One part of the difference in cultures is the tendency of military officers to operate by giving commands. One Senior Executive Service (SES) member spoke for many in expressing his discomfort with this approach: "The military, primarily the senior military, come very often to the job with the mind-set of issuing orders, and very often they're dealing with a civilian workforce, whose job expertise far exceeds their own. And consequently, orders are not the most effective way to get the job done, in many instances."

Further, civilian managers feel that in some cases they are not listened to or trusted by the military. A first-line supervisor articulated the clash of cultures that sometimes occurs: "There seems to be, at least from the perspective that I'm at, a hesitancy on the side of the military to trust the civilians. They don't understand the rules and regulations that govern civilians. They think that we are just weird because we don't wear the same uniform every day and salute them. They take it as a personal affront when you point out that civilian rules and regulations prohibit what they are about to ask you to do. They just have no concept at all."

Of course, not all military-civilian relations are so negative. While few people talked about positive interaction with their military superiors, I observed one example when an interview was interrupted by a crisis and the "team" kicked into action. A military officer dropped in and brainstormed strategy with the civilian, each speaking in the kind of shorthand that comes of a positive working relationship governed by mutual respect.

On the other hand, when military command is exercised in a way that is perceived as cruel or insensitive, the effects can be disastrous. A manager who reports directly to a military officer told me a story about such an event in her office:

> I would make it mandatory to make officers take a course in how to manage civilian personnel. Too many times, they act like we are enlisted personnel. They are too abrupt; they act with no forethought. We have a person with a new baby who she needs to take for doctor visits. She commutes from Frederick [a considerable distance away]. She brought the baby in, just for the morning. She had a friend who was going to take the baby home. And [the military officer] came out of his office and said to her, "Don't you ever bring that baby into the office. You get out of here and take that baby home." She didn't do any work for two or three weeks, and she is very interested in getting out of the office. You just do not treat people like that.

The differences in management style are compounded by differences in formal personnel systems between the military and civilian sides of the Navy. Many managers see the military commanders as uninformed about the civilian system and uninterested in learning. The SES members I spoke to have often dealt with this by cutting a deal in which their military boss in effect cedes authority over civilian personnel to them.

Navy officers, like political appointees, are "birds of passage," normally rotated every three years, if not sooner. Many managers saw this as disruptive. One described the tensions created this way: "Frankly, I think the turnover of military management hinders the job. They're here for three years. You spend a minimum of a year training your bosses. Then it takes them another year to where they get to be useful, then they have another year and you start all over again. You're lucky to get a fifty-fifty split on good ones and bad ones."

Military leaders are seen as people who are trying to make their mark quickly. As one manager described it, "For the most part, the military rotation system brings in people with an inadequate background of the organizational culture and at the same time a mandate to do something, to become visible to make the next promotion." The result is that newly arrived officers are biased toward making changes—a bias that can undermine rational planning. From one perspective, the tendency of new military officers—like that of new political appointees—to want to move the organization in new directions can be seen as healthy, as it prevents organizations from becoming ossified (Ingraham and Ban, 1986; Aberbach, Putnam, and Rockman, 1981).

For career managers, however, the costs of such frequent midcourse corrections can be unreasonably high. One Navy manager, who complained that he had to "reinvent the wheel" every three years because of new commanders, shared his frustration: "You've expended all this money. You're going in this direction, and for some ungodly reason, I can't convince this person that he's not doing us any justice if he tells us to go in that direction now, and I've already spent a couple of million dollars going in this direction, and now he starts all over."

The bottom line is that the Navy is always going to be a military organization, its priorities and values set by military leadership. Sometimes, this gets articulated with startling frankness by the military, as in the conversation a manager had with an admiral, who told him, "You civilians would be a lot better off and a lot happier if you realized that your only purpose in life is to make your officers look good for their next assignment." The tension between military and civilian managers was much more obvious at both NAVSEA and SPAWAR headquarters than at Portsmouth, but in general, we can conclude that for civilian managers in the Navy, working for uniformed superiors is often a source of frustration and can act as one more constraint on their ability to manage.

External Pressure for Change

Both because of its size and history and because of the dominance of the traditional military culture, the Navy looks very like the hierarchical culture, which values stability and is dependent on formal communication and standard operating procedures. Changing that culture in response to a changing external environment is a bit like turning an aircraft carrier: it can be done, but not quickly or easily.

While some of the pressure to change could be felt at headquarters, it was very much in evidence at the Portsmouth Naval Shipyard. On the one hand, the shipyard has a strong sense of tradition. It is almost two hundred years old, and a sense of history hangs over the place. (In 1905, the Treaty of Portsmouth was negotiated there.) Even though it is large, it has a close-knit feeling, since for years it has been the only major employer in the region. Frequently, several generations of the same family have worked at the yard. One person described it as "family-knit," saying: "Personally, I really like it here. They better not shut the gates. I don't know what I'd do. My dad works here, and my sister works here, and my mother-in-law works here, and my friends work here. I don't know where people would work if they didn't work here."

On the other hand, this speaker articulated the fear, spoken or unspoken, that permeated the interviews at Portsmouth: what is the future of the Portsmouth Naval Shipyard in the new Navy? The Navy as a whole is shrinking, and thus there is a reduced need for new ships. While the existing fleet must be maintained, reduced demand is pitting one shipyard against another, and yards operated by the Navy against commercial yards, in a race for business that is also a race for survival. In short, although they are public organizations, Navy shipyards are being required to act like commercial corporations—that is, to adopt a market culture in order to stay afloat.

In fact, one of the reasons I chose Portsmouth as a site was that these pressures were very real there and had recently precipitated a reduction in force (RIF)—government jargon for a layoff. While I was there, rumors were circulating about another RIF the following year. (These rumors subsequently proved to be well-founded.) But as the previous quotation makes clear, the real, underlying fear was that the whole yard would be shut down.

The high level of uncertainty about the future sometimes made planning impossible, as one Portsmouth manager explained:

> The unknowns out there affect the shipyard, because there's no way the managers can predict what's coming. The shipyard commander would go down to Washington and get one story, and by the time he got back it had changed. . . . There are so many proposals floating around Washington that it just made it virtually impossible to manage. All those unknowns, and we keep hearing about further budget cuts and cuts in nuclear armaments. We don't handle the armaments, but we work on attack boats [nuclear submarines]. Our workload will be affected. To do a five-year staffing plan is a joke, in reality.

Given this uncertain background, managers particularly recognized the importance of improving efficiency and boosting production in order to remain competitive with other yards. Changing the way work and people are managed was seen as vital, because, as one person put it in the plainest terms, "Our jobs are at stake."

Total Quality Management

For the Navy as a whole, adjusting to the post–Cold War environment requires wrenching change, and top management has recognized that doing business as usual is no longer possible, that the Navy needs to change both how it works and its underlying culture. As a result, implementation of Total Quality Leadership (TQL), the Navy's version of Total Quality Management (TQM), has been mandated throughout the Navy, from the top down. TQM is a complex approach to management, and there are a number of different versions of it. But most authors would agree with Dean and Bowen (1994), who list as the core concepts of TQM a customer focus, continuous improvement, and use of work teams. The values underlying these three concepts lie in different quadrants of the competing values model. Continuous improvement in production, which relies on the use of statistical process controls, draws on elements of the market culture. The focus on customer relations is central to the adhocracy and market cultures. The use of teams of employees to analyze and improve work processes fits well with the clan culture. TQM deemphasizes the values of the hierarchy culture, with its stress on stability, top-down leadership, and formal rules.

After several years, it remains unclear how extensive the effects of TQM have been, but the approach has by no means been uncritically accepted within the Navy (Ban, 1992).

Under the dual impact of changes in the external environment and internal attempts to reform the culture, the Navy is now an organization in flux, clinging to some extent to the old ways of doing things but also grappling with the need for change.

The Environmental Protection Agency: A Nontraditional Culture

The contrasts between the Navy and EPA are dramatic, both on objective dimensions and in cultural terms. EPA is relatively small, as Table 1.1 shows, and relatively young. It was created as an independent agency—by amalgamation of various programs that existed in other agencies—in 1970. At headquarters, it is divided into offices dealing with air, water, and other categories of pollution. The agency also has a strong regional structure; almost half (49.5 percent) of its staff members are in the regions. EPA's general mission—the protection of the environment—is clear. But the interpretation of this mission has changed over time and is the subject of ongoing debate, both inside and outside the agency. Among the contentious issues is how to balance environmental goals with those of economic development. More than in the other organizations studied, such debates have taken place in public, under intense scrutiny from Congress; from active, vocal interest groups; from the media; and from the courts.

EPA's resource picture also differs from that of the Navy. While the Navy is currently facing severe cutbacks, EPA's budget has grown significantly over the last ten years (see Table 1.2). But this growth has not been uniform across the board. At one end of the spectrum is the Superfund, whose expansion has outstripped all other programs. At the other end are programs that have actually been reduced in size.

Definitely Not Your Average Agency

As we have seen, the traditional view is that all government agencies fit the model of the traditional bureaucracy, or—in competing values terms—the hierarchical culture. While EPA certainly has some elements of the traditional bureaucracy, it is overall far less bureaucratic than the other agencies in this study. Its culture is complex and includes elements of all the other quadrants in the competing values model.

First, a central theme in EPA culture is a strong commitment to the agency's environmental mission. This came up frequently in the interviews and was supported by an internal study of the agency culture conducted by Region Three (U.S. Environmental Protection Agency, 1988). As one regional manager expressed it: "A lot of people work here because they have a true devotion to improving the environment. They don't see it just as a job, but more as a cause."

This strong commitment to mission clearly affects the agency style. One of the first things that struck me when I started conducting interviews at the agency was the high energy level. EPA is a place that hustles. When you walk through the rather dingy halls of its headquarters in southwest D.C., you notice that people in the halls are really moving, not just strolling. As one person said, "EPA is a dynamic, exciting place to work." And in the group interviews, the decibel level was dramatically different from that at the Animal and Plant Health Inspection Service (APHIS), where I was holding group interviews at the same time. EPA people are not shy about expressing their ideas, often at full volume and in no uncertain terms. This is not a soft-spoken agency. Employees relish what they see as a style that sets them apart: "You're expected to speak and have opinions and be energetic and be entrepreneurial. I'm not sure I'd be happy working anywhere else in government. We have a mission, and people care about it. We have an elitist attitude of looking at places like [the Department of] Agriculture and saying you can hear the squeak of the wheelchairs in the corridors."

While the analogy to a market culture does not fit EPA perfectly, since regulatory agencies do not face external competition, EPA employees' high energy and their strong commitment to the organization's mission are both highly congruent with the underlying production values of that quadrant in the competing values model.

EPA as an Adhocracy

While some elements of the EPA culture fit the production or market model, others are much closer to the adhocracy. These include the attitudes toward change and toward formal regulations, as well as the external focus and political environment of the agency.

Although some EPA old-timers bemoan the fact that the agency is growing, aging, and becoming more formal and thus more like just another government agency, it is still a relatively open, informal organization, willing to experiment with new approaches and savoring a reputation for being on the cutting edge. For example, parts of EPA were pioneers in the application of Total Quality Management. Furthermore, TQM spread informally from below, rather than being imposed from above (Ban, 1992; Cohen and Brand, 1993).

The same values permeate the agency's attitudes toward formal rules and regulations. The combination of EPA managers' strong commitment to mission and the agency's freewheeling, still somewhat countercultural atmosphere, results in a management style which is consistently described as individualist, entrepreneurial, and independent in thought. Here, too, EPA staff like to compare themselves with the rest of the federal government; they see EPA as relatively less bureaucratic, rigid, and rulebound than other agencies:

In DOD [the Department of Defense], everything is by the regulations, and everything is slow. That's somewhat a function of old versus new organizations. When I first came here, I was aghast at how they put a contract through. It's less structured and less controlled than at DOD. Also, everyone here is known by their first names, up to the administrator and deputy—it's Bill and Hank. That gives a certain informality to it. In DOD, it's Colonel this, and Captain that. The DOD culture is sort of stuffy and staid. Here it's not that this culture doesn't have its bureaucracy, but it's a little easier to take, if you have a certain personality. If you like structure and rules, you'll be happier in DOD.

However, as several people pointed out, the looser EPA environment is not everyone's cup of tea. One told of hiring a person from the DOD who could not adjust and who left after six months: "He said that he simply couldn't deal with the lack of structure. He couldn't find his bearings in the place, he didn't think that there were any rules, that everything had to be made up as you went along, and he just found it disconcerting. He didn't fault it, you understand. He thought the people were very nice, but he just couldn't live with that."

Not only does EPA have fewer rules, but it clearly has less respect for those it does have. Several people expressed an attitude that combined a willingness to push the rules to the limit with an unwillingness to take no for an answer. The fact that managers do not work by the book is not lost on the personnel staff. In one of my first visits to the agency, I talked to a senior manager in human resources who told me: "This isn't the kind of place where you can tell people what to do, where you can say, 'You will follow the following twelve steps.' My job may be harder than someone at Navy, because here everyone thinks they're an expert after ten minutes. I have no authority. I have to use persuasion to get people to do things."

A Political Environment

The EPA culture resembles the adhocracy also because of its focus on external relations. The high energy level at EPA comes not only from internal commitment to the agency mission but also from an extraordinary level of outside pressure and scrutiny—from the courts, the press, the public, and particularly Congress. EPA managers frequently mention how it feels to be on the receiving end of all these pressures. Discussions focus on both "the incredible, intense, and continuous congressional scrutiny, the number of hearings, the number of committees that get involved in any one law," and the level of public concern, often "a very emotionally involved public, on issues like siting, like various forms of pollution control."

The other key aspect of this pressure is deadlines—deadlines that managers know are unrealistic. As one explained: "The outside pressures affect our daily lives a lot, because a lot of our laws are really structured to give us a lot of deadlines that we can't meet. We don't meet them until someone sues us to meet [them]." Not surprisingly, the unrelenting pressure leads to crisis management, or as one person put it, "In [this] agency . . . we have lived and died by crises." As we shall see in later chapters, this crisis-management style puts pressures on the personnel staff as well.

The fact that the EPA environment is so political necessarily affects the nature of political leadership at the agency. In the Navy, as we saw, there is considerable tension between the military leadership and the civilian managers. At EPA, the tensions are between political and career managers. EPA is more politicized in a partisan sense than either the Navy or the Department of Agriculture (or at least the branches of the department I studied). This is a reflection of the controversial nature of its mission. The years under administrator Ann Gorsuch (Burford) in the early 1980s were an example of such politicization at its most extreme, and current employees still tell stories about that period.

Although EPA does not have an unusually high number of political appointees, they occupy highly visible positions. For example, most assistant administrators (AAs), who head the major divisions of the agency, are political appointees. They are not universally loved by the career people. While in the Navy problems were caused by the rapid turnover of military officers, at EPA, people griped about the turnover of political appointees and about their uneven quality. A senior manager expressed concern about the administrative competence of the political appointees at the top of the organization as well as about their sheer numbers. As she put it: "This place has enormous numbers of political appointees. It's crawling with them. It's a lack of stability or of a long-term commitment to things like personnel management or management systems."

Region Three: A Clan Culture

While griping about political appointees was common at EPA headquarters, it was nonexistent in Region Three, except as part of general complaints about headquarters. The region has only one political appointee, the regional administrator (RA). At the time of the study, the incumbent was respected by the regional staff, who perceived him as sincerely committed to the environment. And his deputy was not just respected but genuinely admired. Far more than at headquarters, the values of the region appear to be those of the clan culture. Top management was seen as experienced, able, and committed. One senior manager described the region as "a very nurturing place." Indeed, Region Three prides itself on being an open environment, where there is "still enough room for a manager to come up with new ideas." The regional leadership is also seen as genuinely caring about good management. As one manager expressed it: "I think there is a real concern for management here. We have a good group up there, who really look for ways to improve management. We have a good RA—we've generally been blessed with good RAs."

In general, direct conflict with political appointees is likely to be less in the regions, simply because almost all such appointees (except the regional administrators) are at headquarters. But Region Three staff also saw a difference in style between the region and headquarters. At headquarters, competition sometimes led to deadlock. In the region, by contrast, managers perceive less turf-guarding and less blocking by veto. Or as one manager put it, "We have a bias for moving forward in the region."

The Department of Agriculture: A Holding Company

The Department of Agriculture is the most loosely structured of the agencies in this study. I was interested in looking at a "holding company" to examine both structural issues—such as the level at which personnel policy is set—and cultural issues. Is there a department-wide organizational culture or management style? Or are organizational identity and organizational culture formed at the lower, agency level?[1]

The Department of Agriculture is an old organization, founded in 1862 and established as a cabinet department in 1889. It is much larger than EPA, although it does not approach the size of the Navy. The department is also very decentralized in structure, comprising more than forty-three separate agencies with diverse missions and internal structures. The two organizations included in this study, the Food and Consumer Service (FCS) and the Animal and Plant Health Inspection Service (APHIS), illustrate the broad range of functions subsumed within the Department of Agriculture.

The Food and Consumer Service (formerly the Food and Nutrition Service) is the smallest of the organizations in the study, with a total staff of less than two thousand, one-third of whom are at headquarters. FCS is a relatively new organization, founded in 1969 to administer programs such as food stamps, the Special Supplemental Program for Women, Infants and Children (WIC), and school lunch and other food programs.

APHIS is somewhat larger than FCS (see Table 1.1) and much more loosely structured. It has broad-ranging responsibilities, including:

- Detecting and monitoring agricultural pests and diseases
- Excluding exotic agricultural pests and diseases (including port-of-entry quarantine and inspection)
- Protecting the welfare of animals in a wide range of settings, including zoos, circuses, and laboratories
- Overseeing the growing industry in biotechnology and biologics (Animal and Plant Health Inspection Service, 1989)

The diversity of these functions means that just as the Department of Agriculture is a holding company so is APHIS. The separate parts of the organization function independently and even have their own field and regional structures.

Although the resources of the Department of Agriculture as a whole have grown significantly, there are substantial disparities among its component agencies. Of the two in this study, FCS, which administers welfare-like programs, was cut drastically in the Reagan years, while APHIS, which provides services that protect American farm production, has remained steady and has even grown slightly.

The FCS Family

FCS managers, more than those in other organizations in the study, present a consistent view of the organization's culture and consistently use a common metaphor: people talked frequently about the organization as a family. This culture is a reflection of the FCS mission, size, and structure and of the kinds of people attracted to the organization. Agency members see their mission as setting them apart from other agencies of the Department of Agriculture; as a midlevel manager explained: "Every other part of Agriculture is dealing with farmers and agricultural policy, and we're out there with the income maintenance and social welfare. We're urban-oriented, whereas agriculture is rural-oriented—even if it is not crops, it's rural developmental kind of stuff. [FCS] has almost nothing to do with agriculture except that it has to do with food."

The small size of FCS and its clarity of mission contribute to a relatively open, informal organization, where people use first names, even up to the top levels. (The administrator of FCS was always referred to as "Betty Jo" rather than "Ms. Nelson.") Managers stressed the ease of both horizontal and vertical communication. As one described it: "It's not the strict chain of command type setup in which you don't go to the next chain unless you report to the first line. It's more of a relaxed environment, in which the first-line supervisors can feel free to go to the branch chief, can feel free to go to a director if necessary."

Some participants in the group interviews felt that the food stamp side of the organization, which is governed by extensive rules, was somewhat more hierarchical. There was also some friendly rivalry between food stamps and special programs. For example, the final shot in a disagreement over performance appraisal standards in a group interview was, "Well, you know those food stamp folks. They're weird." But in fact, the programs are quite permeable, with people moving fairly easily from one program to another.

FCS managers do not express the same impatience with rules and regulations as do EPA staff, nor is there the same drive to be on the cutting edge of new approaches. But within the FCS "family," there is a tendency to look for informal solutions to problems. This was particularly apparent, as we shall see in Chapter Eight, in strategies for dealing with problem employees.

FCS Political Leaders, Past and Present

In the Navy, we saw tension between military and civilian leadership and, at EPA, tension between political and career executives. At FCS, there was some griping about inexperienced short-timers who were too low in the organization. But overall, the current level of tension between career managers and political appointees at FCS is far less than at other agencies. In fact, one senior manager praised the appointees, saying, "We've never had anyone as competent as the Bush people." The political leadership appeared to reinforce the caring values of the clan culture and to downgrade somewhat the values of traditional hierarchy.

Relations with political appointees have not always been so warm. One of the stories that has passed into the folklore of the agency features the past administrator (described by one person as a "full-bird colonel"), who was clearly uncomfortable with the FCS culture and referred to the agency in an open meeting as a "country club." People are still smarting from that comment, and still feeling the need to explain why it was inappropriate. The following observation from a regional manager, discussing the country club label, sums up nicely the differences between a formal, rigid military culture and the more informal style of FCS:

> There's about two thousand people or less here. . . . The only way you can run this agency is to be very, very flexible. Inflexible people cannot get the job done. . . . So the fact that people are fluid, they're moving back and forth, they're doing things, they're being creative, that's the only way you can cover all of our programs, all of our responsibilities, with the number of people we have here. So if someone would come from Defense, where he saw people pigeonholed down the line and wired into little tiny cubicles . . . with little tiny jobs, and pyramids from top to bottom, and then come into an agency where he can't track what everybody is doing every day, because people are working on five or six different projects, then basically, it's not a country club, it's just a very advanced form of management, getting the most out of your people.

The political leadership at the time of the study obviously had much more respect for the career staff. However, the administrator was trying to make some changes in the agency, and change is never easy. Nelson, who had been at the helm for about a year when I began my research, was seen as trying to open up an organization that was already fairly open and informal compared with other government agencies; her aim was to make it less hierarchical and more participative in management style. The policy was received better at the bottom than at the top. In the group interviews, the change in style elicited mixed reviews. As one first-line supervisor described it: "[She] is trying to open the system up . . . by trying to at least give the impression that she is trying to include everyone in decisions that are important to the agency, and doing that with a lot of very positive feedback, especially to supervisors. I think she's concerned about the individual a great deal."

Another first-line supervisor talked about the administrator's expectation that lower-level staff who had worked on a policy participate in meetings. As he put it: "When you take the staff with you to the administrator's office, wow, that's pretty darn good! They'll even put a suit on for that!"

But the first-line supervisors encountered resistance to change at the levels between them and the administrator. As one of them summed it up while the administrator was trying to make changes, "How open an environment is depends on who's right above you, who's two steps above you, who's three steps above you."

The changes are seen as threatening by some top managers. One senior manager commented: "If you have a new management style, then you have to retrain managers or replace them. . . . That's why the paranoia."

However, such tensions did not show up in the regional office I visited because the regional administrator, who had been in that position for sixteen years, seemed to epitomize an open management style. Rarely have I heard such unanimously warm comments about a top manager. People characterized the culture there as open and participative, and they saw the regional administrator as "very accessible." One person described his style this way: "He walks around, and you will see him on the floor within the units a couple of times a week, maybe. And so literally everyone has an opportunity to talk to him. Indeed, they take advantage of it. And [he] takes his time. He knows the people, he talks to them, and he's open to comments and suggestions. It can be friendly chitchat. . . . He will ask them what they are working on currently, or he will ask them about an issue."

The openness of the FCS culture, both at headquarters and in the region, was very evident to me as a researcher. The friendliness and warmth of its managers at all levels, including political appointees, were striking. Even though resources were very tight, this was a close-knit, mutually supportive group of managers. I saw much less of the competition or conflict between parts of the organization, or between political and career managers, that I found in other organizations. In short, the top leadership supported and reinforced the organizational norms of a clan culture.

A Holding Company Within a Holding Company

APHIS is the hardest agency to describe in cultural terms; its own managers, in the group interviews, had trouble articulating what they considered to be the common elements of an overall organizational culture. At both the midlevel-manager and SES levels, they focused first on the organization's diversity. As we saw, APHIS has an unusually diverse mission. The agency's staff carry out a wide range of activities, from checking luggage at ports of entry for everything from fruit to sausages, to eradicating medflies, to overseeing the biotechnology industry, to protecting animal welfare. The diversity of these functions means that, just as the Department of Agriculture is a holding company, so is APHIS. As an SES member described it: "APHIS, rather than having a single mission, is really a conglomeration of a number of programs and activities. Many agencies do have a single mission. When we talk about ourselves as being regulatory, that gives the impression of having a single primary mission. We really are a conglomeration of small programs."

The two largest parts of the agency are Veterinary Services (VS) and Plant Pathology and Quarantine (PPQ). Traditionally, they were very separate organizations. One senior manager in VS described both the separateness of the organization and its stability over time: "Going back and looking at the segment that I've been in, Veterinary Services, we really were organized as the old Bureau of Animal Industry, way back in the 1880s, and when you go back and look back from the 1880s up until three or four years ago, there wasn't a whole lot of change in our organization, really, and Veterinary Services' leadership pretty much ran their own organization, answering to the administrator."

The separation between the two sides of the agency is still so great that the organizations maintain completely separate regional and field structures. A recent reorganization, in 1988, was designed to improve coordination, provide better scientific support, and reflect new missions, at least in part as a response to outside criticism. Many functions that had been contained within major programs were spun off into new organizations in such areas as science and technology; biotechnology, biologics, and environmental protection; and program development. But the changes were quite unpopular, particularly within the old-line sections of the agency, which lost resources to the new units.

There were also tensions between headquarters and field offices, which is probably inevitable in an organization where a lot of the hands-on work is done out in the field. And at APHIS, they mean "hands-on" literally: "I've been out there and gotten dirty. It helps so much, I think, to have people come up through the structure, start in the field, start out there with coveralls, you know, and get knocked around by the cows, and having to do the dirty work, so that when they get into the upper positions they know what the problems are to the guy out in the field doing the work."

Here, too, tensions reflect competition for resources, with several people reporting that the field was the consistent loser. As a headquarters manager described it, "When funds get tight, it's the resources available for field delivery of services that get tightened, and headquarters feels it less."

If there is a common culture among so much diversity, it appears to most closely resemble the traditional hierarchy, focusing on stability and tradition and changing only slowly and with difficulty. The first-line supervisors, in particular, described APHIS as "conservative" and "conventional." While individual units, particularly some of the new ones, appear to be fostering innovation and looking for new approaches to the agency's mission, the feeling in the agency generally was very much one of business as usual, with heavy reliance on standard operating procedures and hierarchical decision-making structures. It is interesting that although one small part of APHIS successfully implemented TQM, the method had not spread spontaneously through the organization nor was it supported by top management (Ban, 1992). The movement to TQM may have been too great a jump for such a traditional culture, absent the intense external pressure faced by the Navy.

Political Environment at APHIS

While APHIS and its programs have nothing like the visibility of EPA, for example, APHIS does have strong political support from those served by its programs. It is also subject to stringent oversight (seen by those inside the organization as meddling) from Congress. Managers complain about increased politicization, decrying the role of political appointees and the intrusion of political considerations into the policy process. This is particularly resented by managers with scientific backgrounds, as one articulated: "The politics are becoming more and more a factor. It's coming down lower to our level. We didn't notice it in the past. We had things we wanted to do in the field. Now it seems the direction comes the other way. Scientific considerations are diluted more by political considerations."

What was really striking in analyzing the APHIS interviews was how infrequently people mentioned the top leadership of the agency. Not only was the leadership failing to articulate a consistent culture, it was nearly invisible. This was in marked contrast to both FCS (which is much smaller) and EPA, where people referred frequently to Administrator William Reilly as "Bill" and to Deputy Administrator Henry Habitch as "Hank." Even in the Navy, people often talked about the admirals who headed the major SYSCOMS and occasionally about the current or past secretary of the Navy. But at APHIS, members of the top leadership were shadowy figures who apparently had little direct influence on people's lives. The only interviewees who presented a different picture were SES members (who obviously had more frequent contact with top management), and they were quite critical. One described the current administrator as "weak in leadership skills." Another told me, "Most of the managerial decisions are made on the basis of personality and close relationships with some of the unit heads, as opposed to issue management or management to the benefit of the organization." He saw the lack of strong leadership as having a negative effect throughout the organization.

I should note that the administrator just referred to was removed during the course of the research. As one person described it: "Glosser . . . has resigned. There was some scandal about vehicles. So he's going on the shelf. There's some program where he'll stay on the payroll and go to the University of California and be an honorary faculty member and give two lectures."

Not only the administrator seemed detached from the daily lives of first-line supervisors. With only a few exceptions (mainly the heads of some of the newer sections of the organization), SES members chose to have their offices not at APHIS headquarters, a somewhat dingy office building in suburban Hyattsville, Maryland, but at the Department of Agriculture headquarters in downtown Washington. This may have improved communications upward in the departmental hierarchy, but it cut off the managers from easy informal communications within their units. I did not hear many stories of "management by walking around" at APHIS.

Conclusions

What is most striking about these findings is the sharp differences between the agencies, not only in their size, missions, and histories, but in their organizational cultures. Of course, none of the four agencies are pure types, and all have elements of each of the four cultures described in the competing values model. But there are clear differences of emphasis, with APHIS falling most closely into the traditional hierarchy mold, the Navy attempting to move from a hierarchy to a market model (particularly at the shipyard), EPA placing strong emphasis on the values that exemplify an adhocracy, and FCS epitomizing a clan culture.

These cultural differences have a significant effect on the attitudes and behaviors of managers within each organization. As we shall see in Chapter Two, they affect both the kinds of people hired into managerial positions and the messages they are given about the appropriate role for supervisors. The cultural differences also directly affect the norms that develop within the organization about bureaucratic constraints and how to cope with them.

It is important to note, as we look at the effects of organizational culture on management style, that even in organizations with a strong culture, there are likely to be significant variations, including subcultures that may support values counter to those of the wider agency. One of the key issues we will turn to in Chapter Three is the culture of the personnel office and the extent to which it is congruent with that of the agency as a whole.

Chapter Two

The Different Roles
of Public Managers

The last chapter focused on the organizational environments in which managers work and on how these environments affect the organizational cultures. In this chapter, we turn our attention to how the organizational differences shape individual managers.

The first question addressed is: who are the managers in these agencies? Do differences in agency mission and culture affect the kinds of people hired or the career paths they follow?

The second major set of questions concerns what I call role conflict and role definition. I am looking here at the relationship between managers' backgrounds and their behavior in their managerial positions. First, I turn to the specific challenges posed for technical specialists who are promoted into management positions but who, in many cases, must continue to play their technical roles. I explore two variants of this role conflict: the worker-manager and the pseudo-supervisor.

Finally, I examine how managers conceptualize the management role, given their backgrounds and the role conflicts they experience. This analysis builds on the competing values model introduced in Chapter One.

Who Manages?

The kinds of people hired by an organization depend in part on its mission. This is clearly true of the four organizations in our study. Let us consider, for example, educational background.

At three of the four agencies, the most common educational

background is technical, reflecting the specific nature of the agencies' work. In the Navy, the most common degree was engineering, mostly at the B.S. level, but with several M.S. and Ph.D. degrees, mostly in scientific fields. At APHIS, most of the managers in the Veterinary Services (VS) had degrees in veterinary medicine, while most other supervisors had either B.A. or B.S. degrees, often in such fields as plant pathology. There were only a few with master's or Ph.D. degrees. EPA had the highest education level of the agencies in the study; about a third of the managers at headquarters had Ph.D. degrees and almost as many had master's degrees, usually in scientific fields, but a few were lawyers or had M.B.A. or M.P.A. degrees. I did not ask what schools people had attended, but at EPA they often volunteered their school, and many had attended prestigious colleges and universities such as Harvard, Princeton, and Johns Hopkins.

While the specific backgrounds in these three organizations differ, what they have in common is the predominance of technical training. In contrast, the work of FCS is less technical, and this is reflected in the wide variety of educational backgrounds of its managers. Only a handful had degrees in food-related fields; most had B.A. or B.S. degrees in the humanities or social sciences.

Another pattern that emerges across the four agencies is that educational levels are generally higher at headquarters than at the field and regional level, where fewer people have advanced degrees, and more have only a high school education. For example, at the Portsmouth Naval Shipyard, about half the white-collar supervisors I interviewed had B.S. degrees, and half had only a high school diploma (though frequently supplemented with additional training).

What are the effects of these different educational backgrounds? Does it matter, in terms of management style, whether an individual was trained as an electrical engineer, a lawyer, a veterinarian, or a social worker? It is obvious, both to the managers and to the people who work with them (such as the personnel staff), that each profession attracts a particular type of person and that this may affect how they manage. A recurring issue is how well technical training prepares someone to move into management. For example, several people at Portsmouth discussed the problems engineers have in managing people, and some questioned whether engineering was the best background for management. At APHIS, people raised similar concerns about veterinarians, who are well-trained in veterinary medicine but not necessarily in management.

One of the most striking findings is how few managers had formal training in a program designed to prepare them for management, such as an M.B.A. or M.P.A. program. Almost all had either technical training in a field such as engineering or veterinary medicine, or (particularly at FCS) a bachelor's degree. In other words, the vast majority had not set out at an early age to become managers. Rather, most moved into management from a base in the technical work of the agency. We turn in the next section to a consideration of their actual career paths.

Growing Your Own Versus Lateral Entry

Managers' backgrounds differ not just in terms of their education but also in the career paths that led them into management. There is a traditional image of how one gets ahead in government: you come in at the bottom and work your way up the ladder, usually in the same agency and often within one narrow division of the agency that makes use of your technical specialty. This pattern came under some attack in the late seventies, when the federal government was considering civil service reform. The traditional path was criticized for producing managers with narrow technical perspectives who lacked the breadth of vision to see how policy issues affected the government as a whole (Ban, Goldenberg, and Marzotto, 1982a). Thus, one of the original goals of the Senior Executive Service (SES) was to create an elite cadre of top-level managers who had formal training in management through executive development programs and could move easily from one assignment to another, even across agency lines. (Huddleston, 1992, has a thoughtful discussion of this and the other, often contradictory, goals of the SES.)

Have agencies moved away from the traditional model of "growing their own"? It depends on which agency you look at, for this is another area where organizational culture plays a role. As we saw in Chapter One, the competing values model, as applied to organizations, has a dimension showing the extent to which the organization has an internal or an external focus. We might expect agencies with a stronger external focus to be more likely to hire people from outside the organization—particularly at higher levels—both because there is more interaction with potential employees in other organizations and because knowledge of the external environment is valued.

And in fact, there are marked differences in the extent to which agencies grow their own versus bringing in experienced people. EPA, with its strong adhocracy culture (see Chapter One), is clearly the most permeable organization of those studied; on average, managers at EPA headquarters had the fewest years in their agency (under twelve) than any other group. The majority of EPA managers I interviewed, both at headquarters and in the region, entered with significant prior work experience, most commonly in the private sector. Many had been employed by contractors or consulting firms that did business with EPA; others came from universities and nonprofit organizations, as well as from other federal agencies.

While the tight clan culture at FCS has an internal focus, programs such as food stamps are actually administered at a state level, so FCS employees work closely with their state counterparts. This is reflected in hiring patterns; people typically enter FCS from organizations with similar social service missions, mainly other federal agencies and state government, bringing both transferable skills and familiarity with FCS programs. But the severe cutbacks suffered by FCS in recent years have produced a gradually shrinking workforce rather than an expanding one. Thus, the majority of employees at managerial levels have been at the agency for many years—on average, about fifteen to sixteen.

Although the Navy is trying to move its culture toward more external, market-oriented values, this is not yet reflected in the backgrounds of its managers. In the Navy, the old traditions still live: most of the current crop of managers at headquarters came in either directly from school or from the active-duty military. About a third came from private industry, but usually fairly early in their careers. Only one person I interviewed came to the Navy from another agency. Similarly, at Portsmouth, most people came in directly from school or from active military duty, with small numbers moving from other shipyards or from private industry. Most managers had put in long careers with the Navy: at headquarters, the average was more than twenty years; at Portsmouth, about seventeen. The Navy's recruitment patterns—which are difficult to change during a period of layoffs—make for a tightly knit organization that is somewhat insular and that values stability.

APHIS, too, tends to fall at the internal end of the internal-external dimension in the competing values model. Whether APHIS is seen as hiring from outside depends on which organizational lines are considered important. Most APHIS managers moved to the agency from somewhere else at some point in their career, but almost half came from other parts of the Department of Agriculture. Should such moves be considered simply as transfers within a single agency? Not if the definitions of organizational identity are drawn narrowly. At least one person told me of hiring new staff from "outside," then mentioned another part of the Department of Agriculture.

The career paths at APHIS reflect the attempt to change the organizational culture via reorganization. In the field, most managers interviewed had served long careers; the average was over twenty years. But at headquarters, the picture was more complex. As we saw in Chapter One, the agency reorganized in the late

1980s and hired several senior managers from outside APHIS to head its new organizations—and, presumably, to spearhead cultural change. The resulting pattern was bimodal: either managers had worked for many years at APHIS or they had been there only two or three years. Not only was there an influx of new blood at high levels, but many of the old-line managers were moved to new positions. Consequently, at APHIS headquarters, the average time managers had been in their current positions was less than three years, lower than anyplace else in the study, while in the field, APHIS managers had been in their current positions, on average, for eleven years, the longest of any organization studied.

Does it matter whether a manager has spent his or her entire working life in an organization or has come in from outside? There are pluses and minuses in each case. On the one hand, the person who has been grown from inside probably has a strong sense of organizational loyalty and has been well-socialized into the organization's norms and culture. The Navy managers, for example, talked about managing "the Navy way." And at FCS, the fact that many of the current management had entered the agency in its early days and worked their way up produced a very close-knit group that saw FCS as being "like a family."

On the other hand, managers with more diverse backgrounds give the organization a broader perspective and bring with them experience of how things are done elsewhere. They may, for example, be familiar with new management tools such as Total Quality Management. EPA employed a number of managers who had private sector experience, which provided a useful reference point, though not always in the way many would expect. One of the funniest moments in a group interview came when an EPA manager who had come in from a corporation surprised and shocked his peers by telling them that he liked working in the government because it was so much *easier* to fire incompetent employees—clearly not what they expected to hear.

These recruitment and promotion patterns reflect the relative values the organizations assign to stability and change. Stability can foster close working relationships and in-depth knowledge of the technical work of the agency, but it can also lead to stagnation or to bitterness about lack of opportunities for advancement. Mobility within the agency can be a symptom of institutional instability, but it can also be a sign of rapid progress up the career ladder or of opportunities for lateral movement.

The critical question is: what are the effects of these various patterns of recruitment on individual management style? We have seen, in the previous chapter, that the four organizations have very different missions, structures, and cultures. Partly as a consequence, they hire distinct kinds of people, who follow quite different career paths. Does this variation in environment and background have an impact on how people define their roles as managers? Or do the similarities in the day-to-day work of management create a uniformity of approach that transcends organizations? The answer to both questions is yes. We start by looking at some of the similarities and then turn to the differences between agencies and between cultures.

Common Problems in the Transition to Management

As we have seen above, while there are differences both in the backgrounds people bring to their agencies and in their career paths, there are also some overarching similarities. Most people came into government as technical experts and moved up the technical ladder inside their agency before moving into a management position. Most had technical educations, and few had previous management experience before joining the agency. Are the people selected for management suited to it, and does their agency adequately prepare them to be effective managers?

Many of my interviewees felt their agency was not selecting the right people for promotion or adequately helping them make the transition to management. Reading over the notes from the interviews is like hearing an extended "nature" versus "nurture" debate.

A sizable number of respondents felt that good management can be learned, but they faulted their agencies for giving managers inadequate training. Some saw this as a general problem. For example, an EPA manager told me: "There might have been a little bit more aggressive training of managers. A lot of what goes on appears to be training by pushing them into the deep end of the pool. I think it should be in two parts. It should be the theory—how to deal with problem employees, to allocate assignments. Then there's the nitty-gritty nuts and bolts. What's in the union contract? What can you ask in interviews? What is sexual harassment?"

Many others addressed the issue in much more personal terms. Several told me that they had had to wait a year or more to get any supervisory training or that they had signed up for a course but it had been canceled. One first-line supervisor in the Navy blamed crisis management for his difficulty in receiving training; he told me that just the day before the interview, he had been supposed to attend a course, but had been yanked out to deal with urgent requests for information. He saw this as a reflection on the organization's management style, but it also clearly reflects the value placed on training.

Although coverage is uneven, every agency in this study does provide formal training for new supervisors. And on the basis of my interviews, it would appear that one positive effect of the creation of the SES was to focus more attention and resources on training for people at the top. But several interviewees mentioned that midlevel managers are falling through the cracks. A senior executive at APHIS highlighted this problem: "We are deficient on midlevel management training. We train them originally, and then we put them out and say, 'By golly, you're trained now, you go out and do your thing.' And we never come back and try to retrain them and see how well they're doing. We train new entry levels, and we train for technical things, but we very rarely do the management training."

The dearth of adequate training means that many people have

to learn how to manage informally, on the job. None of the supervisors mentioned any formal on-the-job training or mentoring relationships. It is clear that, in the absence of such formal training, people are likely to model their behavior on what they see around them, which may or may not be a positive example. As a supervisor at the Portsmouth shipyard explained, "For individual managers, [management style] all depends on how you have come up through the ranks, who was your supervisor, and then whether it's a person who leads by example and is a team player or 'you're going to do it my way.'" His perception was that the latter was still the more typical approach, perhaps reflecting the persistence of the hierarchy culture at Portsmouth.

The other danger, of course, is that new supervisors, as well as more experienced ones, never really get a firm grasp on the complex personnel system. Even after years, it may remain something of a mystery to a manager. Many managers would agree with a midlevel manager at FCS regional office who told me that the formal civil service system was never covered in his training and that he had had to pick it up on the job. He concluded, "I've been in government for twenty-three years, and I still don't understand the classification system. I've had several classifiers explain to me how they do it, and each one does it differently."

One might speculate whether the problem here is adequate training of management or adequate training of classifiers, but he is not alone in feeling that there is insufficient instruction in the formal aspects of the civil service.

However, the fault lies not only with the agencies. Managers themselves told me about offers of training that were deferred, usually because of the press of time. Further, even the best of training does not always "take," particularly if the skills learned are not used frequently, as one Navy SES member pointed out: "I'm not sure what authority I have. . . . I've taken courses. I forget the information. One way or another, I've accomplished what I need to accomplish."

While the "nurture" crowd focused on training, there was also a sizable group that emphasized "nature"—that is, a person's talents and skills prior to promotion. They criticized the tendency to promote employees into management primarily on the basis of technical expertise, and they expressed concern about inadequate screening for managerial experience or potential. Managers in several agencies agreed with the APHIS supervisor who felt that the problem was not just adequate training. As he put it, "When you become a supervisor, you're pretty much set in your lifetime patterns. We need to be more careful in assessing the supervisory potential of people prior to selecting them."

As numerous interviewees pointed out, good technical people do not always make good managers. Or in the pithy language of an EPA regional manager, "[In the past,] we had a supervisory cadre of the best engineers in the region, and some of them couldn't manage a lemonade stand."

Why then do agencies keep promoting their best technical staff? I heard two explanations. A few people said it reflected the fact that management was not really valued in the organization. More frequently, the explanation was tied to the classification system: if someone is at the top of the technical ladder, the only way to get a promotion is to move into management. We will look in more detail at some of the dysfunctional aspects of the classification system in Chapter Six. Here, the important issue is why people are moved into management and whether they are both suited for management and motivated to be managers or merely want the accompanying pay raise. Of course, some of these individuals adjust to the new role and find satisfaction in it. But too many made it clear that there was some degree of mismatch.

Particularly revealing were several interviews in which supervisors candidly told me that they disliked their role. For example, an EPA respondent who was still listed officially as a supervisor—and hence made it onto the list from which I sampled—had recently asked to step down from a supervisory position. He explained: "I really found that I did not like supervising, and that meant that I was not particularly good at it. I felt I was acting like a grad school professor—'Here's your assignment. If you can do it, fine. If not, that's too bad.' It worked well when they were self-motivated but not when they weren't or weren't honest. I found giving orders difficult."

To confront the problem of mismatch by seeking a transfer takes guts. More frequently, the disgruntled manager suffers through, unwilling to give up the higher pay. The largest group of unhappy supervisors I encountered was at FCS headquarters, where close to a third of those interviewed expressed dissatisfaction. One told me his goal as a supervisor was to retire and said, "I'm probably not a great manager. I'm more of a doer than a manager." A particularly disaffected first-line supervisor said: "What scares me is I've got another twenty years to go [before retirement] and I'm not sure I can make it. I definitely want out of supervision if I can get out of it."

Obviously, most cases of mismatch are not as serious as this one. But a survey of first-line supervisors in the Department of the Army is particularly telling; it reported that fully a quarter of respondents said that they would rather not be a supervisor (U.S. Army, 1985).

Needless to say, not all technical experts lack a talent for supervision. And supervisors do need to have the technical grounding to understand the work their staffs are doing (although there is a debate both in the literature and among my respondents about the managerial levels at which this remains true). But aside from the problem of extreme lack of fit, the preponderance of technical managers leads to two forms of organizational pathology. One is what I term the *worker-manager*, and the other, more severe, problem is the *pseudo-supervisor*. Let us look at each in turn.

The Worker-Manager: Leading and Doing

The worker-manager is usually (but not always) a first-line supervisor. He or she manages a staff but at the same time remains responsible for hands-on technical work. This happens, in many cases, because of cutbacks and staff shortages. The phenomenon was mentioned frequently at FCS; one midlevel manager stated that the problem was "not having enough staff in general to get the work done that's demanded. The managers, therefore, have to do the staff work."

But the blame falls not just on the organizations. Managers who have spent their careers developing technical expertise still identify themselves primarily as technical experts and get their greatest satisfaction from technical work. One of the most telling questions was, "What do you like best about your job?" Particularly at the more technical sites (EPA, APHIS, and Navy), I repeatedly received responses like the following:

> I'm most comfortable with dealing with the technical aspects of our program [APHIS].

> What I like best is I have my own projects, and I like to do them by myself [Navy].

> I guess the technical portions of the job are the most enjoyable. After all, that was my background [Navy].

These managers do not want to let go of the technical work. One might question how well they can delegate to staff, and indeed, some recognize this as a problem. But the central issue is simply that in the press of a busy day, time spent in technical work may mean less time spent in managing people. This fact is by no means lost on managers themselves. While the problem of worker-managers was mentioned in every agency, it came up most frequently at FCS (both at headquarters and at the regional office) and at EPA headquarters. At both agencies, managers expressed considerable frustration at being pulled in two directions.

One EPA supervisor estimated that first-line supervisors "probably spend 70 percent of their time doing staff work." Another said there was "just . . . no one to delegate it to. You can't be a branch or section chief. You don't have the time to spend."

This sense of frustration was also heard at the Food and Consumer Service: "It's been my experience, although I think it's governmentwide, that people aren't rewarded for good supervision. They're expected to be good technical people first. Maybe it's because we're a crisis-oriented organization, or because most of us come up from technical positions. But we're all trying to do too much, and if we have to make a choice, it usually falls on the product, not the people."

These are just a sample of numerous comments on this subject. Several people told specific stories of giving difficult supervisory tasks short shrift because of the pressure of being a worker-manager. In particular, they were sometimes unwilling to take the time to deal with a problem employee (a subject to which we return in some detail in Chapter Five).

The Pseudo-Supervisor

The problem is exacerbated when the supervisor is actually a pseudo-supervisor. We have seen above that technical people are sometimes promoted to supervisory positions in order to give them a raise and to help retain them. In the extreme, this method of circumventing the limits of the classification system leads to the assignment of sham supervisory jobs, carrying minimal supervisory authority; in fact, these "supervisors" are still working primarily as technical specialists. In such cases, the real authority remains with the person who is formally the second-level supervisor. One second-level Navy supervisor was quite frank about the arrangement: "There are eight people on the staff. We are broken down into branches, but that's only a formality. To get better grade levels, we've broken it into branches. Officially, there are branch heads. They do the performance appraisals, but they minimally act as supervisors."

Not all second-level supervisors are so open about the process, but many first-level supervisors complain that authority is held at too high a level, that they have little real authority, or that they are unsure what authority they do have.

Understanding that some first-line supervisors are really pseudo-supervisors helps make sense of the striking findings in a recent Office of Personnel Management (OPM) report on delegation of personnel management authority. The report found that the amount of personnel authority delegated to first-level supervisors varied dramatically among government installations, and that "there is no 'standard' set of personnel authorities formally delegated to first-level supervisors in the Federal Government" (U.S. Office of Personnel Management, 1992b, p. 13). In a number of cases, first-line supervisors had "recommending authority only." While the more basic supervisory functions, such as approving sick leave or annual leave or determining training needs were more apt to be delegated, few installations let first-line supervisors make decisions in such functions as reassigning employees, taking disciplinary actions, making performance awards, and classifying positions (p. 17).

Even more notable was the OPM finding that when supervisors were formally delegated the authority, many did not believe they could actually exercise it. In many cases, the differences between the formal delegations and first-line supervisors' perceptions of their actual authority were stark. For example, 60 percent of the installations reported that supervisors had the authority to certify "position descriptions," but less than 20 percent of supervisors perceived that they had that authority (U.S. Office of Personnel Management, 1992b, figs. 6, 7; pp. 20–21). The report concludes that "although they may have formal authority to take certain actions, many supervisors see themselves in a recommending role rather than a deciding role" (p. 22). This suggests that despite formal delegations, a significant amount of control is exercised by higher-level management or the personnel office, and that installations are not allowing supervisors and managers to manage resources with the degree of autonomy portrayed in their written guidance.

OPM gives a number of explanations for the discrepancy between managers' formal authority and their perceptions of their actual authority. It talks, for example, about "tighter controls" being "placed on inexperienced or poorly performing managers or supervisors" (U.S. Office of Personnel Management, 1992b, p. 26). But it does not go so far as to explore the possibility that some of the people interviewed might be pseudo-supervisors and that second-level managers have intentionally retained authority because their subordinates are supervisors in name only.

A study of first-line supervisors' competence, conducted by the U.S. Merit Systems Protection Board (MSPB) had very similar findings. They, too, found a pattern of promoting the best technical employees to supervisory positions. And they, too, found that first-line supervisors were given very limited authority:

> Many Federal organizations do not delegate much authority to first-line supervisors to make decisions and take actions. This leaves supervisors out in the trenches with very little authority to do the things that they deem necessary for the effective and efficient operation of the work unit. Concomitant with a lack of authority, some first-line supervisors also feel that their supervisors are watching over them very closely, and making decisions that the first-line supervisors themselves should be making. (U.S. Merit Systems Protection Board, 1992a, p. 27)

Another MSPB study puts the onus on managers themselves and reports that "when we asked managers what personnel authorities they had, they reported astonishingly few, when in actuality they had many." The study reports further that "there was not much agreement or clarity about the manager's role. . . . When 32 percent of managers responded that they did not have the authority to initiate a personnel action, a question arises as to whether such managers should even be classed (and paid) as supervisors (U.S. Merit Systems Protection Board, 1993, p. 33).

The Consequences of Worker-Managers and Pseudo-Supervisors

What difference does it make, for individuals or organizations, if managers are also workers or if supervisors are closer to pseudo-supervisors? First, neither bureaupathology can be blamed solely on poor managers; both are systemic problems. For example, while MSPB (U.S. Merit Systems Protection Board, 1993) is critical of managers who do not fully accept the responsibilities of management, we may discern (reading between the lines) at least some cases where authority may be conferred on paper but in reality is held at a higher level—in short, cases of pseudo-supervisors. Similarly, while some managers have trouble letting go of their technical work, others feel forced to continue to do it because of staffing shortages and recognize that the management side of their job suffers as a result.

Managing well is a demanding job in and of itself. Combining two jobs puts a heavy, sometimes an impossible, demand on worker-managers. In fact, research done at the University of Michigan found that "effective leaders did not spend their time and effort doing the same kind of work as their subordinates. Instead, effective leaders concentrated on supervisory functions, such as planning and scheduling the work, coordinating subordinate activities, and providing necessary supplies, equipment, or technical assistance" (Yukl, 1981, p. 114).

The problems caused by worker-managers are especially severe in the public sector, where managers have to work within the complex constraints of the personnel, budget, and procurement systems. In such an environment, the most severe constraint many managers face, particularly if they are worker-managers, is the press of time. As we shall see in later chapters, this affects the coping strategies they develop for working within the constraints of the formal systems.

The phenomenon of pseudo-supervisors may create even greater problems. The studies cited here are a warning that in many cases, second-level supervisors are unwilling to give up authority to their subordinates, leaving first-line supervisors unsure of their authority and unwilling to take risks. While my discussion has focused on first-line supervision—where these problems are most acute—there are indications in the interviews that agency leaders expect even highly placed executives to continue to be hands-on technical experts. Furthermore, even midlevel and upper-level managers sometimes do not have full authority delegated to them; they have to go up one level or more for review of personnel actions and certainly of related budget actions. Lack of time is bad enough, but lack of authority can paralyze lower-level supervisors or lead them to pass the buck when confronted by difficult challenges. In the worst scenario, it is not clear just where authority (or responsibility) really lies, and the hard problems, such as dealing with problem employees, get shuffled back and forth or are simply ignored.

Organizational Culture and Management Roles

We have been looking at a problem common to all agencies and to all managers: how do people make the transition to management? In particular, how are they selected and trained, and how much authority do their superiors give them? While there are common elements in these transitions, it is clear that individuals learn management skills, and management styles, within an organizational context.

Management is a complex task, involving a number of different functions. How a manager approaches the task of managing people will depend, to some extent, on how he or she weighs the importance of different functions. These weights are, at least in part, situationally determined. Managers learn by watching those who manage them and seeing "how things are done" in their organization. Their decisions are also based on incentive structures, on what is valued in their organizations. As a result, we can expect some differences in how managers define their roles to reflect varying organizational values.

There have been a number of attempts to catalogue the functions of management, going back to the early days of public administration (see, for example, Gulick and Urwick, [1937] 1973). More contemporary scholars, such as Katz (1955) and Mintzberg (1973), have developed a variety of schemas for thinking about management functions. The competing values approach to analyzing managerial functions is particularly useful for several reasons. First, it facilitates movement between an organizational level of analysis and a focus on individual managers. Second, at both levels, the competing values model highlights the fact that the functions performed by managers reflect values that, at least on the surface, are in conflict with each other: stability and change, internal and external focus, control and flexibility. The model's emphasis on conflicting values provides a nonjudgmental basis for the conceptualization of management; it helps us understand that there are many valid ways to define the management role.

Figure 2.1 is a graphic representation of the model. The axes of the model when it is applied to individuals are the same as those for organizations: internal versus external focus on the horizontal axis, and control versus flexibility on the vertical axis. The resulting quadrants are described in terms derived from classic management theories: the internal process model, the rational goal model, the human relations model, and the open systems model. Each quadrant includes two specific management roles, such as mentor and group facilitator within the human relations quadrant. The parallels between these models describing individual behavior and the quadrants describing organizational cultures presented in Chapter One are obvious.

The competing values model has been used extensively in

Figure 2.1. Competing Values Model of Managerial Roles.

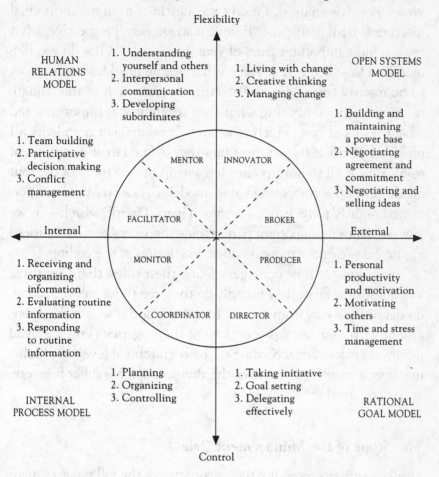

Source: Adapted from Faerman, Quinn, Thompson, and McGrath, 1990, p. 17. Used with permission.

studying management, both in the public and the private sectors. (See, for example, Quinn, Faerman, Thompson, and McGrath, 1990; Quinn, 1984; Giek and Lees, 1993). Much of the previous empirical work has relied on an extensive closed-ended questionnaire covering the kinds of tasks that fall within each of the eight roles. One recent exception is the research by DiPadova and

Faerman (1993), which utilized individual and small-group interviews. For this analysis, I used two questions from my individual interviews with managers: "From a management perspective, what are the most important parts of your job?" and, "What do you like most and least about your job?" What people liked least turned out to be mainly things external to themselves, such as inadequate resources. But combining what they thought was important and what they liked best (which were strongly related but not identical) provided a fairly good picture of how they defined their management role. Almost all their responses fell within one or more of the four quadrants of the competing values model. (Those that did not pertained mainly to technical, nonmanagerial work, which—as we saw—remains an important part of some managers' responsibilities.) Figure 2.2 presents a more detailed description of the coding.

In looking at how managers define their roles, there are three key questions. First, how broadly do they see those roles? Second, do definitions vary from agency to agency, and if so, are they congruent with managers' perceptions of their agency's culture? And finally, do roles vary according to the hierarchical level at which a manager is working? If so, does this division of labor differ from one agency to another?

The Scope of the Management Role

Ideally, managers recognize the importance of the full range of management functions. However, in the present study, most managers spontaneously mentioned only one or two of the quadrants in the competing values model when describing their jobs, and very few mentioned all four. Previous research has shown that managers typically have at least one quadrant in which they are weak (Quinn, 1988). Managers who view their roles too narrowly may ignore, or perform poorly, essential job functions.

Further, as Table 2.1 shows, the overall pattern differs significantly by organizational level. Almost a third of first-line supervi-

Figure 2.2. Coding of Managerial Responses.

HUMAN RELATIONS (HR)	OPEN SYSTEMS (OS)
Mentor: Focus on working with individual employees—coaching, training, employee development. Includes performance appraisal, discipline. *Group facilitator:* Focus on working with groups. Emphasis on commitment, motivation, group morale.	*Innovator:* Focus on creative approaches, being at cutting edge, managing change, involvement in broad policy issues. *Broker:* Focus on acquiring resources and on external interactions—with clients, constituents, other agencies, Congress.
INTERNAL PROCESS (IP)	**RATIONAL GOAL (RG)**
Monitor and coordinator: Focus on routinization, setting up SOPs, monitoring performance, internal communication; setting work priorities, scheduling work, distributing resources, handling routine paperwork.	*Producer and director:* Focus on getting the job done, productivity, output, setting clear goals; accomplishing technical work through others; work planning.

Note: Technical nonsupervisory work (that is, staff work personally performed by a supervisor or manager) is not coded here.

sors mentioned only one quadrant as a central part of their role, compared with less than 20 percent of higher-level supervisors. At the other end of the continuum, higher-level supervisors were much more likely to mention issues in three or four quadrants than the first-line supervisors. This may reflect the reality of their differing worlds. Second-level and higher supervisors may, indeed, be called on to perform a more varied range of functions than those at lower levels.

However, DiPadova and Faerman (1993) argue that although there were differences in managerial behavior across organizational levels, managers at all levels actually performed functions that related to all four quadrants. The difference between our findings may reflect different research methods, or it may be that higher-level managers, with more experience, are more articulate when discussing the complexities of the managerial role. But the difference in findings may also reflect the fact that agencies are not all alike in the emphases they place on the various managerial functions or in the divisions of labor that have evolved within their organizations.

Competing Values in Managerial Roles and Agency Cultures

Do managers in different agencies define their roles differently? If so, do these definitions reflect the agencies' cultures? The answer to the first question is a resounding yes. Managers' responses varied,

Table 2.1. Complexity of the Managerial Role.

Number of Quadrants Mentioned	Supervisory Level			
	First Level (N = 54)		Second Level and Up (N = 58)	
1	17	(31%)	11	(19%)
2	27	(50)	24	(41)
3	7	(13)	18	(31)
4	3	(5)	5	(9)
Mean	1.9		2.3	

sometimes dramatically, across agencies. The relation between individual managerial behavior and organizational culture is more complex. Figure 2.3 shows the responses from each agency in the four competing values quadrants. For the Navy and EPA, the responses from headquarters and the field site have been separated out, both because the numbers were large enough to permit separate analysis and because, in each agency, headquarters and field showed clear differences. At both of the Department of Agriculture sites, FCS and APHIS, headquarters and field responses have been combined, as they showed quite similar patterns. Quadrants mentioned by two-thirds or more of respondents in an agency were labeled "high," those mentioned by at least one-third were labeled "medium," and those mentioned by fewer than one-third were labeled "low."

The most striking overall finding is that in only three sites was there a single dominant quadrant; in the others, responses were more evenly divided among three of the four quadrants (although not the same three). Let us look first at the cases where one quadrant predominated.

At two sites, the Navy shipyard and APHIS, the most frequently mentioned management functions fell in the rational goal quadrant; they included getting the work done, stressing productivity and output, and meeting deadlines. It is not surprising to find that this is how managers at the Portsmouth Naval Shipyard see their job. The shipyard is a large, production-oriented organization, with large numbers of blue-collar workers. It combines a lot of routine work with high-level technical tasks, all performed under tight deadlines. Most managers at the shipyard have an engineering background. Production aspects dominate, with some emphasis also placed on the internal process quadrant, which includes monitoring performance, setting work priorities, and establishing or following "standard operating procedures" (SOPs).

There was a high level of agreement among Portsmouth people about what was important. Many of them echoed the individual who said that the most important thing was "to produce a quality

Figure 2.3. Managerial Role Definitions Using
the Competing Values Model.

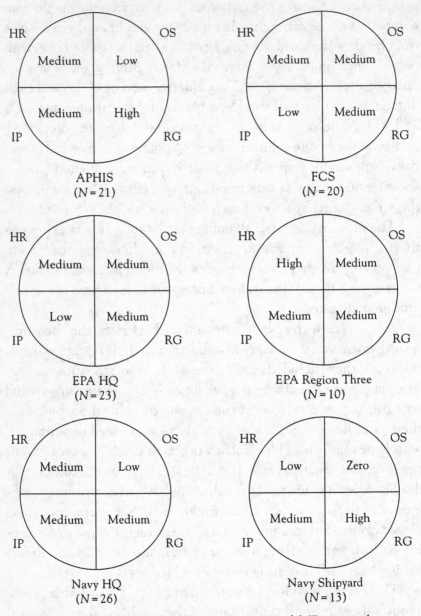

Key: HR = human relations model; OS = open systems model; IP = internal process model; RG = rational goal model.

product, on time, and either on or under costs." Portsmouth managers tend to be results-oriented and to like technical problem-solving. They only infrequently mentioned human relations tasks as important parts of their job, and none of them saw the more external, entrepreneurial, and innovative open systems functions as either central or enjoyable.

This picture, based on the responses of managers in individual interviews, fits well with the image of the organization's culture gleaned from responses in group interviews. As we saw in Chapter One, the external pressure to compete in order to survive was driving the traditional hierarchical culture of the Navy to move more toward a market culture. This culture is clearly reflected in how managers define their jobs.

The other organization with a strong focus on the rational goal quadrant was APHIS. There, too, at least two-thirds of those interviewed stressed the functions of that quadrant, with its focus on the producer and director roles. But APHIS managers were more balanced than those at Portsmouth; they rated medium on both the internal process and human relations models and low only on the external, entrepreneurial roles of the open systems quadrant. Again, these are people with technical backgrounds. Some are directing research, others are supervising the employees who work in the field. Many are worker-managers and still see themselves as technical experts first. Several mentioned planning and developing a strategy to approach a problem as parts of the job that were particularly satisfying. Conversely, they are uncomfortable with the functions within the open systems quadrant; they rarely mention them as important or enjoyable, and when asked what they dislike, they often cite the political aspects of the job, including the budgetary process.

The fit at APHIS between individual managers' role definitions and descriptions of the organization's culture is less exact than at Portsmouth. That may be, at least in part, because managers had a less clear-cut sense of overall APHIS-wide cultural values. The agency made a conscious attempt to change the organizational culture to support the value of innovation, but it does not appear to have taken hold; managers' perceptions of their roles, particularly their dislike of the functions within the open systems quadrant, are consonant with a rather traditional bureaucratic culture.

In only one of the organizations I studied did managers place greatest emphasis on the human relations aspect of their jobs: the EPA's Region Three. This is in line with its strong clan culture, as well as with the priorities set by its top leadership, which has made the management of people a high priority. The bias may also be reflective of an organization that is doing better than most in selecting people on the basis of management potential and not just on technical skills. The emphasis on the human relations quadrant came through clearly in the interviews. For example, this is how one second-level manager responded when I asked her what the most important part of her job was: "It would be, I think, leading people. Motivating them. Making sure that they have good, interesting, challenging work. Creating an environment that allows them to do their best work."

At the same time as EPA regional managers emphasized the human relations quadrant, they were not neglecting the other parts of their job. In fact, they present a very balanced profile; they are the only group that rated at least medium on all four quadrants.

In the remaining three sites, no one aspect of the job dominated. Rather, the managers' responses were more widely dispersed across three of the four quadrants. In many ways, the more balanced pattern found in these three organizations is a positive finding, particularly if it reflects a more complex approach to the job. But it is interesting to note that at each of these organizations, there was one quadrant that was more neglected. Managers at FCS, EPA headquarters, and Navy headquarters were rated medium on three quadrants and low on a fourth. For both EPA and FCS, the weak quadrant was internal process, which includes coordinating, monitoring, and routine record-keeping. Both organizations had cultures that valued flexibility more highly than control; FCS exemplified the values of a clan culture and EPA headquarters the values of an adhocracy. Managers at Navy headquarters scored low in the open systems quadrant, which is congruent with cultural values that emphasize hierarchy (the opposite quadrant).

To summarize: Managers do emphasize different parts of their job according to the organizations they work in, and these differences are, to some extent, consistent within organizations. In most cases, there is considerable congruence between the functions that individual managers see as important and their perceptions of their organizations' cultural values.

Management Role and Rank

In some cases, the relatively even distribution of responses for an agency as a whole masks significant differences among subgroups and particularly among supervisors at different levels. As managers move up the ladder from first-line supervisor to middle- or upper-management positions, do their definitions of their managerial roles change? Some people maintain that there is a division of labor, with first-line supervisors focusing more on the internal roles and higher-level managers having more external responsibilities. But others believe that each role applies to all levels of supervision, though the exact nature of the work will change (DiPadova and Faerman, 1993). Further, Faerman and Peters (1991) posit that, as people move up the supervisory ladder, the eight separate roles become less distinct. In comparing managers at different levels, I am therefore interested in two questions. First, are different roles emphasized at different supervisory levels? Second, are there differences in the complexity of the role definitions at different levels of supervision? The simple answer to both questions is yes.

Let us look first at what aspects of their jobs managers stress. Figure 2.4 takes the information in Figure 2.3 and breaks it out by supervisory level. For three of the four organizations, I have made the simplest division: first-line supervisors and everyone else

Figure 2.4. Managerial Role Definitions by Supervisory Level.

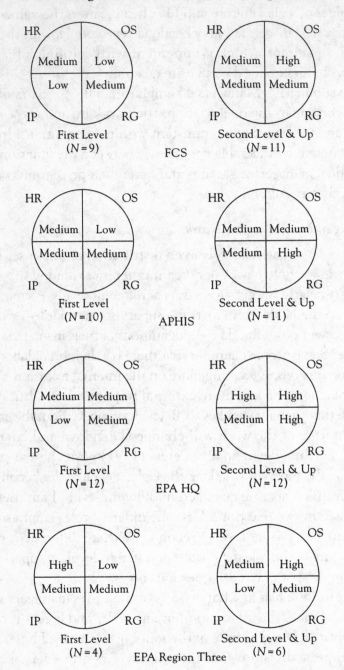

FCS

First Level
(N = 9)

Second Level & Up
(N = 11)

APHIS

First Level
(N = 10)

Second Level & Up
(N = 11)

EPA HQ

First Level
(N = 12)

Second Level & Up
(N = 12)

EPA Region Three

First Level
(N = 4)

Second Level & Up
(N = 6)

Figure 2.4. Managerial Role Definitions
by Supervisory Level, *continued.*

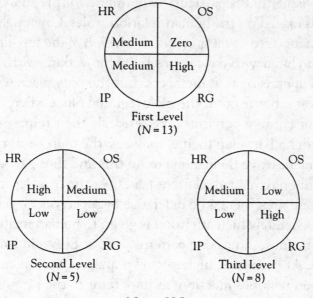

First Level
(N = 13)

Second Level
(N = 5)

Third Level
(N = 8)

Navy HQ

Key: HR = human relations model; OS = open systems model; IP = internal process model; RG = rational goal model.

(second, third, and fourth levels). For the Navy, although the numbers are small, I have divided the sample into three groups: first level, second level, and third level and up. I did so because combining the second- and third-level groups hid an interesting pattern.

One clear finding is that, in almost every organization, the external, entrepreneurial, innovative roles are seen as more central to mid- and upper-level managers than to first-level supervisors. At two sites, the difference is quite dramatic: at both FCS and the EPA region, it is the least-mentioned role by first-level supervisors, but is most frequently mentioned by higher levels. At almost every other site, it comes up more often for mid- and upper-level managers; although in the Navy, it is apparently more important for midlevel managers than for their superiors. The one exception to this pattern was Portsmouth, where no one at any level mentioned as important anything that fell into the open systems quadrant.

One issue that is particularly germane to this analysis is the emphasis placed on the human relations roles. One might expect these functions to be most central to the job of the first-line supervisor, who has day-to-day responsibility for working with, developing, and appraising staff members. But the only place where this prediction is borne out is the EPA regional office where, it would appear, first-line supervisors take seriously their responsibility to work with and develop their employees; the more senior levels of management leave them alone to do this and thus pay somewhat less attention to human relations issues. At the two Department of Agriculture sites, there is no difference by supervisory level; at both levels, moderately high attention is given to human relations concerns. The most interesting patterns were at EPA and Navy headquarters. At both sites, higher-level managers were *more* likely to see human relations functions as important to their jobs. At EPA, I combined the figures for second- and third-level managers because they did not differ; human relations issues were rated high at both levels. But in the Navy, the second-level supervisors focused more on human relations than did the higher levels.

What is going on here? One possible explanation is that the data reflect the phenomenon of the pseudo-supervisor. Particularly in the Navy, one finds first-level supervisors focusing primarily on technical production issues while their immediate superiors center their efforts on human relations tasks and place very low emphasis on the rational goal quadrant. This makes most sense in a situation where many personnel functions are not delegated to the first level but are actually held by the second-level supervisors.

Conclusions

Looking at managers' backgrounds and at how they define their roles helps us to understand how they approach the challenges of management, particularly within the complex environment of the federal system. It also helps us to think more broadly about constraints on managers. Managers usually talk about constraints as forces external to themselves and often blame the formal system, the civil service rules and regulations, for tying their hands. But in fact, the formal system is not the only constraint they face. Their own limits as managers may constrain them even more.

First, we have seen that recruitment and promotion patterns sometimes result in a lack of fit—in managers without aptitude for or interest in management. Some of these individuals grow into the job, but others remain frustrated and unhappy. This frustration is even greater when there is no clear separation between the role of worker and of manager, when a person is trying to do two jobs and feeling that he or she is doing neither well. For worker-managers, the greatest constraint may simply be lack of time to carry out even basic management functions.

Still others are limited by a lack of formal power or authority. Officially, they are supervisors, but actually, they have little power to do anything and are really pseudo-supervisors, afraid to act or to take risks for fear that they will overstep the bounds of their limited authority.

Finally, some managers are limited by overly narrow views of their roles. They may be unaware of the full range of management responsibilities, or they may choose to ignore parts of the job that they find difficult or distasteful, thus limiting their effectiveness.

Are there ways to address these problems and to improve the quality of management in federal agencies? Reform proposals have focused on a variety of issues.

Some have proposed changes in the way the government recruits and trains managers. For example, while a research report by the U.S. Merit Systems Protection Board (1992a) concluded that "federal first-line supervisors see themselves and are seen by others in the workplace as being of fairly high quality overall" (p. 1), it recommended overhauling federal supervisory selection systems to do a better job of identifying people who were qualified based on "core supervisory tasks and abilities," rather than basing selection primarily on technical capacity (p. 3).

Observers of the federal government have long been calling for better training of federal managers. (See, for example, National Academy of Public Administration, 1983; National Commission on the Public Service, 1990; U.S. Merit Systems Protection Board, 1992a, 1994.) New supervisors need training to help them make the transition to management and to give them a broad understanding of their role; lack of training may contribute to the overly narrow role definitions we saw above, particularly among first-line supervisors. But training is also needed—and rarely given—to help people as they move up to higher levels of management and need to rethink their role. Further, as we shall see in later chapters, lack of training in the specific rules and procedures of the civil service makes managers fearful of taking action because they do not feel they really understand the complexities of the formal system. But committing the needed resources to training becomes ever more difficult as budgets are squeezed.

While some reformers have focused on individual managers and their recruitment and training, others have recognized the need to change the incentives built into the classification system. It is these incentives that drive the need to move people into management jobs to justify a pay increase. In fact, some movement in this direction was visible in the four agencies studied. Two agencies, FCS and EPA, were experimenting with nonsupervisory tracks to promotion, which would enable them to reward and retain their top technical staff without forcing such individuals into supervisory positions. This was seen, by and large, as having a positive effect on the quality of supervision. However, it is not an easy solution to sell to some personnel offices. As we shall see in Chapter Five, it goes deeply against the grain of traditional classification values. Indeed, at APHIS, managers were still bemoaning the fact that they have not succeeded in establishing an alternative, nonsupervisory career path.

Revamping training and making changes to fine-tune the requirements for promotion are relatively modest changes. The Clinton administration is engaged in far more drastic attempts at reform. As we saw in the Introduction, the National Performance Review (NPR) recommended deregulation of government and decentralization of responsibility from control agencies and units to line supervisors. The NPR also advocated delayering: reducing what it saw as redundant layers of management. Both reforms were used as justification not just for moving people out of management positions but also for massive cuts, justified by the reduction both in managers and in staff for such oversight functions as budgeting, personnel, procurement, and auditing.

Undoubtedly, if my analysis is correct, the creation of pseudo-supervisors means that there are indeed extra layers of supervision that could be eliminated. But often, these people are actually the best of the technical staff. It would be ironic if past attempts to reward them made them appear redundant and thus placed them in danger of having their positions eliminated today. In fact, the manner in which some agencies are coping with the requirement to reduce the number of management layers may actually compound the problems discussed in this chapter. They are reclassifying their first-level supervisors as "team leaders" but are not significantly changing their job assignments (Ban, 1994b). Since they are still responsible for day-to-day supervision of staff and for performance appraisals, there is a likelihood of even greater confusion about supervisory authority than in the past.

But agencies are not merely relabeling positions. The implementation of the NPR calls for massive cuts, with a goal of reducing the federal workforce by 252,000. This figure was later raised to 272,900, and even broader cuts were proposed following the Republican congressional victories in 1994. As Kettl points out, "About 55 percent of the cuts . . . were to come from the ranks of middle managers, although neither the report nor subsequent discussion made clear exactly who was in the 'middle'" (1994, p. 7). Rather than deregulate first, then determine actual staffing needs and decide what could be cut and who should be redeployed, the administration began with the cuts. As Kettl put it, "By committing itself to an arbitrary reduction, the NPR eliminated any chance that a serious look at the composition of the work force and the skill mix of government would drive the reductions" (p. 8). The net effect in many agencies has been to further reduce workforces that were already cut to the bone in the Reagan-Bush years, putting even more pressure on managers to do more with less (or, as we shall see later, do less with less) and to stretch themselves too thin by serving as worker-managers.

In short, there have been some modest attempts to improve the quality of management through better selection and training, but the actions taken to flatten and downsize organizations following the 1993 NPR reports may, ironically, add to the constraints on managers rather than reduce them.

Part Two

How Public Managers Cope with the Civil Service System

Chapter Three

The Personnel Office:
Friend or Foe?

In Chapter Two, we examined constraints on managers that come from within—from their own backgrounds and experiences and from their own definitions of their role as managers. But managers also labor under very real external constraints. At the top of their lists of things that make their lives difficult are the formal rules and regulations that they see as limiting their discretion and creativity. And high on this list is the civil service system. When I asked managers in the focus groups to characterize the system, the most common adjective they used was "cumbersome," but many of their comments were more colorful, and included such words as "illogical," "inflexible," "confusing," "encrusted," "ponderous," "out of date," and "irrelevant." At the EPA, where people do not mince words, one manager in a group interview summed up the consensus view bluntly: "It sucks!" Most would tend to agree with the federal managers and personnelists interviewed for a recent Merit Systems Protection Board (MSPB) study, who felt that "the tens of thousands of pages of personnel laws, rules, regulations, and written procedures that encrust the Federal personnel system are too much, too prescriptive, and counter-productive" (U.S. Merit Systems Protection Board, 1993, p. viii).

A major theme of this book is that the rigid formal system so deplored is actually used and interpreted differently from one organization to another. Thus, we need to look at (and perhaps reform) not just the formal rules as they appear in the books, but the ways in which they are interpreted and applied in practice. And the key people in this process are the personnel staff in individual agencies.

They are given great power by the current system. How they work with line managers depends on their own organizational culture and on whether or not that culture is congruent with that of the managers. This chapter examines the backgrounds and cultures of the personnel offices and the ways managers choose to work with (or around) their personnel staff.

The analysis has direct bearing on the reform debates of the mid 1990s. First, reformers advocate deregulation of the personnel system, arguing that the rules have become a straitjacket—limiting discretion, causing inefficiency, and forcing managers to spend inordinate amounts of energy trying to beat the system. Second, reformers argue in favor of decentralization, which would delegate authority to line managers as far down as possible in the organization, rather than to staff offices (National Performance Review, 1993a). Both reforms would change the roles of personnel staff and their relationships with line managers.

The organizations in this study provide us with a range both of structural arrangements and of cultural values and styles in personnel operations, allowing us to decouple personnel roles from formal structures and to look at the effects of each. This chapter begins with a general discussion of the role conflicts that personnelists face and of the backgrounds that most personnel specialists share. We then examine both the structures and cultures of specific personnel offices and the effects of each on the relationships between personnel staff and line managers.

Conflicting Roles of Personnel Staff

For well over twenty-five years, research has documented the fact that personnel staff have traditionally felt torn between two roles—control and service (Krause, 1979; Nalbandian, 1981; Straus, 1991; Ban, 1994a).

Traditionally, personnel staff placed strong emphasis on the control role and defined their job as upholding the rules. Given the history of the civil service and its emphasis on preventing abuses, this is understandable. Personnel staff saw themselves as the "keepers of the flame," charged with preserving merit in the merit system—a probably accurate reflection of congressional intent. This view of their role was also instilled by their socialization, both inside most agencies and particularly in training given by the Office of Personnel Management (OPM) and its predecessor, the Civil Service Commission (CSC), which reinforced in budding personnelists an adversarial view of the system. They were conditioned to see managers as the people asking them to break the rules—to violate the merit system. They were supported in saying no, and many of them used the threat of OPM or CSC oversight to keep managers at bay.

For many years, personnelists have been exhorted to deemphasize the control function and to define their role more in terms of service, helping managers find ways to solve problems rather than simply enforcing the rules (Ban, 1994a). Changing the orientation of personnel staff was a major theme for the drafters of the Civil Service Reform Act (CSRA) of 1978. Alan Campbell, who spearheaded the effort for CSRA and became the first head of OPM, told personnelists that they "must be a part of management, rather than either servants of management or policemen of the civil service system," and he excoriated them for "rigidity, inflexibility, and a turn of mind . . . that thinks in terms of protecting the system; can't do, rather than can do" (Campbell, 1978). The same message was echoed by scholars who called for personnelists to move "from compliance to consultation" (Nalbandian, 1981). As we shall see, some personnel offices have successfully made this leap and redefined their role primarily as one of service. But this is by no means universally true (Ban, 1994a).

One can speculate about why many personnel offices have not succeeded in changing. Certainly, part of the answer is in the laws and regulations themselves, which impose, at least to some extent, a control function on personnel staff. But another part of the answer lies in the traditional mind-sets of personnelists, reflecting values that are resistant to change.

In fact, personnel staff often feel that they are walking a tightrope in attempting to balance the two roles. A study by the U.S. Merit Systems Protection Board (1993) found that "many of the personnelists felt torn between conflicting demands. On the one hand, they felt strong pressure to help the manager achieve the desired result by 'getting around' the system. On the other hand, they felt strong pressure to enforce strict compliance with the rules, often obstructing the desired result" (p. 28).

The inability of many personnel offices to resolve this conflict puts considerable psychological pressure on individual personnelists. It may also help explain the divergence between the way personnel specialists view themselves and the way they are viewed by line managers. For example, the report by the U.S. Merit Systems Protection Board (1993) cited above found that, in all areas of personnel work, personnelists rated their own performance much more positively than did managers.

The continuing failure of personnel staff to please their customers has led to sustained pressure for change, most recently from the National Performance Review (NPR). The NPR report on OPM stressed the need for formal deregulation, but also urged OPM to change its culture to emphasize service and to act as a model for similar changes throughout the government (National Performance Review, 1993d). Looking at the personnel offices of the organizations in this study helps us to see the extent to which personnel staff have succeeded in making this culture change and what the effects have been on their relationships with managers.

We look in the next section at the backgrounds of the personnel staff, which shed some light on the tension between personnelists and managers. We then turn to the distinct cultures and approaches of personnel staff in individual agencies.

Personnel Staff: Moving Toward Professionalism

If the personnel staff control many of the key personnel processes, then their competence is critical. If, for example, hiring a new staff member takes months longer than it should because the personnel specialist handling the process has mislaid the papers or made a technical error and thus has to redo critical steps, line managers certainly have a legitimate gripe. Managers' views of personnel staff vary greatly, as we shall see below, and many feel that they get excellent service from their personnel office. To the extent that they have unfavorable views, these may be based either on actual negative experiences or on differences in backgrounds and in rank and power relationships.

The backgrounds of personnel staff are indeed different from those of line managers. On the one hand, as we saw, line managers typically move into management after working as technical experts. Most have a college education, and a sizable number have advanced degrees. Although the number of women and minorities at management levels is increasing, line managers are still primarily a white male group, particularly in the higher echelons.

The personnel function, on the other hand, has not traditionally required a college degree prior to government service.[1] While the number of personnel staff with college degrees, and even advanced degrees, is increasing, many personnel specialists started out in low-level government positions; personnel has been a route to upward mobility for these people. Among the agencies I studied, there was some difference in educational background of personnel staff members. For example, at FCS, almost everyone I talked to had at least a B.A., and several people had advanced degrees, while in the Navy, less than half of those I interviewed had completed a B.A., but 50 percent were currently in college working toward a degree. Overall, of the personnel specialists interviewed, 60 percent had completed at least a B.A. or B.S. degree. This is slightly higher than the figure found by the MSPB. In the four federal agencies MSPB studied, 53 percent of personnel specialists and 8 percent of personnel assistants held a bachelor's degree or higher.[2] Personnelists themselves recognize the increasing need for a higher education. As a senior personnel manager at the Navy told me: "The role of the personnelist is changing, and yes, it does require a different person with different training. At one point, people just evolved into the personnel office. Education is going to become more important, if only because most people are walking around with a college degree. It has to be more than just, 'I like people.' When people say that, I always say, 'Do you like paper?' "

Personnel staff also followed a quite different career path from those followed by managers. The personnel function is quite transferable, and very few personnel specialists I talked to got their start in their current agencies. At each agency, only one or two people were hired right out of school. Most had moved from another federal agency. What is striking here is that none of these agencies consistently grows their own. As we saw in Chapter Two, agencies differ in the extent to which their managers came from outside the organization. But on average, personnel staff are considerably more mobile than managers because their knowledge of the federal personnel system is easily transferable to any federal organization.

The U.S. Merit Systems Protection Board (1993) found a relationship between career path and education. Most personnel staff hired from outside government came with a bachelor's degree or higher academic qualification (86 percent), but only 39 percent promoted into personnel positions internally from personnel assistant or clerical positions had a bachelor's degree.

The personnel staff also *look* different from management. They are much more likely to be women or people of color. Personnel has traditionally been a field open to women, and that continues to be the case. In each of the four agencies, women made up approximately half of the people I interviewed, and they were often in leadership positions in personnel offices. Representation of people of color was more uneven, reflecting to some extent the labor pool in the area. At EPA and FCS, in particular, there was considerable diversity. At FCS, close to half the personnelists interviewed were African Americans or Latinos. On balance, the personnelists were a much more diverse group than the managers in their agencies.

These demographic differences raise the difficult question of whether some of the negative views of personnel staff held by line managers are based on negative gender or racial stereotypes. Not surprisingly, given that they were being interviewed by a woman, no managers expressed sexist views to my face. But one manager did explicitly link the racial backgrounds of personnel staff to his perceptions of their competence, and a few others made more guarded comments that could have been interpreted similarly. For the most part, managers' negative comments focused on lack of education rather than on race or sex explicitly. Managers sometimes disparaged the backgrounds of personnel staff and particularly their lack of technical training and their inability to understand what the organizations they worked with were actually doing. The recent MSPB study uncovered similar reactions. According to that report, "A number of managers expressed concern . . . that many personnelists with whom they had worked were not as capable and competent as they needed to be, in part, because they lacked adequate career development training or some type of formal preparation such as that gained through a college education" (U.S. Merit Systems Protection Board, 1993, p. 29).

Differences in background and in demographics are compounded by the fact that managers clearly outrank personnel specialists, particularly those who are not supervisors. Supervisors are used to seeing differences in rank as meaning differences in power. The personnel system, however, gives power over managers to people whose rank is often several grades below theirs. And when such people say, "No, you can't do this," the managers often question the decision on the basis not of the personnelists' knowledge or competence but difference in rank.

To summarize: Looking at the backgrounds of personnel specialists does not tell us a great deal about their actual abilities (some of the ablest people I talked to, for example, did not have a college degree). But it does help us understand how the personnel staff are viewed by the line managers who work with them. While managers' views of the personnel staff are certainly shaped by their actual experiences, they may also be colored by the differences in backgrounds between the two groups and by the values managers place on education, on race and gender, and on rank.

Personnel Office Cultures and How Managers Cope with Them

As we have seen, personnelists face conflicting pressures. On the one hand, their socialization and their formal responsibilities emphasize their control function. Their responsibility to uphold the values of the merit system can easily become a tendency to emphasize process and compliance with formal rules. On the other hand, they have been exhorted for years to shift their orientation toward service, so that they help managers find ways to do what they feel they need to do, carving out a broader, strategic role as consultants to management rather than simply saying no.

Personnel offices have responded to these conflicting pressures quite differently. Several of those in the agencies included in this study have, as a result of strong leadership, changed their cultures to stress the service function. Others are still uncomfortably attempting to balance the two, while still putting considerable emphasis on the control function. The structure of personnel offices ranges from quite decentralized to highly centralized. As a result, they provide good case studies of what happens to the relationship between personnel offices and line managers both when values are relatively congruent and when they diverge; the different structural arrangements supply an additional dimension of comparison. We look first at two cases where the personnel staff are conflicted about their role and then consider cases where the personnel office has more successfully internalized the service approach.

Coping Informally with a Traditional Personnel Office

On the continuum from control to flexibility, the FCS personnel office was further toward control than the other personnel offices in this study. Individual personnel specialists were quite aware of the role conflict between their service and control functions and struggled with the task of balancing them. While they wanted to help managers, they tended to put adherence to the rules (or protecting the system) first. As one told me, "Upholding the integrity of the merit system is the more important role. That is what you were hired to do."

Conflict also exists for those in the area of employee relations, who work on disciplinary cases. As one explained: "Yes, there is a conflict. . . . We are the disciplinarians, but also we are the counselors to troubled employees who have grievances. We give advice to managers, but also we assist or give guidance to employees seeking redress. . . . I don't think one is more important, but, on the other hand, personnel is management. But the other role is more satisfying and provides opportunities to help people."

While the balance is slightly more toward the control side at FCS, individual personnelists vary in how they choose to resolve this conflict. That variance appears to reflect the lack of a consistent message from management about how personnelists should define their role. As we shall see, some personnel offices have radically redefined their role in recent years and have developed a strong internal culture. That has not happened at FCS. Indeed, two managers in the personnel office responded very differently in discussing the problem of balancing different roles. One of them strongly stressed service and was trying to change the personnelists' role definition while still recognizing the need for balance:

We are responsible for upholding the integrity for the rules and regulations. But we are a service organization. We are preaching that you can do both by knowing the rules and being creative in their interpretation. The classifiers see themselves as policemen: "We control this, and if you want to do something, you have to do what I tell you." I'm trying to change that. If [managers] come and say they want a [grade] 12 for this person, if it's legally possible, they should get it. It's a scratching, screaming, kicking, drag-me-along approach [to get people to change]. If you can get someone new and train them, it's easier. But there's not a lot of turnover.

But in contrast to that strong message of culture change, the other manager, while recognizing the "pressure between conservative and liberal classifiers," told me that "we don't encourage them to take either role. We are neutral. We have moved . . . away from compliance to technical assistance, but we do very little with the classifiers."

Lacking either strong leadership from inside or concerted pressure from outside (that is, from line managers) in the direction of change, the FCS personnel office remained fairly traditional, striving to give managers good service but also staying very mindful of its role as protector of the merit system. The culture of the personnel staff in the regional office that I visited seemed quite similar, with the difference that, given the small size of the office, relationships were even more informal than at headquarters. The FCS personnel operation was also quite traditional in structure, with a staff serving headquarters and making general policy and separate regional staffs enjoying a moderate amount of independent authority.

How do FCS managers view their own personnel office, and what strategies have they developed for working with it? Reactions to the personnel staff directly reflect the role conflict the personnelists express: managers sense that the personnel office lacks consistency, both in quality and in values, and many see the office as emphasizing control. One manager stated it very directly: "Personnel is not service-oriented. They see themselves as the guardians of the system. The personnel office thinks we want to abuse the system, and their role is to prevent us from doing whatever we want, because we must be trying to get around them." Managers in the region were much more likely than those at headquarters to see their personnel staff as responsive to their needs.

Where personnel is not seen as actively getting in the way, it is perceived as passive—as willing to help when asked but rarely taking the initiative to identify problems and help correct them. It is also seen as not very creative or innovative. For example, in the area of recruitment, one person noted, "I think we recruit the way we recruit because we always recruited that way. They're not looking for new ideas."

Managers' perceptions of the competence of the personnel staff they worked with were also decidedly mixed, with less than half of those interviewed rating them as good or pretty good. Again, ratings in the region were higher. A typical assessment stressed the wide variation in quality: "In some cases, they're not very competent. The quality of service leaves something to be desired. Routine actions are slow. Their tracking system doesn't always work, so you can't even tell whose desk it's on. You get the runaround. On the other hand, sometimes they're very prompt. It has to do with their workload, and if the individual feels like going out of his way. . . . It varies a lot, depending on the circumstances—what the issue is, who said they would do it, what the competing priorities are."

Managers attribute variability in the quality of service to several causes. First, some recognize that FCS has failed to define a clear mission for the personnel office, thus permitting considerable personal variation. Second, some attribute the problems in personnel either to understaffing or to lower grades in the personnel office. Third, they recognize how severely personnel staff are constrained by the civil service system itself. As one manager put it, "I sort of see them as captive too. I think their captivity has tended to douse the flames of their creativity." Finally, they wonder to what extent the control orientation at FCS is a reflection of the Department of Agriculture's conservative style or a response to department direc- tives to hold the line in such areas as classification.

FCS managers' strategies for working with the personnel office reflect both their diagnosis of the problem and their own cultural values. As we saw in Chapter One, FCS is a small organization with a clan culture. Given these values, managers tended to rely on informal solutions rather than direct confrontations or challenges to the system. Since many recognized wide variability in the com- petence and responsiveness of personnelists, their preferred ap- proach was to develop a personal relationship with an individual personnel staffer whom they saw as responsive and reasonably com- petent and to work as much as possible through that person. As one first-line supervisor told me: "I think the key is individuals, and we know the person to go to and that individual is helpful. . . . There are some in personnel that are not helpful. I think it's the person. We've been dealing with one or two personnel staffing people that are just excellent. And no matter what the problem is, they seem to resolve it, or get the answer. You always go to that person."

To summarize: The most common strategy that managers use reflects their organizational culture and the way they deal with each other—using informal networks and building personal rela- tionships. This is not a group of managers that, by and large, is aggressively challenging the system or demanding a greater role in personnel. Rather, they have learned ways to work more or less comfortably within the confines of the system by establishing infor- mal relationships with the individual personnel specialists they find most helpful.

EPA: Tough Customers

Structurally, EPA looks like FCS: a human resources staff at head- quarters and quite autonomous regional offices. But particularly at

EPA headquarters, the approach of the personnel staff and their relationship with line managers differ sharply from those at FCS. EPA personnel specialists would fall quite far out toward the flexibility end on the control-flexibility dimension. But some individual personnelists appear uncomfortable and conflicted about how far they have gone in that direction. One possible reason is that they have done so in response to pressure from outside, particularly from managers. As a result, they sometimes conveyed the impression that their behavior had changed, but their beliefs and values had not, which resulted in considerable internal conflict.

I found a similar reaction at other agencies, particularly among classifiers, but EPA staff expressed it most pungently, often with black humor. A typical example: "Yes, there's conflict. It's time for a joke. A couple of days ago, the queen of England decided to watch the Baltimore Orioles play baseball. I said to my office director, 'If those umpires worked here, they would be in deep trouble for not letting the Orioles win so as not to embarrass the queen and the president.' My office director said, 'At least they should have been winning at the time the queen left.'"

As we shall see in more detail later, in some cases, the vehicle for changing the culture of the personnel office was the adoption of Total Quality Management (TQM). At the time I visited EPA headquarters, TQM was being implemented in some parts of the agency, and personnel was just starting to adopt it. The skepticism that certain staff members expressed about TQM was related directly to concerns about their role conflict. As one explained, "The TQM focus on the client doesn't deal with clients who have unreasonable demands. You can't go to Burger King and ask for a Big Mac."

While one can attribute this awareness of conflict to the difficulty personnelists have in giving up traditional values, a critical source of conflict is the managers themselves. One sometimes gets the feeling, talking to managers, that no matter how far the personnel staff goes in bending the rules, it will never be enough to please them. Particularly at headquarters, their assessment of the personnel staff is mixed to negative. This appears to be a reflection not just of some real problems in the exercise of the personnel function, but also of the fact that EPA managers are really "tough customers"—they are impatient with the niceties of personnel rules and regulations and demanding of immediate service. This is congruent with the EPA adhocracy culture, discussed in Chapter One, which values innovation and risk-taking far more highly than stability or compliance with formal rules.

EPA managers certainly recognize that some of their problems with personnel are a function of the rigidity of the regulations that the personnel staff must navigate. As one manager explained it: "I think I've dealt with excellent people in personnel and some not so good people, like any organization. I think the big problem [comes] back to the rules. They are so arcane and cumbersome and don't fit—a lot of them were written maybe twenty or thirty years ago . . . and personnel people have every right to try and help us, but they have got to live within those rules. And I think that that is the root source [of the problems]."

The rules notwithstanding, what EPA managers want and expect is service—a strong customer orientation. Their assessments of personnel staff, positive and negative, focus entirely on this dimension. Some see the personnel staff as very responsive. As one put it, "They take this dinosaur set of rules, and they've got them stretched right to where they're going to break." Others see the quality of service as varying across different parts of the personnel office. One person explained the differences in terms of the history of the personnel function. He felt that, in the past, "they were not helpful. It used to be that it was the kind of place where you traditionally had to know what you wanted to do and then come in and tell them how to do it." EPA then commissioned a study on the personnel function from the National Academy of Public Administration (NAPA) (1984). "The agency took the NAPA study to heart and created a human resources (HR) office, which coexisted uneasily with the existing personnel office, and eventually HR won and took over the personnel function." But even though the two functions have theoretically merged, this person saw the human resources office as "fairly proactive," but the personnel office as "totally reactive."

Many of the negative comments portrayed the personnel staff not so much as unresponsive but as stretched too thin and uneven in quality. Several people recognized that while they were asking the personnel office to do more, the office's resources had not increased to handle the greater workload. Further, some felt that, as one person put it, "several [people in the office] are service-oriented, but overall the ability to get the job done is poor. Volume is a very important aspect of it, but it's also the knowledge of the [personnel staff]."

Expressions of concern about quality were often accompanied by stories, some quite detailed, of getting the runaround from personnel. There were complaints about receiving contradictory advice from different personnelists and about sitting in a meeting where a personnel supervisor told the managers they could do something but the supervisor's staff "quietly said, 'No, we can't.'" Several stories focused on the problem of what one interviewee called "sequential information requests." As this person explained it: "You do it, and they come back and have you do it again. It's very hard to get all the steps done the first time if they don't give you all the information." One specific area of conflict, which came up frequently, was the competence of the personnel staff to review the qualifications of job candidates in highly technical fields. We will return to this problem in more detail in Chapter Four.

The strategies that EPA managers use when they are in conflict with their personnel office differ dramatically from those at FCS. Particularly at headquarters, there was far less emphasis on building personal relationships. Rather, what managers describe most often is a strategy of confrontation and escalation. As one person summarized it, "Unless you're willing to push, you're just blocked all the time in the people you want to hire." EPA managers do not easily take no for an answer. They are quite willing to take a disputed matter to the individual's supervisor or even to the highest levels if they think the issue is important enough. Given the outspoken EPA style, some managers are not above bullying the personnel staff. One described the process as seeing if they are going to provide the services you need, and "if they aren't going to be responsive, you go to the second phase—of clubbing them; no, cajoling them." Another told a long story of a conflict with personnel. Even the edited version gives a clear flavor of his personal style:

> I've read the classification manuals. I mean, I'm a goddamn scientist, and a goddamn manager, I shouldn't have to read the goddamn classification manuals. I have to quote chapter and verse occasionally. I pull the goddamn manual over to the goddamn personnel specialist. I have taken a classification course, so that I'm more facile in it. Ironically, if you read the OPM regulations, they are reasonably flexible. But I talk to "beebee brain"—I call her a "beebee brain" to her face—I had to yell at a section chief so much, my whole goddamn branch cleared out, they were afraid of what was happening. That's what it takes to get people on. . . . My time has been spent more in trying to get around them than in working with them. [*Describes a specific conflict over hiring.*] That's where I was quoting chapter and verse, and that's where I went over with the manuals that I had underlined. It was like interpreting the Bible, for Christ sake. It was ridiculous. That took me, literally, three person-weeks, full-time. I didn't do any thing else. I mean, my branch went to hell.

What is striking about this story, apart from the language, is the lengths to which this manager has gone to learn about the system in order to take an active role in the personnel process, and the amount of time and energy he devotes to taking on the personnel staff. This is clearly not a passive consumer of services.

A second, less confrontational strategy for dealing with personnel conflicts emerged from the interviews: offering to give the personnel staff additional resources to deal with extraordinary demands. Several people mentioned trying this approach, with mixed results. One person who found it effective described a situation where his unit was given increased resources for a large number of new positions and "ended up detailing people over there to help them get our people processed." On the other hand, another person shared a similar story that had a different outcome: "One time, I even hired an AARP [a person in a special program for hiring retired people] and a clerk-typist and another person and gave them to personnel and said, 'I'll double your staff if you give me better service.' And I gave them a computer. When I asked for better service, they said, 'That wouldn't be fair. We have to treat everyone the same.'"

To summarize: Despite a fairly strong customer orientation among the personnel staff, there remains a significant amount of conflict between personnelists and managers, with managers pressing the personnelists to go further, do more, and move faster. EPA managers are not content to be passive users of personnel services; they tend rather to push the system and the personnel staff aggressively to meet their needs.

A Human Resources Success Story

While headquarters presents us with a mixed picture of considerable conflict and of a personnel office struggling, not always successfully, to meet the demands placed on it, the picture in the region is remarkably positive. In both the individual and group interviews, managers consistently rated the service they received from the personnel office as good to excellent. While there were some complaints about timeliness, most people saw their personnel staff as responsive and helpful. A number of factors explain the differences. One is size. In a smaller organization, more informal relationships develop, and people frequently talk about having "friends over there" who are helpful. Another factor may be differences in management styles and cultural values between headquarters and the region. In the region, I heard few stories about direct confrontation. A typical interviewee was one who told me that the service he received was excellent, saying, "I guess that's because I've worked with these people for so long. If you were nice to them when they were a staff person, when they are personnel officer you have it made."

Finally, managers feel that, as one person put it, "personnel got better in the last few years in helping people." This person attributed the change to leadership: "I think it's due to one or two individuals that came into personnel that made a great change."

While leadership plays a role here, so does structure; the relatively loose EPA structure allows regional offices considerable autonomy, which permits different cultures to develop there, among both line managers and personnelists. In the case of Region Three, these cultures appear to be both congruent and quite positive.

TQM Comes to Personnel Management

Both the culture and the structure of the personnel function at APHIS are in marked contrast to those at FCS, even though both are parts of the Department of Agriculture. First, APHIS has centralized most of the operating personnel functions (as well as some other administrative functions, such as procurement) in a single office, the Field Servicing Office (FSO), which serves all APHIS offices nationwide from Minneapolis. FSO provides an example of dramatic culture change—driven primarily by strong internal leadership—based on the newest management reform, Total Quality Management (TQM). A central value in TQM is service to the customer. The director of the FSO had discovered TQM about five years before this research was conducted and had moved aggressively to implement it, with consulting assistance from 3M Corporation. When I arrived, TQM had been up and running for some time, and its values permeated the organization. As the director himself articulated it, "Here, we've been able to communicate to people that customer service was the priority, and it will stay the priority." His staff had gotten the message loud and clear, and most of them liked it just fine. As one of them described it: "TQM does affect me. We've made a tremendous amount of improvement. . . . I come out of a stodgy environment at the [Veterans Administration]. This is a more open environment. I think it's really helped here. We are very involved here. We as individuals work really closely together."

When I arrived, FSO had taken the next step and was starting to pilot self-managed teams, in which groups of employees would work together to provide coordinated services to the customer. Each group would also, in many respects, manage its own activities. While the first group had just been formed, the energy and excitement of the members were contagious. Overall, FSO felt like an organization on the cutting edge—one that had moved well beyond the traditional role definition of the personnel office and was actively exploring future roles and structures for the personnel function.

I should note, however, that changing an organizational culture, even with strong commitment at the top, is not without costs. The organization devoted considerable resources to training all staff in TQM, a process which took two or three years, and even hired a full-time TQM coordinator. Some staff members were unwilling to make the needed changes and went elsewhere or retired. While FSO sent a clear message to its employees that the dominant value should be one of service, it was impossible to completely eliminate the conflict between flexibility and control. One employee expressed discomfort about the balance being tipped so far toward the service function and described the operating style as "fast and loose" and as "totally out of control." While most FSO staff would not agree with these characterizations, it is clear that control is downplayed as much as possible. As another staff member explained, "We do as much as we can for them without violating the law or the merit system."

How do APHIS managers rate the service they receive from this centralized, service-oriented personnel staff? Their reactions are surprisingly mixed. First, one senses a distinct cultural gap. APHIS management has been reluctant to adopt TQM. In some cases, there has been active hostility on the part of the top leadership. This is a management approach that challenges many of the values of a traditional, hierarchical culture.

Second, many line managers have very little direct contact with FSO staff. They tend to work through administrative officers (AOs) in their own organizations or through regional personnel staff who handle liaison with FSO. Managers in Washington also sometimes have direct contact with the small Washington "Customer Support Office" set up as an arm of FSO.

APHIS managers told few stories of open conflict with FSO. This may simply reflect the fact that conflict is mediated through the AOs or regional offices. It appears also to be a reflection both of the service orientation of FSO and of the fact that the APHIS management style is more laid-back and less confrontational than is typical of EPA, for instance. Further, the Department of Agriculture as a whole is seen as rather conservative on personnel matters, so while conflicts (over classification, for example) sometimes get referred to the department level, this is not a safety valve that is often used. Thus, while APHIS managers grumble frequently about the constraints of the personnel system, they tend to blame the formal rules and regulations more than the personnel staff and to be resigned to living within the limits of the rules.

In spite of FSO's service orientation, some managers are still uncomfortable with the logistics of a centralized personnel function. They would prefer to walk down the hall and talk face-to-face with someone than to call Minneapolis, particularly on complex or delicate personnel issues. As one manager explained it:

Now, the [staff at the] Field Servicing Office [are] supposed to be the ones who counsel all employees in the agency, whether headquarters or field, about retirement. It's been my experience that employees here at headquarters are very reluctant to get on the phone and talk to someone about their retirement. They would like to just go into an office, sit down, and have someone counsel them on their options, forms to fill out, and so on. But the way we are structured, that doesn't exist. . . . I think that is a real failing in the agency— thinking that all things can be done impersonally over a phone or through a fax or telecommunications.

FSO created the Customer Service Office at headquarters to respond to this need for personal "hand-holding," but most actions still need the approval of FSO staff in Minneapolis.

The issues related to centralization are complicated by a fair amount of structural confusion built into the personnel function at APHIS. While the operating personnel function is located with FSO in Minneapolis, the human resources policy function is the responsibility of a separate organization (Human Resources, or HR), which has remained at headquarters. To further complicate things, recruitment programs, as well as training and development, are managed by a third office, also at headquarters (Recruitment and Development, or R&D), created in the late 1980s to cover functions that were falling between the cracks. As a result, management dissatisfaction is sometimes a result of confusion—of not being sure whom to call for what.

While centralization does cause some problems in communication, most (though not all) managers recognize and appreciate FSO's service orientation.

Two Naval Victories

While reform at APHIS came largely through the internal impetus of strong leadership, my sense is that change in the Navy's

Consolidated Civilian Personnel Office (CCPO) in Crystal City, Virginia, was the result both of strong leadership and of serious customer dissatisfaction. I had expected, when I began this study, that centralized personnel offices would be less responsive; evidently, CCPO in the past had fit this description. Several years ago, the personnel function had been taken away from a number of separate Navy organizations, all clustered in a strip of buildings in Crystal City. Not only did the individual organizations lose control of the process, but they were quite dissatisfied with the service they received from the new organization. Navy managers may not be quite as outspoken in style as the average EPA manager, but there was no doubt that they made their dissatisfaction known.

When the current director took over in 1989, he began a process of culture change that had close parallels to the FSO story, with the same strong emphasis placed on service to the customer. He sent people regularly to meet with line managers in their offices; upgraded training for personnel staff (and in more recent years, added specific TQM training); and integrated the staffing and classification functions, to try to improve service. When I arrived, CCPO was also starting to experiment with an integrated team approach. Further, in large and small ways, the director tried to improve the professional image of the office. As a rank-and-file staff member told me, "[The current director] has made a big thing about looking professional—how you dress, how you act, eating at your desk. We never could get a lunch room. Now we have one, and that is where you are supposed to eat. The cleanliness issue in the office was a big cultural issue."

At CCPO, as at FSO in APHIS, there was some initial resistance to the changing culture. Some people could not adjust and left, but most of those who remained have embraced the focus on service, as one person explained: "I think Navy has come a long way from when I first started working with them. Probably [because] they got rid of the old classifiers [*laugh*]. The whole role of the personnel office has changed. I try to assist managers in getting whatever they want. Before, it would just have been *no*. We definitely stress customer service more. The relationship had started to change six years ago, and [the current director] put even more emphasis on it."

The picture is slightly different at the Portsmouth Naval Shipyard. The personnel office there is called the Industrial Relations Office (IRO), a reflection of the distinct culture in a heavily blue-collar production organization. This is an office with a very positive reputation within the Navy. When I asked its director how he managed to serve such a large organization with such a small staff, he gave considerable credit to the "strong New England ethics" of his staff. Their esprit de corps was evident when I visited. While Portsmouth's personnel office seemed less innovative than CCPO, at least in terms of adopting TQM or a team structure, the sense of customer orientation was (with one possible exception) obvious. In contrast to CCPO, IRO staff tried to avoid working directly with line managers—of whom there were over one thousand—preferring to work through administrative officers in each part of the organization, who served as liaisons with the managers. We will return more generally to the role of administrative officers later in this chapter.

Managers served by CCPO gave it the most consistent high marks of any personnel office in this study, and they frequently drew comparisons with the past. Navy managers were very aware of the difference between a control orientation and a service orientation in personnel. As an SES member explained it, "Personnel people tend to be a lot like ADP [Automatic Data Processing, that is, computer] people and a lot like travel people. They've got rules and some of them can help you find the way to get the job done within the rules, and some can throw up a thousand ways that can prove to you that you'll never get anywhere. . . . So it's a function of whether your personnel people are helping you get the job done within the rules, or whether they're trying to throw rusty mufflers and tail pipes in front of your car as you go down the highway."

Almost everyone I spoke to saw the current CCPO staff as helpful, cooperative, and going out of their way to provide service. They were seen as knowledgeable about the rules and how to work within them. Managers credited the turnaround of CCPO to its current leadership. As one person explained it: "You have one individual who has a decent view of what's going on. He's come in, he's tried to motivate the organization, and he personally, I believe, has done a great deal to turn the organization around. . . . Of course, he would have been hard-pressed to make it worse, in terms of his predecessor!"

Some of the comparisons with the preceding leadership were rather droll: "I accused a former head of CCPO of being a Russian mole, because they had absolutely brought us to our knees. Even though we could hire, we found people and we couldn't get them in the door, because the people in the personnel office didn't know how to hire anybody."

The positive relationship between Navy managers and CCPO staff is quite apparent. Managers told me remarkably few stories about conflict with personnel. There was much more extensive discussion of conflict inside their directorates (the major operational units) with the people who controlled the purse strings. This makes sense in an agency going through major cutbacks (an issue discussed in more depth in Chapter Seven). Permission to hire, even on a replacement basis, is very hard to obtain, and the process may take months. Once approval is granted, working with personnel is a snap by comparison.

The one area where some tension persists is that classic area of conflict, position classification. Interviewees raised concerns over the level of knowledge of personnel staff in highly technical fields. The difference in backgrounds and grade levels between managers and personnelists clearly rankles some managers. One said of personnel staff, "If they had any college-level degree or anything, it often might be in psychology or some other thing." Another complained about the frequent rotation of classifiers and the fact that "classifiers are not experts and do not hold the series of the jobs they classify. And I really think that's a problem, because they are trying to classify something they really don't have a feel for."

This conflict is less severe than in other agencies, because in much of the Navy, the managers hold the final authority on classification, and personnel's role is advisory. Chapter Five will look at how this has worked out in practice.

Managers' assessments of the service they received from the personnel office at the shipyard, IRO, were somewhat more mixed. Most of those interviewed gave the office positive ratings and saw it as both helpful and competent. But close to a third gave mixed or negative responses. Among the sources of tension were the conduct of a recent reduction in force (RIF) and subsequent battles over plans to reorganize the staff and upgrade some classifications as people took on new responsibilities. (See Chapter Seven for a discussion of the RIF process.)

But managers at Portsmouth had much less direct contact with IRO than did Navy managers at headquarters with CCPO, because, as we saw, IRO has followed a strategy of working with the administrative officers (AOs) in each office rather than dealing directly with supervisors. The implications of working through AOs are discussed later in this chapter.

Overall, the Navy, like APHIS, provides a positive example of a professionalized, service-oriented personnel office. Unlike FSO, it has not resorted to national centralization; given the size of the Navy, this would probably be unworkable. But CCPO is an example of moderate centralization, providing service to a large number of Navy components in one geographic area.

Culture and Structure of the Personnel Function

As we have seen, the personnel offices in the four agencies differ both in their culture and values and in how they have chosen to structure the personnel function. Comparing them allows us to make some generalizations about the effects of culture and structure on the relationships between personnelists and line managers. One of these is that cultural differences between the two sets of actors can increase friction. In the case of EPA, even though the personnelists perceived themselves as extremely service-oriented, they were still criticized by managers as not going far enough. It is questionable whether they ever could go far enough to suit EPA managers. The staff role in an adhocracy will probably always be uncomfortable, because the values of that management culture are antithetical to the traditional bureaucratic respect for rules and standard operating procedures that are the underpinning of the formal personnel system. However, the Field Servicing Office at APHIS was implementing a culture change, based on TQM, that may have taken the office out in front of its line managers, who still strongly adhered to traditional hierarchical values. As we shall see in later chapters, these cultural differences affected such issues as the proper division of labor between personnelists and line managers.

Unintended Consequences of Centralization

Two key structural issues emerge from our earlier discussion: the advantages and disadvantages of centralization, and the use of shadow personnel offices.

Scholars and practitioners have debated the pros and cons of centralized and decentralized structures for years. One private sector source, speaking to researcher Fred Foulkes, described what happens when one decentralizes personnel: personnel "becomes much closer to the action, really learns to understand what pressures line people are under, and becomes actively involved in working with line managers to meet their goals." However, this same source recognized that "from a corporate standpoint, this results in a somewhat fragmented personnel function. The separate groups tend to function independently, and as a result, much effort is spent in reinventing the wheel. It is very difficult to coordinate with this type of organization" (Foulkes, 1986, pp. 166–167).

Two of the four organizations in this study had centralized the personnel function, at least to some extent. In the Navy, the centralized organization serviced offices in one geographic area, while at APHIS the centralization was nationwide. Centralization does have certain obvious advantages: it permits some specialization, and it may provide adequate resources for development of a truly professional staff. Moreover, as we have seen, it allows a strong manager to instill a consistent culture—something much harder to do if the function is decentralized. Nonetheless, my expectation was that managers would resist centralization, and that they would rank the service they received less positively than did managers in agencies where the function was more decentralized. This simple prediction was not borne out. In fact, CCPO got the highest marks overall from the managers it serviced.

One obvious difference between CCPO and its APHIS counterpart, FSO, is geographical. At CCPO, although the personnel office is not down the hall from managers, it is within a ten- or fifteen-minute walk. Furthermore, CCPO has assigned teams to work with specific offices. These teams spend a considerable amount of time in the offices they service; they meet personally with managers and often hand-carry paperwork to speed things up. Managers are very appreciative of this service. As one midlevel manager described it: "The people who support me physically come over a couple of days a week and are working out of our administrative spaces. It's worked well. They do know the organization. They try to tailor responses to the organization."

In spite of this hands-on service, a few Navy managers still felt that they got better service at Navy installations that had their own personnel office, which would pull out all the stops for them in a pinch. One told of bringing in over sixty people in less than a year, through extraordinary effort, and concluded: "I cannot imagine, in my wildest dreams, ever getting CCPO to help me do something like that. Never." Still, most managers would agree that the level of service they get from CCPO is more than adequate to meet their needs.

The more mixed reactions to FSO at APHIS may reflect, in part, the greater physical distance between the service provider and the customer and the preference for informal, face-to-face communication on complex or sensitive issues.

In short, while centralization works pretty well in most cases, some managers are still uncomfortable with it, and they cope with the problems it creates in ways that may be functional for them but have dysfunctional consequences for the organization as a whole. At APHIS headquarters, managers tended to look "throughout the building" for informal experts who had some personnel knowledge and could help them. Even though FSO added a small office at headquarters, it did not meet all needs.

Managers' discomfort with a centralized office arises from more than just their communication styles and preference for personal interactions. Moving the personnel function further away from them removes it from their direct authority (particularly if they are senior managers) and increases their fear that it will be used to constrain what they can do. Stressing the service function, as both these centralized offices do, goes only so far in alleviating this anxiety. One of the most common reactions to the anxiety, as well as to the distance of the personnel office, is the creation of "shadow" personnel offices.

The Shadow Personnel Office

The existence of shadow personnel offices is a phenomenon that, as far as I can tell, has never been discussed in the academic literature. Yet they are fairly commonplace in organizations, and they play an important role in mediating between the line manager and the personnel office proper. Most frequently, the person or people playing this role are termed administrative officers or administrative assistants. The line between staff support and a shadow personnel office is a fine one. On the one hand, most managers rely on a staff member for such routine clerical functions as filling out the forms necessary to process a personnel action. But when the AO's responsibility includes strategic planning of staffing needs, detailed knowledge of the civil service rules, and finding creative ways around the rules, the function mirrors, at least to some extent, the activities of the official personnel office. This may be seen as usurping the personnel office's functions or as getting it off the hook because it no longer needs to provide these services, but the net effect is to develop shadow offices that report directly to line managers.

In the four agencies, there was fairly widespread use of shadow personnel offices. Only the Food and Consumer Service, which is quite small, made no use of them. At EPA and at NAVSEA and SPAWAR, the pattern was mixed, while at the naval shipyard and at APHIS, virtually all managers worked through an administrative officer, who was often clearly functioning as a shadow personnel office.

Why create a shadow personnel office instead of working directly through the official one? For managers, it is a way of bringing the personnel function back under their direct control. Their perception is that the new office will be more understanding of what they do and more responsive to their needs. Further, the shadow office relieves them from having to learn the nitty-gritty details of the personnel system. For example, the shadow office takes care of such details as filling out forms and even writing job descriptions—tasks the official personnel office usually will not do for managers.

Rather than seeing shadow offices as competition, personnel offices often prefer to work through them for the same reason: the personnel office responsibility for providing certain services to managers is reduced. The arrangement also shields personnelists from direct pressure from managers; they may prefer to work with an administrative officer, who often comes from a personnel back-ground and speaks their language.

But creating shadow personnel offices has its downside, too. For one thing, it is to some extent duplicative. If one of the goals of cen-tralization is to provide economies of scale and to reduce the over-head spent on staff functions, extensive use of shadow offices undermines this effort. Further, the shadow offices created to make life easier for managers can actually create one more hurdle and slow things down. Managers now need to worry not just about the skills and values of the personnel staff but also about those of the shadow staff. To what extent are the shadow staff keeping up with changes in the personnel rules? Are they really giving their man-agers the best possible advice? Finally, while saving managers time, shadow personnel offices may also increase the tendency of line managers to see the personnel process as someone else's responsi-bility and not central to their own role.

Conclusions

Personnel staff in both official and shadow personnel offices play an important role by:

- Providing services directly—for example, recruiting job candidates
- Interpreting the formal rules and telling managers what they can and cannot do
- Coaching and counseling managers—for example, on how to deal with a problem employee

How managers perceive the personnel staff—whether they see them as sharing their values or as competent—will have a power-ful effect on how managers cope with the constraints of the per-sonnel system. Are the personnelists allies, helping to find ways around the rigidities of the system, or are they "part of the problem"? In subsequent chapters, we will examine this relationship in more detail.

The findings presented in this chapter also shed light on the issues raised by the current movement for administrative reform. Reformers, including the National Performance Review, have advocated formal deregulation of personnel as well as of budgeting and procurement. For example, the entire *Federal Personnel Manual*, which gave detailed guidance to personnelists, has been eliminated (although what this means in practice is not yet clear). At the same time, the NPR stressed the need to change the culture of personnel and other staff offices to emphasize the service function and to downplay control. The four agencies in this study are located along a range of this dimension; three of the four already give strong emphasis to providing service to management. Although personnelists, like managers, are hampered by having to operate within the constraints of rigid civil service procedures, strong support from top management has enabled many of them to give managers considerable assistance in finding whatever flexibility the system possesses. Deregulation of the system would not only give managers more discretion, it would also lift burdensome requirements from personnel staff and enable them to provide better service to line managers.

Defining their customers as line managers and focusing on the provision of better service are vital first steps. But what is missing, even in some of the more service-oriented personnel offices, is a focus on *strategic human resources management*. This focus aligns the human resources function with the core mission and the strategic planning processes of the organization (Anthony, Perrewe and Kacmar, 1993). The client becomes not the individual manager but the organization as a whole, and the human resources function is closely integrated with planning, budgeting, and other management functions. While the private sector has been moving in this direction for some time (Miles and Snow, 1984), the concept is still quite new for public sector organizations (Perry, 1993). Moving to a strategic focus will require a different role for the Office of Personnel Management. For example, the National Performance Review report on OPM envisions it as providing "planning for development of the workforce of the future and identifying strategies for providing the training essential to achieving culture change" (National Performance Review, 1993c). The agency personnel offices in the present study, even those providing good customer service, have yet to make the leap to strategic human resources management. As we shall see later, human resources functions have yet to be fully linked to budget and planning functions in many government agencies. Strategic human resources management is particularly important as organizations make the hard decisions needed to downsize; without use of appropriate workforce planning methods, cuts may have seriously adverse long-term consequences.

The National Performance Review also raises interesting questions in linking deregulation and an increased focus on customer service with structural change; the NPR has a clear bias in favor of decentralized structures. But looking at the four agencies in this study leads one to question such a linkage. The personnel function is not always more responsive if it is decentralized. The centralized personnel offices we have looked at are highly professionalized and service-oriented. In fact, a new organizational culture may be more easily instilled in a more centralized organization.

One way that centralized personnel organizations have been able to provide high-quality service is by moving away from structures based on narrowly specialized functions and toward work teams that provide coordinated service to managers. In such organizations, the need for both flexibility and coordination has led to operations structured "around core points of integration, not based on subfunctions such as classification and pay" (Perry, 1993, p. 66). Crosstraining has also been conducted, so that individual employees, often working as teams, can handle both staffing and classification.

One issue that is ignored by many proposing reforms—as well as by academic observers—is the role of shadow personnel offices. Yet many of the reforms proposed could have the effect of increasing reliance on shadows. That will be the case if personnel functions are overcentralized and the centralized offices are not seen as providing adequate customer service. Sharp cuts in the staff of formal personnel offices may lead to reduced levels of services and, hence, increased reliance on shadow personnel offices. But greater dependence on shadows is also the likely outcome if responsibility for personnel functions is delegated to line managers who do not want it and are unsure what to do with it. Reformers need to look carefully at the costs, both in dollars and in quality of service, of using shadow personnel offices that duplicate the functions of existing personnel staff.

Chapter Four

The Labyrinth of
the Hiring Process

In previous chapters, we have examined the context within which managers operate—the culture of their organizations, their backgrounds and training, and their own definitions of their roles. We have also looked at the backgrounds and role definitions of the personnel staff with whom they work. In the next five chapters, we turn to how managers deal with specific challenges and how the context we have discussed affects their responses. While our main focus will be on personnel issues, it is important to remember that the formal systems governing management in the public sector do not operate in isolation; personnel, budgeting, and even procurement systems are linked in a variety of ways, so few issues are wholly civil service issues. The two we begin with, hiring in this chapter, and firing in Chapter Five, are largely personnel problems, but even here, as we shall see, budget considerations intervene. In the later chapters, we explore issues where these linkages are more direct: setting pay, use of contractors, and cutback management.

The System Managers Love to Hate

As we saw in Chapter Three, the formal civil service is hardly well-loved by managers. They see it, accurately, as having been designed to limit their discretion. Managers resent the fact that they so obviously are not trusted, and they find that working within such constraining rules means that everything they attempt requires more of their energy and time than it should.

It may be argued that this formal system is, in reality, only a minor constraint, because aggressive, astute managers find ways around it. They learn how to manipulate the system to get what they want. The manipulation may entail significant transaction costs, but in the end, effective managers will achieve most of their goals, despite the formal constraints. This chapter explores the question of how constraining the civil service system actually is and how managers cope with those constraints, examining the part of the system most frustrating for managers, the hiring process.

One might expect that most managers in the government have, over time, learned how the hiring process works and have discovered ways, formal or informal, to work within or end run the system. In fact, as I talked to managers in the four organizations in this study, I found that the picture is more complex. Rather than seeing common patterns of coping in all four organizations, I found that organizational context makes a difference; managers in the four agencies defined their roles in the hiring process differently. As a result, they had disparate perceptions of how constraining the system was, and they developed very different coping strategies.

I begin with an introduction to the complexities of the hiring process in the federal government, to give the reader a sense of the formal constraints within which managers have to work. I then turn to a discussion of the differing roles that managers and personnel offices play in the hiring process in the individual agencies, and finally, I show how these differences have led to very distinct managerial strategies.

The Formal Hiring System

The formal system for hiring federal employees is quite complex. An individual can be hired in a wide variety of ways. This complexity can be a source of confusion both for managers and for job applicants (U.S. Merit Systems Protection Board, 1994), but it can also be an asset to creative, aggressive managers seeking to manipulate the system. The various hiring procedures (technically referred to as *hiring authorities*) differ in their degree of centralization, in their criteria for selection, and in whether they are designed to hire individuals or whole groups of new employees. Let us look at each dimension in turn.

At the most centralized end of the hiring continuum are the tests administered nationwide by the Office of Personnel Management (OPM) for entry-level professional positions, known as Administrative Careers with America (ACWA).[1] Applicants apply directly to OPM, which tests them and sends a list of the top candidates to the agency doing the hiring. (For a more detailed description of both ACWA and other entry-level hiring methods, see U.S. Merit Systems Protection Board, 1994).

External hiring at more senior levels (such as GS-11 and GS-12) of these same occupations is generally also controlled by OPM, which announces openings in an agency and reviews the qualifications of applicants.[2] The review in this case is based not on a formal written test but on the background of the applicant (known in the personnel field as T&E, for training and experience) as reflected in his or her SF (standard form) 171. When OPM advertises a specific opening and rates candidates on the basis of qualifications for that position, the process is referred to as *case examining* (that is, it is done on a case-by-case basis).

When the process of examining is controlled by OPM, the agencies and individual line managers play a smaller role. Even if they successfully recruit a candidate, for example, they may have trouble actually hiring that candidate if he or she does not turn up at the top of the list generated by OPM.

On the other hand, for some positions, OPM has given authority to agencies to manage the process themselves. Increased decentralization of the hiring process is one of the legacies of the Civil Service Reform Act of 1978 (Ban and Marzotto, 1984). Particularly for those occupations that are unique to a specific agency, individual agencies are delegated authority to advertise positions and to conduct an unassembled exam, that is, to review applicants' qualifications and to rate and rank the applicants without going through OPM. In such cases, the responsibility—and workload—of the agency personnel office increases dramatically, and there is greater potential for line managers to play an active role in the process.

Hiring methods also differ in terms of the selection criteria that are applied. For the ACWA, people are ranked on the basis of their scores on a written test. In case examining, a person's education and experience are assessed. At the time of this study, the latter process still made use of the SF-171, which was employed throughout the federal government. In either case, candidates are compared and placed on a ranked list. The *rule of three* is applied, meaning that managers can choose only from among the top three names on the list. Veterans preference also applies, giving veterans extra points and thus placing them higher on the list.

But there are a few methods that permit the hiring of a person if he or she meets some minimum qualification, without any requirement to compare that individual with others. These methods are designed to be simple and fast. First, in occupations where there is a shortage of applicants or in geographical areas where the government is having trouble recruiting, agencies can receive what is known as *direct hire authority*. Direct hire means that candidates who meet the qualifications for the job can be hired on the spot, without any competition. This approach is predicated on the assumption that there are more openings than applicants, so that all qualified applicants can be hired.

In the past, direct hire authority was frequently tied to job fairs; at such fairs, agencies could make offers on the spot or even for some period of time after the fair. But during the time of the study, at least partly in response to criticism from the U.S. General Accounting Office (1990a), OPM tightened up the procedures for job fairs. Agencies were no longer allowed to hire on the spot; rather, they had to conduct an unassembled exam (that is, to rate the candidates identified at the job fair) and to apply veterans preference.[3] This change greatly increased the workload of agency personnel offices participating in job fairs and wiped out the primary advantage of such fairs, the ability to hire people quickly.

Another route for hiring that does not require comparison among candidates is the Outstanding Scholars Program, which allows agencies to hire without any additional examination a qualified entry-level applicant who has a 3.5 grade point average from college or who is in the top 10 percent of his or her graduating class. This program was mandated by the courts as an affirmative-action vehicle, to make it easier to hire minority candidates.

Similar in their effect are *special appointing authorities*, which are designed to increase the hiring of such groups as disabled veterans, the mentally retarded, the physically handicapped, and students at predominantly black colleges. There are over a dozen such special appointing authorities. Among the less well-known are programs that allow agencies to hire noncompetitively people leaving the Peace Corps or leaving staff positions in Congress or the federal judiciary.

Hiring methods that do not require ranking a group of candidates have several advantages. Speed is one. Another is the ease with which managers can recruit individuals and then bring them on board. However, these methods raise questions about how well the principle of open competition is being honored and about the potential for abuse, for hiring friends or political cronies.

Finally, while most hiring is of individuals to fill specific slots, there are a number of programs designed to bring people into entry-level positions as a group. The method of selection may be traditional (that is, a test or unassembled examination), but recruitment—by either OPM or agencies—is done broadly, and when the group is hired, they may be trained formally as a *class*. One of the best-known of such programs, the Presidential Management Internship (PMI) program is managed centrally by OPM, which interviews candidates and selects the finalists. The shortlisted candidates then interview with specific agencies, which make the final selection. These are fast-track trainee positions designed for people who have just completed master's degrees; they typically include rotation through several positions, as well as seminars that bring together the "PMIs" from all participating agencies. Several agencies have designed similar programs for their own use; the agency hires a whole class of candidates at one time, trains them as a class, and often rotates them through several positions to give them broad exposure to the work of the agency. I will discuss some of these programs in more depth below.

Who's on First? Recruiting and Hiring

These bare-bones descriptions give little sense of how each hiring mechanism works in practice. The key issue here is: what are the respective roles of the line manager and the agency personnel staff in the hiring process? One thing that is clear from my research is that, in the absence of formal, systemwide guidance specifying who does what, each agency has developed its own approaches to the tasks of recruiting and hiring. And there is some indication in prior research that this unclear division of labor is causing problems. We saw in Chapter Three that personnelists rate their own performance more highly than do the line managers in their agencies. Nowhere do these perceptions differ more than in the area of recruiting and hiring. Seventy-eight percent of personnelists interviewed by the Merit Systems Protection Board rate the service they provide in these areas as good or excellent; only 36 percent of their clients, the line managers, agree (U.S. Merit Systems Protection Board, 1993, p. 15). At least some of this dramatic difference may be a result of confusion about the appropriate roles of managers and personnelists in the recruiting and hiring process.

Who is responsible for going out and finding good candidates? Many of the formal mechanisms, particularly those that require centralized testing by OPM, are essentially passive: OPM posts openings in its own offices and in employment offices—either locally or nationally, depending on the openings. Or OPM periodically offers a formal test, such as ACWA. This approach, in contrast to direct hiring, assumes that there are so many people who want to work for the government that aggressive recruiting is unnecessary. But many observers see this approach as dangerously outdated. They point to the declining number of people entering the labor market, to the increased competition for employees with technical training, and to the growing pay gap between the public and the private sectors. All these factors are making it harder for the federal government to attract the people it needs (Levine and Kleeman, 1986; U.S. Office of Personnel Management, 1988; National Commission on the Public Service, 1990). Even though, at the time of the study, some agencies were laying off employees, others were experiencing difficulty in finding good entry-level staff.

Another factor led to agencies becoming directly involved in recruiting. Prior to 1980, OPM administered a single examination, the Professional and Administrative Career Examination (PACE) for entry-level hiring into more than one hundred professional and administrative positions. That examination was dropped in the closing days of the Carter administration in response to a lawsuit charging that the exam discriminated against minorities. But the new ACWA tests were not introduced until 1990. As a result, for close to a decade, agencies were permitted to use a special hiring authority, Schedule B, for entry-level hiring (Ban and Ingraham, 1988). Under Schedule B, agencies were able to do their own recruiting and to rate and rank candidates using unassembled exams that worked much like the delegated examining process described above.[4] Thus, at the same time as agencies received broad delegated examining authorities for technical jobs, they also were able to use a similar process for entry-level positions. In short, for the first time, they were responsible for finding their own job candidates. Even though this authority has since been taken away, it gave agencies and line managers years of experience with a decentralized, flexible approach to hiring.

Agencies, then, were faced with two questions: whether to recruit candidates aggressively and how to assign responsibility for that task. An examination of the four organizations in this study shows that agencies answer these questions very differently, and that the answers depend on a number of factors. The organizational culture and management style of the agencies, as well as the culture of their personnel offices, play an important role. But the answers to these questions are also driven by resources; in organizations that are cutting back, aggressive recruiting is not a high priority.

Further, organizational responses are determined in part by the external labor market. If an adequate supply of job candidates is finding its way to the agency's doors without active recruiting, then, not surprisingly, there is little demand to increase recruiting. Active recruiting is therefore likely to focus on those specific occupations or geographical areas where the agency is having trouble filling positions.

Conflicting Perceptions of Recruiting Activity

Agencies may make a formal decision to assign primary recruiting responsibility to the personnel office, to line managers, or to both, or a division of labor may emerge gradually over time. Both line managers and personnel offices may be either active or passive in relation to recruiting. This produces four possibilities or models, as shown in Figure 4.1. In model 1, both managers and personnelists play a passive role. If no one actively recruits, then either the agency is not hiring or it is making do with those applicants who either see the formal job announcements or take a standard test, such as ACWA. Model 2 is to assign the task of recruiting to personnel specialists. Managers then hire from the lists of candidates the personnel office has generated. Model 3 is for the managers to take the lead in recruiting. The role of the personnel office in this case is to process the papers or to help in finding ways to actually bring on board the people identified by the managers. Model 4 is

Figure 4.1. Agency Division of Labor in Recruitment.

		Personnel Office Role	
		Passive	Active
Line Managers' Role	Passive	Model 1 Personnel passive Managers passive (FCS)	Model 2 Personnel active Managers passive (APHIS)
	Active	Model 3 Personnel passive Managers active (EPA)	Model 4 Personnel active Managers active (Navy?)

for both managers and personnelists to play active roles in recruiting, either in partnership or, if they have not coordinated their efforts, possibly falling over each others' feet.

Do we see clear patterns, with agencies falling consistently into one of these cells? This question proved to be somewhat harder to answer than I had expected. On reviewing all the discussions about the hiring process that had taken place with both managers and personnelists, I found that the two groups have, in some cases, almost diametrically opposite views of who is doing what. I call this a *mirror-image phenomenon*, and it comes through most clearly at the two Department of Agriculture sites. Specifically, at FCS, most managers say that they are actively recruiting, but the personnelists are mixed in their views of the managers, with a majority saying that managers are not actively involved in recruiting. Conversely, personnelists feel that they are taking an active role, but managers strongly disagree and feel that the personnelists are not doing enough. At APHIS, the same mirror-image pattern holds true for the managers; a majority see themselves as actively involved, but personnelists do not see it that way. However, both groups are in agreement that the personnel office (or a specialized unit) does play an active role in recruiting.

At EPA, in contrast, virtually no one sees managers as passive; everyone recognizes that managers are actively recruiting. But there is disagreement over the personnelists' role: they see themselves as actively recruiting, but the managers see them differently. There is so little hiring going on at Navy that there are few mentions of active recruiting and it is hard to classify the agency. But the mirror-image phenomenon is not evident there; both groups tend to mention active involvement in the process—currently almost entirely internal recruiting—by both managers and personnelists.

Model 1: Passive Recruiting

It is clear from my interviews that in several agencies, there has never been a formal assignment of responsibility for recruiting. What has sometimes emerged is a system where each side has unclear and conflicting expectations of the other, where each side points at the other and says, "Why aren't they doing what they should?" This is particularly true at FCS, which, from the vantage point of this outside observer, falls more closely into cell one in Figure 4.1 than any of the other agencies. Neither group is consistently taking the lead in recruiting, and neither is particularly aggressive in its recruiting efforts. This is not to say that there is no recruiting going on at FCS, but that, compared to other agencies, FCS is not particularly active or innovative in its approaches.

That situation does not necessarily call for criticism. FCS is a small agency that has shrunk significantly over the past decade, taking its cuts through attrition rather than layoffs. Consequently, hiring has been at a very low level for a long time—often below replacement. In such an environment, an attempt to develop major recruitment programs within the personnel office is unrealistic. Most managers, for their part, have had little motivation to expand their own recruitment efforts. FCS managers most often spoke about taking an active role in trying to recruit secretaries, who are in very short supply at all agencies. Particularly at headquarters, managers explained this specifically in terms of the market: "In recruiting for the clerical and administrative types, the walk-in candidates usually are of such poor quality that you often waste your time if you don't go out and start looking yourself. We make fun of a manager here who goes to K-Mart and hires clerk-typists because that was his only solution. So, well, . . . some of them worked out."

Further, managers at FCS were not terribly knowledgeable about the intricacies of the hiring system. For example, one of the participants in a group interview for midlevel managers told me: "I found out this morning that we had something new, the ACWA, or something. That's the first time I heard of it. What I know about it I read in the *Washington Post*, not from our personnel people."

It turned out that most of his colleagues were no better informed. These are not, on the whole, savvy managers who have learned how to manipulate the system. Some of them do know about the Outstanding Scholars Program and have made use of it. And FCS has taken advantage of the hiring authority that allows noncompetitive hiring of ex–Peace Corps volunteers (as is quite evident by the Peace Corps posters and artifacts decorating a number of offices). But overall, FCS managers are not aggressive about recruiting. A staffing specialist told me that she could usually get a line manager to go along on college visits, but that "just in very rare situations do they recruit on their own." The long hiring freezes have had the expected effect on such college visits. As a manager in the personnel office explained, "We still try to get out and make contacts with colleges, but it's hard when you can't hire."

However, those managers who expect to have significant numbers of openings are using more active approaches. One person told me about recruiting at public policy schools, going to conferences and job fairs, and networking with colleagues at universities. But the same person explained that one of the main reasons there were not more such efforts was the problem discussed in Chapter Two— the worker-manager. As this person put it, "It takes time, and we do a better job when we're not quite as heavily loaded up with our program work." Managers who are stretched thin doing the work of the program often do not have the time or energy to build networks, even if they can come up with the travel money to go to the conferences. Successive waves of attrition only make the problem worse, because as organizations become more short-staffed, pressures on managers to take on more program work become even greater.

To summarize: The contradictory perceptions of who is actually recruiting at FCS are understandable. Recruiting is spotty, both because so little hiring is going on and because the agency has not given clear signals to managers (who are often worker-managers) that this is part of their job. A rather passive approach to recruiting has probably not been dysfunctional for FCS over the past decade, but if any parts of the organization have to grow rapidly in the future, the lack of agreement on whose job it is to recruit could cause serious problems.

Model 2: Active Recruiting by the Personnel Office

As the previous discussion mentions, there is some confusion within APHIS about who actually does recruiting as well as about who should be doing it. Nonetheless, from the vantage point of an outside observer, APHIS falls, albeit with some exceptions, into the cell in Figure 4.1 that shows an active role for the personnel office and a more passive role for managers. However, there is an interesting wrinkle: a special unit that is not a part of the personnel office, Recruitment and Development (R&D), has a major responsibility for both external recruitment and employee development. My guess is that in the past APHIS actually fell into cell one (both parties passive), because people told me stories of how recruiting had been "falling between the cracks" and how a recognition of this problem led to the formation of the R&D unit during the large-scale reorganization discussed in Chapter One. The unit was given the mission of increasing the agency's external visibility and improving the quality of new hires.

R&D has been quite successful in creating a range of innovative recruiting and training programs. Two of the most notable programs involve group hiring, one for secretaries and the other for entry-level veterinarians. The first, labeled Operation Jump Start, was designed because of the critical shortage of secretaries and the poor quality of many new secretaries in the agency. The program aggressively recruits potential secretaries, hires them as temporaries, and puts them, as a group, through a seven-week formal training program in everything from office procedures to interpersonal skills. They are then placed on a thirty-day detail in an office that has a vacancy. At the end of this time, if the supervisor and trainee are both satisfied, the individual is converted to a permanent position. The program received almost unanimous raves from managers. Their only complaints were that there were not enough graduates to go around, or that people were so good that they were eventually lost to other agencies that could offer higher grade levels. But this is clearly an example of a group hiring program where both aggressive recruiting and the ability to train new hires as a group have led to an improvement in quality in an occupation where competent employees are in very short supply.

APHIS has a similar success story in its program for hiring entry-level veterinarians, another position where quality had been a problem. In the past, when there was an opening for a veterinarian in a local office, the position was advertised locally, attracting more often than not a local vet who might be reasonably competent but who typically was unwilling to accept reassignment later on. The Public Veterinary Practice Careers (PVPC) program made several changes in the hiring process. Recruitment became national, producing a large pool from which to select. Candidates were chosen after an extensive screening process, one of whose criteria was a willingness to accept job mobility. And new hires were brought in and trained as a class.

Most managers see this combination of aggressive recruiting and formal training as having led to improved quality. Further, because PVPC recruits are required to sign a mobility agreement and because the training gives them a broad, agencywide perspective, there is hope that they will be on a fast track and will provide the future leadership of the agency. Further, hiring in groups has made it much easier to take affirmative-action goals into account; the incoming PVPC recruits are more diverse than those hired individually in the past. In short, this program, too, seems to be working. In fact, a number of federal agencies now recruit and train "classes" of new employees.

The role of R&D in recruitment is widely recognized; hence the widespread agreement among managers and personnelists that both the personnel office (that is, the Field Servicing Office and its small D.C. satellite office) and R&D played an active role in recruiting. Where there was more disagreement was over the role of managers in the process. This disagreement reflects two issues: first, the fact that the role of managers is in flux, and second, that the role of a manager varies according to position.

Many managers say they do little active recruiting, but they acknowledge that expectations are changing. For example, one midlevel manager told me, "The agency encourages us to [become active in recruiting]—there's a whole new push in the agency in recruitment." But he said that, in fact, he had done very little.

R&D lays emphasis not just on recruitment for current vacancies but on the development of a long-term marketing perspective that includes building relationships with individuals and organizations that might become sources for future hires. One element of this strategy was a program that trained one hundred managers nationwide as recruiters. The group received a full week of training in recruiting techniques, emphasizing recruitment on campus and through professional organizations. Most of the managers trained in this program have remained active, which has reinforced the view in the agency that managers should be playing a central role in recruitment.

Nonetheless, some managers still do not see this as an important part of their role. Their attitude is not surprising, given what this study has found about the way they define that role (see Chapter Two). We have seen that APHIS managers gave moderate emphasis to the human relations part of their job but put much less stress on the external, entrepreneurial aspects. Yet the latter contain the skills the managers need to go out and sell the agency to future employees. Some personnelists expressed frustration that managers were not picking up this role. For example, one person told me that she had encouraged the area veterinarians in charge, who head local offices, to play a more active role in recruiting, but that "a lot of them just have no intention of getting involved." Further, a number of APHIS managers would agree with the personnel specialist who told me, "My sense is that no matter what we do, the whole system is a mystery to managers." APHIS managers were, in fact, more likely than those at other agencies to say that they did not understand the system and to express lack of confidence in their ability to make a good selection.

Nevertheless, some managers are very actively engaged in recruiting. They are developing their own networks and finding people through a variety of sources, including colleges and professional associations. One explanation is that these people are recruiting for higher-level technical or managerial positions. While they may leave entry-level recruiting to R&D, they often say that neither R&D nor FSO knows how to recruit for technical occupations. Thus, there are mixed reactions, reflective of the role confusion in recruiting; while some managers accept the responsibility for higher-level recruiting willingly, many others gripe that this is not their job and that someone else (either R&D or FSO) should be doing it.

Personnelists, on the other hand, say that managers really should be doing this for themselves. As a personnelist at FSO told me, the overall picture is mixed: "Some programs are good about doing their own recruiting, and others don't. They should. They're the experts. Since we're centrally located, we don't know where to go in their areas. . . . A lot of managers need help in how to recruit."

At FCS, we saw that the role stress experienced by worker-managers affected their ability to recruit. This issue did not come out at APHIS. There, the pattern was somewhat more reflective of the pseudo-supervisor problem: the tendency of top managers to keep control of the hiring process, control which got in the way and slowed down the process. Several people criticized the propensity of top management to micromanage hiring. One supervisor in a group interview described the obstacles his unit is facing in trying to bring on someone from another agency: "We can't get it through the director of HRD [human resources development], because he has to have control over it. And the deputy administrator has to okay it. We have a GM-14 chief that has the authority to make that selection, and he can't do it, because they're not permitted to do it. . . . If you're going to give [someone] authority to run a staff, then why can't you give them authority to hire the people they want to do the work for the staff?"

To summarize: At APHIS, there is aggressive recruiting for some positions by the personnel office (FSO) and by the recruitment and development unit, but considerable variation in the level of activity of line managers, some of whom still do not see recruitment as part of their job.

Model 3: Aggressive Recruiting by Line Managers

Not surprisingly, the picture at EPA is different. As we saw earlier, both managers and personnelists agree that EPA managers play a very active role in recruiting but have some disagreement about personnel's role in the process. Why are EPA managers so active?

There are several possible explanations. One is rooted in the culture of the agency, discussed in Chapter One, and in the typical management style at EPA, discussed in Chapter Two. EPA managers have a deep commitment to the environmental mission of the agency. They are also subject to intense pressure, both from externally imposed deadlines and from the aggressive, entrepreneurial values of the adhocracy culture. Together, these forces lead them to push the recruitment system rather than wait passively for the personnel office to find staff for them. The personnel specialists recognize the pressure on line managers. As one explained, "We have so many vacancies to fill, and they are so under the gun that they are required to be more proactive than [Department of Agriculture] managers."

Further, EPA managers are likely to see human resources issues as important aspects of their job. This was particularly true in the regional office, as we saw in Chapter Two. But we also explored in that chapter the issue of the worker-manager and saw that, at EPA, second- and third-level managers were more likely to mention the human resources aspects of their positions. Recruitment patterns reflect this tendency: it is often the higher-level managers who are most active in working their networks to find candidates.

This pattern of active management recruiting is also a function of the kinds of jobs EPA is recruiting for. The group hiring programs at APHIS, discussed above, are designed to bring in fairly large numbers of entry-level staff. While EPA sometimes hires substantial numbers of staff at one time, it is more often hiring individuals with scientific, technical, or legal backgrounds. These are not easy people to find, and there is a general feeling among managers that personnel either does not know how to find them or does not have the time and energy to devote to active recruiting. In some cases, managers are just as happy to do it themselves, but others gripe about the lack of support from personnel. As one senior-level person put it: "Finding people is up to each office individually, and it takes a great deal of time. I would like them to be going out and recruiting and screening candidates, but it would require them to understand our programs."

This comment goes to the heart of the conflicts over the role of the personnel office in recruiting and hiring. As we saw in Chapter Three, one source of tension between managers and personnelists was that the latter did not always understand the work of the organizations they were servicing. In fact, many personnelists agree that they are not qualified to take the lead in recruiting, particularly for technical positions, and feel that it is quite legitimate for line managers to take on this role. I asked a personnel specialist whether managers identified most of the candidates themselves. He replied: "Yes. Personnel is the last place managers look for people, but why not? They know what skills they need. What do we have to add? . . . OPM feels unless you put [job candidates] through a lottery, and that's what it is, it's going to be tainted. At least 90 percent [of job candidates] are found by the managers."

Some EPA personnel specialists said that they would like to play a more active role in recruiting, and that they had done so in the past—visiting colleges, for example. But several would agree with the person who said, "We've been so busy this year that we couldn't afford to do this."

In fact, most of the conflict between personnel and line managers at EPA is not over recruiting but over the next step in the process: the screening of applicants to determine whether they meet the qualifications for the jobs. Many managers argued strenuously that personnel staff did not have the skill to evaluate candidates for technical jobs. For example, here is the complaint of one first-line supervisor:

> [There are] people at various levels at OPM and then in our office going through [SF-171s] who don't really understand my responsibilities and my job, and I wouldn't expect them to. I mean, how could they understand everybody's job in EPA? And yet they're making a decision on who's qualified. . . . Three or four years ago, I

wanted to hire a program analyst, and the cert [the list of candidates from which the manager can select] comes back, and at the top of the cert is a guy whose job title on his 171 is "loss prevention specialist." Here I am, I want a budget analyst. What is the guy? He's a store detective, out from some department store in the Midwest. The guy's probably capable and intelligent, but he had no experience related to what I was doing, and he should not have been on the top of that list. You end up with results that make no sense.

Yet one could say that personnelists are damned if they do and damned if they don't. Some managers criticize them for doing a bad job of screening applicants, and others for not screening at all. Apparently in response to some of this criticism, personnel is sometimes giving managers more choice than they want. Another supervisor in the same group interview told a very different story from the one just quoted: "My certs came in. Personnel did not rank the candidates; they just kind of shipped over all the 171s, and because I had advertised 5, 7, [and] 9 to 11 [grade levels], I had four different sets of certs. I must have had at least sixty-five applications. . . . I was not happy with [this list] because they were not screened. If there was anything in their 171 about doing administrative work, it was in the cert. But I did get a large amount of candidates to select from."

To summarize: EPA fits the model of active managers well; however, stresses and conflicts arise over the proper role of the personnel office in the hiring process.

Model 4: Active Recruiting by Both Line Managers and Personnel

It is tempting to say that the Navy fits into the fourth quadrant of Figure 4.1, if only for the sake of symmetry. However, the evidence is thin because so little active recruiting has been done during the recent years of contraction. Much of the discussion therefore centers on past practice. Managers at Navy sound more like those at EPA than like Department of Agriculture managers when they talk about recruiting and hiring. They stress that, particularly when hiring engineers and other technical staff, they need to take an active, aggressive role in the process. An SES member described how he operated: "I have never in all my years had a problem in getting staff, because I go out and I beat the bushes in schools, I knock on doors of firms, I do anything I can to steal, impress, whatever is illegal—like the Brits did to us before the War of 1812. . . . I never use CCPO [Consolidated Civilian Personnel Office]. The biggest mistake you could make . . . is to let them do your recruiting for you if you are looking for engineers."

Here, too, much of the discussion of active recruiting came from second- and third-level managers, not from first-line supervisors. This pattern clearly arises from the phenomenon of the worker-manager and sometimes from that of the pseudo-supervisor. But it is also a reflection of current budget constraints. Because of hiring freezes, and because of the Navy's Manage to Payroll (MTP) system, discussed in Chapter Six, authority to approve hiring is held at a high level (at least third level, and often fourth). As a result, most of the gripes from Navy managers were about budgetary controls, not about the civil service system.

Further, during a time of cutbacks and hiring freezes, it does not make much sense to maintain extensive recruitment programs. In the past, the Navy, like APHIS, had developed its own group hiring programs and internships in a number of fields. For example, a number of interviewees praised the Engineer in Training (EIT) program, which has had a very successful track record for a number of years in bringing in talented individuals, training them, and placing them within the organization. There was also a Contract Intern program and a logistics internship. But most of these programs have shrunk in the current hard times. As one person told me, "The EIT program is still up and running, but it's staggering. It's only for those that you have in the program now. Nobody in the program now is going to be dropped from it. But no new people are coming in."

In short, the Navy gives us tantalizing glimpses of what the situation might look like if both managers and personnelists were actively involved in recruiting. On the one hand, such an approach can be very successful if the two groups coordinate their efforts. On the other hand, there is also a risk that they will be pulling in different directions or falling over each other. There was a slight hint of such a problem when personnelists talked about the lack of commitment on the part of line managers to affirmative action in recruitment and hiring. Several people told me about a meeting with top NAVSEA managers at which affirmative action was discussed. As one described it: "They said they did not know what the goals are. I was just floored. Where have they been? Were they asleep? I think they just haven't put much attention on it, but it's going to shift. I think it's going to be put into their performance plans. SECNAV [the secretary of the Navy] said, 'You will do this.'"

Aside from demonstrating the top-down management approach in the Navy, the comment makes clear how hard it is—especially in a very large organization—to get everyone to pull in the same direction when managers are out doing their own recruiting. This independent activity also causes problems for the monitoring and record-keeping that CCPO is charged with: "Yes, [managers are going out and recruiting on their own]. A lot more than we are probably aware of. We were trying to get a handle on that in the meeting last week. There's a lot we don't know about, so it's hard to keep EEO [equal employment opportunity] statistics."

To summarize: If we had been looking at the Navy in a period of growth rather than contraction, we might have obtained a fuller picture of what the fourth model, with both managers and the personnel office taking an active role in recruiting, would look like in practice. Even in the current conditions of cutback management, we can get some sense of both the strengths and strains of such an approach.

Looking across all four organizations, one can conclude that there is no single right or wrong way to divide up the responsibilities for recruiting and hiring. In fact, the divisions of labor that have evolved reflect differences in the organizations' cultures, in the styles and role definitions of line managers and personnelists, and also in market conditions—that is, the supply of and demand for specific kinds of employees. But each approach leads to a very different way of relating to the formal civil service system. It is to this issue that we turn next.

What Happens When the Formal System Gets in the Way?

I began this chapter with an implied question: is the civil service a major hindrance to managers, or have they learned how to manipulate the formal system—either working creatively within it or finding ways to circumvent it—so that it is only a minor annoyance? Our examination of the ways managers and personnel offices define their roles in the hiring process allows a nuanced answer to this question. In brief, what we find is that the formal personnel system is more suited to an environment where the personnel office plays an active role and managers are relatively passive. When managers choose to play an active role, that choice almost inevitably creates conflict with the formal system and pressures for managers to use informal means to manipulate the system.

This difference emerged very clearly in my interviews. When I talked to both managers and personnelists at the Department of Agriculture, there was much discussion about creative, aggressive use of all the formal mechanisms the system provided, but there was virtually no mention of informal strategies for beating the system.

What does the formal approach look like? As we saw, it entails aggressive use of the full range of available hiring methods, including requesting all possible delegations from OPM and using them aggressively, and learning about and using all the special appointing authorities discussed above. Examples include the long-standing use by FCS of the authority permitting noncompetitive hiring of Peace Corps alumni (a mechanism occasionally used also by EPA) and noncompetitive hiring for positions classed as bilingual/ bicultural. An example at APHIS is the development of a co-op program for summer interns from the "1890 colleges" (land-grant colleges serving mostly black students) and other colleges whose students are predominantly from minority groups.

Pushing the formal system to its limits requires a knowledge-able, imaginative, and aggressive personnel staff. While managers may learn about formal mechanisms and may push or prompt personnel, in places like APHIS, the pushing tends to be in the opposite direction; what you are likely to hear are stories from personnelists about how they are trying to sell their managers on such programs as co-ops.

But when the personnel office uses the formal system aggressively and when managers are relatively satisfied with what the formal system gives them and do not accept the idea that active recruiting is part of their job, they do not feel a need to learn the ins and outs of the system in order to find ways around it. Virtually the only discussion of such informal approaches that I heard at the two Department of Agriculture sites touched on ways to avoid use of the universally unpopular ACWA exams. ACWA is disliked by managers because it is seen as too time-consuming and because the candidates referred by OPM are often no longer interested or not suitable (U.S. Merit Systems Protection Board, 1994).

EPA managers, in contrast, have clearly defined their roles as including active involvement in recruiting and hiring, but they constantly collide with a system that is not designed to make it easy to bring in the people they recruit. There is, therefore, necessarily a higher level of conflict with the formal system. Further, as we saw in Chapter One, EPA has a culture somewhat less rulebound than that of other agencies and more tolerant of people who challenge the formal rules. As a result, at EPA one sees moderately high levels of creative manipulation of the system—much of it legal, some of it borderline, and some of it clearly over the line but widely sanctioned (people had no compunctions about discussing it in front of their peers).

The Navy falls between EPA and the Department of Agriculture in this respect. Both because its culture is less freewheeling than EPA's and because it was doing little hiring from outside, there were fewer mentions of informal ways to manipulate the system. But Navy managers were clearly more familiar and more comfortable with such strategies than were Department of Agriculture managers.

What kinds of strategies do EPA and Navy managers use to work within or get around the formal civil service system? They fall into two broad categories: first are a variety of ways to make sure you can hire the person you have recruited; second are ways to get around the slowness of the system.

One of the points at which managers come into direct conflict with the formal system is when they have actively recruited and then come to their personnel office and say, "Now how do I actually get this person hired?" In many cases, the formal system makes this very difficult. If the manager wants to hire the person for an entry-level job, the first response is, "Does the person have a 3.5 grade point average so he or she will qualify as an Outstanding Scholar?" If not, the odds of hiring the person via the ACWA exam are often slim. Individuals who have taken ACWA are ranked by grade, and, when an agency wishes to hire off the ACWA list, OPM sends a cert with the top three candidates remaining on the list, so it is difficult to reach qualified candidates who are lower on the list. In some cases, the agency can send a "name request," that is, tell OPM, "If this person is reachable (that is, meets the qualifications), I want him or her on the list." But that is technically difficult if agencies use the Automated Applicant Referral System to request names from the ACWA list. Therefore, strategy one is to change the grade level of the job so that hiring can be done with mechanisms other than ACWA. If employees are hired at the full-performance level (grades GS-9 or 11) rather than at the entry level (grades 5 or 7), examining authority may have been delegated to the agency. Even if the occupation is one for which OPM still examines, a manager will be able to name request. Of course, there is no guarantee that the person will score high enough to be reached, even with a name request, but the odds may be higher than with ACWA. Technically, this is not getting around the system, since both changing the grade level and name requesting are legal, but the fact that name requesting is not always possible with ACWA has the unintended consequence of encouraging astute managers to hire at higher grade levels, with obvious cost implications.

Managers also change grade levels for other reasons, such as trying to get around a veteran who is blocking a list. Veterans preference requires managers to take a veteran at the top of a list or produce a very solid justification for not doing so. Many managers, even some who are veterans themselves, expressed very negative feelings about this constraint. They see it as making the hiring of women and minorities more difficult and as compelling them to hire people who are not necessarily the best qualified. The issue becomes particularly acute when the list includes a *compensable veteran*—typically, a disabled veteran or certain relatives of a disabled or deceased veteran—who has an extra ten points added to his (or occasionally her) score and thus "floats" to the top of the list even though the actual score may have been barely passing.

Thus, strategies for getting around veterans preference are fairly common. As one manager told me, "I'm having a real battle with hiring entry-level management analysts because they're blocked by veterans all over the place, and we're trying to jury-rig ways around." Some managers will postpone hiring, in the hope that someone else will be forced to take the veteran first. Others will change the grade level of the position, but this can be detrimental to the applicant, as the manager cited above explained: "There's one guy we hired with a master's as a management analyst . . . we advertised as a 9 and it was blocked, and we advertised as a 7 and it was blocked, and he finally took a 5 to come in, and it's taken him years to catch up."

One manager even told me about trying to cut a "two for one deal," essentially agreeing to take the veteran (thus opening up the list for everyone else trying to hire) only on condition that he could hire a second person as well.

In addition to changing the grade level of positions and finding other routes around veterans preference, managers take a number of very direct actions to make sure that the person they want turns up on the lists they receive. One of the most common at the time of this study was coaching the individual on how to fill out his or her SF-171. Certain "tricks of the trade" could be relied on to convince the personnel specialist reviewing the form (not usually a technical expert) that the applicant was, indeed, qualified. One of the first concrete accomplishments of the National Performance Review's deregulation efforts was the abolition of the SF-171, but it is not yet clear what agencies will use in its place and whether coaching will still be needed to make sure applicants put the right buzzwords on their résumés.

Helping people fill out a form or prepare a résumé is both legal and commonplace. More in the gray area of legality is the practice of tailoring the job description to the specific qualifications of the candidate. As we saw in the quote at the beginning of the Introduction, this device is far from unknown.

Further, as we have seen, the system permits managers, in most cases, to name request, that is, to make clear to the personnel office or to OPM, who is the preferred candidate. More controversial is the practice of sending back a list (that is, not hiring) if the person the manager wants does not appear on it. When this stratagem was raised at a group interview with EPA first-line supervisors, a heated debate ensued.

First Speaker: I'll be very honest, since I know this is confidential. When I get certs that have been advertised, if I don't see my person's name on it, my first reaction is to cancel the cert and I'll try it again.

Second Speaker: I just throw out to you, though, what if on that cert there happened to be a person who was better qualified than the person who you thought of? Why do you just throw it out?

First Speaker: Because my experience has been that that's not the case. Yes, it may be, but nine-tenths of the time I get a list of people back, and I talk to them, and they have no business being on that cert. . . . I don't bother any more, because it's a waste of my time.

As this discussion makes clear, there is significant disagreement among managers, at EPA and elsewhere, about the legitimacy of ignoring the requirement for real competition. The debate centers on the question of whether it is fair to conduct a "wired" search—that is, a sham search undertaken when a candidate has already been preselected.

The second major front on which managers have developed coping strategies is in the area of procedural delays. This was a source of constant frustration at all agencies, but particularly at EPA. Estimates of how long it took to hire someone from outside government ranged from four months to eight, with the mean about six. This is considerably longer than the average time OPM found in a recent study for appointments of candidates from outside the government from a civil service certificate (a list of candidates provided by OPM or the agency personnel office) (U.S. Office of Personnel Management, 1992b). OPM reports an average time of almost three months (86.5 days) for such appointments across all the agencies surveyed, but 97.7 days in Department of Defense agencies. One reason managers may perceive the process taking longer is that they include in their estimates the time needed for internal agency approvals from higher-level line managers or from budget offices. In fact, when resources are tight, obtaining budget approval may be a much higher hurdle than going through the formal civil service hiring process.

Whatever the reason for hiring delays, they mean that a position remains unfilled for months, thus increasing the workload on everyone else in the unit. The effort required to bring on outstanding individuals is particularly great because they have to be convinced to wait around for months. Even the most aggressive managers have not always succeeded in getting around this roadblock, and they gripe about the good candidates they lose because of it. Of course, not all delays are caused by the civil service or by slow processing in the personnel office.

Managers deal with the long delays in the hiring system in several ways. First, as one personnel specialist put it, "they make a beeline to direct hire" or to use any other ways they can find to speed up the process. For example, many interviewees mentioned bringing in recruits through job fairs. For some time, OPM was giving agencies direct-hire authority so that they could make an on-the-spot offer to anyone who came to a job fair and met the qualifications for a position. This authority was fairly generous: the agency often had a ninety-day window after the fair in which it could hire a suitable candidate. Naturally, managers who wanted to hire a particular individual would tell him or her to wait until there was a job fair, at which point the hire could be made, sometimes without the individual's actually attending the fair. The changes in the job fair process described earlier in this chapter have, from the manager's perspective, eliminated most of its timeliness.

In general, managers will look not just for direct hire opportunities but for the path of least resistance in hiring. For example, in the Navy, one manager told me that since it had become harder to hire nonengineers (in part because of ACWA), positions were now designed for engineers. Other managers try to "game" the system by figuring out which method is fastest at any time—promoting from within, moving people laterally (either inside the agency or from another agency), or hiring from outside. Several interviewees told me about limiting a search to internal candidates to speed up the process, and one described bringing someone in laterally from another agency, which took about a month.

A different set of strategies focused on ways to bring people on immediately while waiting to find a way to hire them. One that was mentioned by several sources was to hire people as secretaries; once they had met the time-in-grade requirement of ninety days, they were eligible to compete for professional positions. Another strategy is to bring the person on as a temporary while waiting for a permanent position to open. The individual, meanwhile, gains useful experience that will help him or her qualify for the permanent position. But while it is perfectly legal to bring people in as secretaries, hiring them as temps in the hope of then being able to hire them permanently is considered an improper use of the temporary authority, and furthermore, it does not always work. I heard of instances where the manager was unable to convert the individual to permanent status and lost that employee.

Finally, a couple of interviewees at EPA told me about a strategy that is even further over the line: getting a contractor to employ someone while he or she is waiting to be hired by the agency, so that the person can begin work immediately in the guise of contractor staff. Managers recognize that this is an abuse of the system, but they feel driven to it in order to get the job done. In fact, one person told me that his organization was under investigation by the inspector general's office because of abuses of contracting procedures.

To summarize: At agencies where managers take an active role in recruiting, the rigidities of the system virtually force them either to learn how to stretch the system to its fullest limits or to find ways around it, some within the letter (if not the spirit) of the law, a few clearly illegal, and some in a gray area in the middle.

Conclusions

Proposals to reform the hiring process address many of the problems discussed here. The National Performance Review report *Reinventing Human Resource Management* (1993d) defines the "greatest failing of the hiring system" as "lack of managerial involvement in the front-end recruitment and evaluation of candidates for employment—in other words, lack of accountability" (p. 11). From the National Academy of Public Administration report of 1983 to the National Performance Review of 1993, reformers have emphasized the need for maximum delegation of hiring authority to the agencies. In fact, the National Performance Review proposes abolishing central registers and standard application forms and letting agencies establish their own recruitment and examining programs for any position, under broad guidance from OPM. While most of these proposals will require congressional action, OPM, as we have seen, has already moved to abolish mandatory use of the SF-171, the lengthy standard application form used for years throughout the federal government.

What light can the analysis in this chapter shed on the appropriateness or likely success of such reforms? First, the current system is clearly interpreted and used differently from one organization to another. The issue here does not center on individual differences among managers—it is not that some are brighter, more aggressive, or cleverer in finding ways around the rules. Rather, managerial roles and methods vary according to organization, in large part because of differences in organizational culture. Reforms that reflect agency differences rather than forcing all agencies to use the same procedures make sense.

Second, the civil service system is a significant constraint on managers, but the managers who chafe under it the most are clearly those who try to play an active role—in this case, in recruiting and hiring. Even if they succeed in finding ways through or around the system, the transaction costs can be substantial. Further, from the managers' perspective, the system often succeeds in limiting their discretion and in creating barriers to the hiring of people they have actively recruited. The more aggressive managers are probably the most effective at pushing the system, but they are also those who will make most use of increased flexibility in a reformed, decentralized system. To assume that all managers are chafing at the bit, eager to take on more responsibility in recruiting and hiring, is unrealistic. If active involvement by line managers is necessary for the success of decentralized systems, then agencies will need not only to train managers in the technical aspects of the process but to redefine the role of managers within the organization. This may involve looking at the problems created by worker-managers and pseudo-supervisors, who have either no time or no clear authority to take on the tasks of actively recruiting and screening candidates.

Further, handing off to the agencies all responsibility for recruiting and testing will increase dramatically the workload of agency personnel offices. In the current budget situation, agencies are unlikely to get more personnel staff to handle the increase (in fact, they are likely to lose personnel staff), so the result could be an overburdened staff and greater delays in processing time. This could be a particularly serious problem at small agencies. The NPR suggests that OPM could continue to provide examining services on a voluntary basis. In fact, the workload issues may mean that many agencies would continue to use OPM services for some time to come.

Reforms that give more discretion to managers also raise the specter of increased abuse. This is not a simple issue. It raises two questions: how effective have the rigid constraints of the current system been in limiting abuse, and how likely is it that abuse would increase if these constraints were eased? In deciding what we should consider abuse, it is useful to apply Shafritz's (1982) distinction between "base fudging" and "noble fudging." Base fudging is classic abuse—the modern-day version of the spoils system, which includes hiring political cronies, personal friends, or relatives. Noble fudging is bending (or even breaking) the rules to cut through red tape and get the work of the organization done—a laudable end even if the means may be somewhat questionable. It is similar to what some scholars have called "bureaucratic entrepreneurship" (Brower and Abolafia, 1994). What the research showed was a fair amount of "noble fudging," particularly in agencies with managers who took an aggressive role in the hiring process. I have said elsewhere that "one of the basic rules of bureaucratic politics is that the more rigid the system, the more imaginative the ways people will find to 'beat' the system" (Ban, 1991b, p. 19). Reforms that provided increased flexibility in the process and greater discretion to managers would reduce the need to game the system and cut the incidence of noble fudging.

But base fudging, which is clearly abuse, is harder to detect, and personal interviews are unlikely to give an accurate estimate of its incidence. Needless to say, no one confessed to engaging in such behavior themselves, although a few people spoke of others in their agency who had hired political cronies or personal friends. But an analysis of survey data collected by the Merit Systems Protection Board (Ban and Redd, 1990) does give one pause. It found dramatic differences among agencies in the extent to which the merit system was abused through such practices as political hiring, the hiring of friends, and race and sex discrimination. While, overall, the percentage of personnelists who reported having seen hiring based on political party affiliation was fairly low—only 7 percent—this figure masked remarkable interagency variation, from a high of 47 percent in the Department of Education to a low of only 1 percent in the Department of the Army (Ban and Redd, 1990, p. 59). In short, the current system, for all its rigidity, has only a spotty record of preventing abuse. In agencies that are highly politicized, or where the culture is tolerant of cronyism, abuse is still far from rare. Once again, the formal system gets used, or misused, differently from agency to agency.

Would loosening the system lead to widespread abuse? The current system has sent mixed messages to managers, but the predominant message has been that any direct involvement by managers, particularly in screening candidates, is seen as potential abuse and is discouraged. This has produced a disconnect: managers are encouraged to recruit actively but are then sometimes unable to hire the people they have recruited. To increase managers' involvement, not just in recruiting but in screening or ranking candidates, would represent a major change. In fact, the U.S. Merit Systems Protection Board (1992b), in a study comparing the U.S. and Canadian public personnel systems, advocated just that. Would managers take advantage of an expanded role to abuse the system? On the one hand, most managers do not want to hire people who are unqualified to do the work. Indeed, the National Performance Review emphasis on holding managers responsible for results makes that even less desirable. But as the NPR (1993d) makes clear, managers will also have to "become even more accountable for adherence to merit principles and for preventing prohibited personnel practices as increased flexibility leads to correspondingly increased performance expectations" (pp. 13–14). The greatest danger for managers is that there may be an increased perception of abuse. For example, an individual passed over for a job may try to hold the manager personally responsible and to charge bias on any one of a number of criteria. The possibility of personal accountability should strongly encourage managers not only to play fair but also to follow agency procedures carefully and to document bases for selection decisions. In short, while there may be a slight increase in real or perceived abuse, a wholesale return to the spoils system is hardly likely.

The question, then, from a policy perspective is: what level of abuse of the system will be tolerated as managers are given more discretion for the purpose of increasing efficiency? The literature on corruption maintains that the optimal level of corruption is not zero, because the costs of eliminating all corruption would be unacceptably high (Klitgaard, 1988). The costs of the current rigid hiring system are so great that providing managers with greater discretion by loosening the constraints of the civil service system is probably worth the risk. However, as we shall see in the following chapters, the civil service system is not the only constraint on managers, and reform of the system will not be the panacea that solves all managers' problems.

Chapter Five

Addressing
Performance Problems

One of the stereotypes about government employees is that they generally do not work very hard and that people can get away with murder because they cannot be fired. It is true that firing a federal employee is not easy; there are extensive legal requirements designed to prevent dismissals based on political beliefs or personal characteristics (Shafritz, Riccucci, Rosenbloom, and Hyde, 1992). These protections are rooted in the underlying civil service value of "neutral competence," which aims to exclude considerations of politics, not just in hiring but also in firing. Nonetheless, it is far from impossible to fire a problem employee or to take other disciplinary action. Some managers shy away from such measures while others act aggressively, either using the formal system or finding more informal ways to deal with problem employees.

What factors explain these differences? Why do some supervisors take action while others do nothing, at least until a situation becomes intolerable? And how do supervisors decide what action to take along the range from very formal to quite informal?

Our discussion begins with a brief examination of the formal system. In the area of performance problems, two of the factors we have previously considered intersect. First, the phenomena of worker-managers and pseudo-supervisors have a bearing on the issue, as do the backgrounds and training of managers. Second, agency cultures and norms for dealing with problem employees influence how individual managers choose to act or not act. These norms are reinforced by the personnel staff known as the employee relations staff, who are responsible for advising line managers how to deal with problem individuals. Both factors help to explain why many managers avoid taking action when faced with such problems, and why managers in different agencies are likely to adopt somewhat contrasting approaches.

Two preliminary points are in order. First, the goal, both for individual managers and for the system as a whole, is not to fire more people but to have a productive workforce. Therefore, judging the caliber of managers or the effectiveness of the system simply on the basis of the number of people fired is invalid (Ban, Goldenberg, and Marzotto, 1982b). Rather, we need to look at the nature of the problem and whether the actions of managers were appropriate to it.

The nature of the problem, in fact, varies dramatically, and that is the second point that must be stressed. In the individual interviews, I asked managers to describe a specific situation they had faced with a problem employee and to recount how they had dealt with it. Not all the responses were easily codable, but of the 128 that were, about 40 percent dealt with what were basically performance problems (that is, work that was clearly inadequate or marginal) and about 22 percent dealt mainly with conduct problems (for example, illegal behavior, sexual harassment, fighting, excessive absenteeism, and other rule infractions). Of course, some of these cases combined elements of both performance and conduct. More surprisingly, close to one-quarter (23 percent) of the problems were personality issues or full-scale mental illness; an additional 12 percent were drug and alcohol abuse cases; and 3 percent were severe personal problems, such as a major illness. Although substance abuse or personal problems may underlie some of the performance or conduct cases, this is still a surprisingly large number of physical, mental, and substance abuse problems.

It is very clear from managers' responses that the strategies chosen by managers for dealing with incompetent employees are different from those applied to cases of chronic illness or obvious personality disorder. We may presume that the formal system is of more help in dealing with some kinds of problems than others. Let us look at how the formal system is supposed to work.

Using the Formal System: Doing It by the Book

By and large, managers do not much like the formal system. Many would agree with an FCS manager, who told me: "The civil service system has probably gone overboard in making it difficult to deal with an employee that doesn't belong. Just to downgrade someone takes a year or a year and a half of documentation and close work with the person. It probably takes a lifetime to fire someone. I can understand needing some constraints, but sometimes it can shackle a supervisor."

In fact, such criticisms of the system are not new. The perception that it was too hard to fire federal employees led to an attempt at reform in the Civil Service Reform Act of 1978, which President Carter sold to the public and to Congress in part by saying it would help to eliminate "deadwood" in government (Ban, Goldenberg, and Marzotto, 1982b). The reform created a two-track system, with different procedures for conduct and performance cases.

Conduct (more accurately, misconduct) cases are technically referred to as *adverse actions*. Offenses range from the minor (occasional absenteeism or lateness) to the very serious (breach of security, theft, or violence). Except for the most extreme cases, when immediate managerial response is possible, the usual procedure is for a manager to follow a process of progressive discipline, both documenting the offense and then moving through a series of sanctions, which are often spelled out in a formal agency table of penalties. These might start with formally counseling the employee. If the problem recurs, the supervisor might then send the employee a formal letter of warning, or a reprimand. A more severe or repeated offense might be grounds for a suspension or demotion. Only after repeated warnings and attempts to get the employee to change could the manager move toward removal.

The process is somewhat different if there is evidence of drug or alcohol abuse or other personal problems. Employees with alcohol or drug dependency may be considered handicapped, and the agency may have a legal obligation to accommodate them (Shaw and Bransford, 1992). In most agencies, supervisors encountering dependency problems are supposed to send the employee for counseling through the agency's employee assistance program (EAP) and to give him or her a reasonable period of time in which to recover (Bruce, 1990).

Most such cases stand up on appeal if there is sufficient documentation of the offense or offenses, if the manager followed the agency table of penalties, and if there is no evidence that the manager was singling out an employee for personal reasons. But documenting a case of excessive absenteeism or lateness, for example, and working through the process step by step can take months.

More problematic is the task of dealing with an employee whose work performance is marginal or unacceptable. The 1978 reforms developed a set of procedures, tied to a new system of performance appraisal, for cases referred to as *performance-based actions*. Under these procedures, agencies developed formal performance standards for the different elements of each employee's job, and some of these were termed "critical," meaning that they were "aspects of each position that are so essential to the job that unacceptable performance of that particular aspect would make it impossible for the employee to perform his [sic] job effectively" (Shaw and Bransford, 1992, p. 84, based on 5 C.F.R. §430.203). Inadequate performance on one or more critical elements is grounds for a performance-based action. In addition, the reforms lowered the standard of evidence for performance-based cases, from the "preponderance of the evidence" standard required for conduct cases to a "substantial evidence" standard, that is, "the degree of evidence which a reasonable person could accept when considering the record as a whole" (Shaw and Bransford, 1992, p. 82).

Did these reforms actually make it easier to deal with poor performers? Some would say yes, because of the lower standard of evidence in these cases (Shaw and Bransford, 1992), but the people I interviewed were not so sure. Most managers still found the process daunting in its length and complexity. And at least some of the personnel staff working in this area felt that the reforms had actually made things worse because the process is now more legalistic. As one told me:

> It was easier to take performance actions under the old system. People had duties under their job description, and if they didn't perform, they were sent a letter detailing what [they] didn't do and given a reasonable period in which to improve. Then you did it. You wrote out the specificity of the charge. It's changed in the sense that standards were not established [before]. Now we have a dozen cases on standards alone, so you have a barrier to get through before you can initiate action. Before, [the Department of Agriculture] had a numerical system for performance appraisal, and it worked out okay, without the complexity of today's justification and evidence. Now it's hamstrung by the regulatory and legalistic process.

Other personnelists I talked to were not quite so negative, but they tended to agree that the new system worked better only if the manager had a solid position description and good performance standards already in place.

As the comment just quoted makes clear, problems are caused not just by the length of the process but also by the need for actions to stand up on appeal. While many problems are resolved informally at various steps in the process, those that go all the way to removal are often challenged. One problem in the law is that it gives employees multiple routes for appeal. They can take their case to the Merit Systems Protection Board (MSPB). They can file a grievance if they are covered by a union contract. Or if they belong to a protected class (by sex, race, age, or handicap), they can file an EEO (equal employment opportunity) complaint. Some bring their cases to the Office of the Special Council, claiming that they are being fired or otherwise harassed because they are whistle-blowers. Employees rarely take their cases as far as formal lawsuits, but all these routes require managers to face protracted and painful processes in which they are forced to defend their actions, and in which their motives are impugned. No manager enjoys facing an EEO complaint charging him or her with discrimination.

In the worst case scenario, an employee threatened with discipline may threaten back. One SES member, a man highly respected as a conscientious and caring manager, told me of the situation he faced.

> I have only dealt with one case, and I wasn't successful whatever. The employee tried to preempt my action through threats. He said, "I can put you through a whistle-blower complaint and cause all kinds of hassles for you." And that happened to me. The person claimed I had taken a personal trip using government funds. And even if you are found innocent, it plants the seeds of doubt. People like this have often worked in several agencies, and they know the system better than the supervisors. They can play it to the maximum, and that has the ability to intimidate supervisors. I don't like that, and it shouldn't be allowed to happen.

There is no doubt that both the procedures for taking formal action and the need to defend that action on appeal are daunting and time-consuming. But it remains the case that some managers still make effective use of both formal and informal procedures to deal with their problem employees, and others do not. How can we explain the difference?

It goes without saying that dealing with problem employees is one of the more unpleasant aspects of life as a manager. Individual managers cope with these situations in a number of ways. Often, they make conscious decisions based on cost-benefit reasoning: "Is it worth my time to deal with this problem?" This calculation may be affected by their perceptions of what is central to their job and what they will be rewarded for (or at least supported on) by their superiors. Both perceptions are powerfully influenced by the problems of worker-managers and pseudo-supervisors.

Worker-Managers and the Dilemma of Time

Most managers are working under time pressure and attempting to balance the many components of their job. As we saw, they are likely to give priority to the components they think are most important (or that they believe their boss thinks are most important). Setting priorities is never easy, but for worker-managers, who are officially supervisors (or even midlevel managers) but who still have significant responsibilities for doing technical work, it is a constant struggle. Often, it is the technical work that they see as most important and that they enjoy most. Management is sometimes seen as an add-on—something they have to put up with in order to get ahead. And the reward structures reinforce the view that time-consuming management responsibilities get in the way of the "real" job.

Managers in every agency, as well as several personnel specialists, saw this as a key obstacle in getting managers to deal with problem employees. As an FCS personnelist saw it: "The real problem is that in the government there isn't the flexibility to be a full-time supervisor. If they could do that, they'd be more involved in what their employees are doing day-to-day. I think it's that the supervisors are stretched so thin. That's the problem, not the procedures."

How do managers cope with the demands of a difficult job and still go through the time-consuming task of dealing with a problem employee, particularly when the formal process is used? According to an employee relations specialist, they give up their own time: "If supervisors weren't so busy being employees as well as supervisors, they might have the time to do the documentation. But as it is, they have to take it home at night to do it."

An EPA manager well aware of the time demands told me his

approach: "I pick one person at a time to focus on, because that's all you can handle." Other managers, including the one quoted at the beginning of the Introduction, have decided that dealing with a problem employee is just not worth the trouble and that ignoring the issue has fewer costs.

Pseudo-Supervisors and the Dilemma of Authority

The problems faced by the worker-manager are exacerbated for the pseudo-supervisor, the technical specialist promoted to a supervisory position, and therefore a larger salary, in order to reward a high level of technical skill. But the pseudo-supervisor actually remains a technical person, with only minimal supervisory responsibilities. The real authority rests at a more senior level. Except in some extreme cases, the line between the pseudo-supervisor and the worker-manager is not clear-cut. Many first-line supervisors feel that the real authority, particularly on a matter as controversial as discipline, lies above them—sometimes several levels above them. In a few cases, this sounds like passing the buck—a strategy for avoiding the hard parts of the job. But in others, there is a sense of frustration or confusion about who is really in charge. Although I coined the term pseudo-supervisor, I'm certainly not the first to identify this problem of unclear authority. When the MSPB studied managers, they found that less than one-third (32 percent) felt they had the authority to take disciplinary actions (U.S. Merit Systems Protection Board, 1993).

In many cases, it may be hard for an external observer to discern where the authority actually rests, since often the first-line supervisor and the midlevel manager work together in developing a strategy for dealing with a problem employee. But examination of a case where there was conflict between the first-line supervisor and his superior helps elucidate the problems caused by confusion over who has the authority to act.

In a small field office (in an agency that will remain nameless to protect confidentiality), I interviewed three people: two first-line supervisors and a midlevel manager who was their boss and headed the office. Each of the three told me his version of the same story, which concerned a conflict over how to deal with a problem employee. What was clear from all three was that the employee in question was technically competent but occasionally quite rude and even abusive in dealing with the public. One first-line supervisor was frustrated because he felt his boss was dragging his feet and avoiding the problem, so when yet another incident occurred, he decided to take matters into his own hands. He took advantage of the fact that his boss was out of town and called the employee relations specialist at the regional office, who got the assistant regional director involved. The first result was that the employee in question received a formal letter of reprimand and was required to meet weekly with her supervisor, who reported a real change in behavior. But while on paper the first-line supervisor had the authority to take the action, doing so violated two unwritten organizational norms: that first-line supervisors need their superiors' approval to take disciplinary action and that they do not circumvent their superiors by going directly to the regional office (let alone make their bosses look bad to their superiors). Challenging both the boss's authority and his reputation had fairly predictable results: the boss, on his return, reprimanded the first-level supervisor (which brought the regional office back into the picture in the latter's defense), and enduring tension was created between the first-line supervisor and both his boss and the other first-line supervisor in the office. While the reprimanded supervisor is clearly something of a maverick, the severity of the reaction makes clear that where authority for taking disciplinary action lies on paper and where it rests in reality may be very different.

To summarize: Managers select their approaches to problems on the basis of their own definitions of their job and also on the basis of their views concerning the most important parts of that job. For worker-managers, it is the technical work that really counts. Or as an FCS supervisor put it, dealing with problem employees "is one of the things that goes by the boards. We're more work-oriented than oriented toward good supervision. We don't seem to have the time to devote to doing that." For pseudo-supervisors, there may be a tendency to avoid dealing with problem employees because of ambiguity about where responsibility for such problems lies.

Managerial Competence and Conflict Avoidance

There may be other sources of avoidance, beyond unclear authority. As I said earlier, managers are rational people who often make decisions in cost-benefit terms. But they are human, and they may also make decisions on more emotional bases. One of the most common and easily understood is that they avoid situations that make them uncomfortable and actions that they do not feel skilled in performing. Both reactions are very common when managers talk about dealing or not dealing with problem employees.

Managers, like most people, tend to avoid conflict. When I asked them what they disliked about their jobs, by far the most common elements mentioned were giving people negative feedback on their performance and dealing with discipline cases. Interviewees often explicitly referred to being uncomfortable with conflict situations. A Navy manager explained that "first- and second-line supervisors, people like us, are unwilling to take hard lines. They don't want to do their job as supervisors, which is telling people negative things. . . . Nobody wants to be a bad guy. Everybody wants to be nice, everybody wants their subordinates to like them. They don't want conflict."

The level of conflict becomes most uncomfortable when the manager has moved past simply counseling the employee and has actually given the employee a poor performance appraisal. At this point, the relationship may shift in the direction of what Rivas (1991) terms "adversarial supervision." As he defines it: "Adversarial supervision occurs when the organization and supervisor determine that an employee cannot maintain his or her performance at an acceptable level or that the organization cannot raise the level in a cost-effective fashion. At this point, the organization prepares for the dismissal of an employee by carefully documenting his or her poor performance. During this time, the relationship between the supervisor and employee may take on an adversarial quality" (p. 193).

Protracted conflict is not only rough on the supervisor; it can be difficult for the whole organization, particularly since the supervisor may be required to keep more careful records on all of his or her staff, to avoid the charge that he or she is out to "get" the problem employee. Small wonder, then, that some employee relations specialists say managers put off dealing with problems until they become unbearable and then want to take instant action, which, of course, is not possible if they have not been keeping records and counseling all along.

To some extent, this tendency to avoid dealing with people problems may reflect the career paths and selection criteria for managers. As we saw in Chapter Two, most managers started out as technical specialists and often were promoted to management positions on the basis of their technical capabilities. Seldom do selection criteria explicitly factor in interpersonal skills or ability to handle conflict. In fact, some managers expressed frustration with these parts of the job; one person asked to be removed from his first-line supervisory position precisely because he found it so difficult to deal with a problem employee.

But managers avoid dealing with problems not just because it is unpleasant. Many managers also feel unprepared. They do not know how to handle a direct interaction that may involve conflict, such as giving negative feedback. And they do not really understand, and thus are intimidated by, the formal process. They know the sequence of actions is complex, and they also know that if they make a technical mistake it can come back to haunt them. The conventional wisdom hurts here, because it reinforces the view that the process is hard and risky, and that a minor goof will likely lead to years of appeals and litigation. In fact, this is much less true than it once was. The current standard says that an agency action will be overturned by the Merit Systems Protection Board on the grounds of procedural error only if the employee can prove that it was a "harmful" error—that is, that the outcome might have been different had the error not occurred (Shaw and Bransford, 1992, pp. 61–62). Nonetheless, the perception persists among managers that some small slip on their part will cause months or years of effort to be wasted and that they will be stuck with an employee who is still incompetent and now also embittered.

Why do managers feel unprepared? One question that came in for considerable debate was how much training managers received and what it contained or should have contained. As we saw in Chapter Two, many managers had no formal managerial training or had received only a brief course in supervision. In theory, all new supervisors are required to receive training. In practice, new supervisors who are in an acting capacity receive no training. One young woman at a group interview had been acting first-level supervisor for only a few months and was faced with taking a formal disciplinary action. As she put it: "I've never had time to sit down and read the *Federal Personnel Manual*. I don't know what's in the regulations. I don't know what my rights are. . . . There are a lot of things [on which] I don't know where I stand. Maybe there needs to be some sort of training for new supervisors."

Of course, there is training, but she will not receive it unless she is permanently appointed as a supervisor, and even then, she may need to wait a year or more before the training is available—much too long for most new supervisors' needs. Moreover, the training provided may be much too cursory to give managers the tools they need for dealing with problem employees. Indeed, some report that there was little or no coverage of performance appraisal and discipline in their training. As a result, it is not uncommon for managers to report that they do not understand the system. Many would agree with the APHIS manager who told me: "My concerns are, first, do I know all the rules well enough to say, 'What you did is wrong, don't do it again,' versus 'What you did is wrong, you just bought yourself two weeks off'? I'm fortunate I haven't had to deal with that yet. I don't know what's going on enough to be sure what I can do, and it's not in my temperament to be a hard guy. I don't like that."

The flip side of this is that, even if the training is available, managers often do not take advantage of it. As an EPA personnel specialist put it: "Managers don't want to learn the system. The evaluation of their performance is based on their scientific accomplishment and program performance, so why should they want to learn about personnel? I don't think the management would want to devote much time to this effort. I don't think they want more in-depth training. In many cases, it is very involved and complicated, and you don't just pick it up."

Some managers recognize the truth in this and admit that if they were not facing a problem, they would probably say, "I don't need that." In other words, managers are not willing to spend the time gaining skills that they do not feel the need of (even though they might at some future time), particularly if they do not see the function as central to their job. One solution might be just-in-time training, making the information available—even self-taught via a written manual or a video—at the point when a manager recognizes the need for it. The danger, however, is that he or she might recognize this need too late in the process.

In point of fact, a major role of a good employee relations specialist is to provide individualized coaching to managers who are going through the process, particularly to those facing it for the first time. As with any challenging task, doing it well on a single occasion will reinforce a manager's belief that it is something he or she can handle.

In several agencies, personnelists told me that they thought managers were starting to do better at dealing with problem employees. Some attributed this to the changed financial situation in their agency and to less tolerance of deadwood when resources were tight. Others saw younger managers as doing a better job.

To summarize: It is natural to avoid things that make us uncomfortable. While there is probably no way to get around the fact that dealing with problem employees is likely to cause conflict, it is possible to improve managers' skills in dealing with conflict and in working within the admittedly complex formal procedures—but only if managers think that developing these skills is important and useful. If they continue to view this task as an annoyance that gets in the way of the "real" work, then they certainly are not going to make the effort to learn how to do it better.

Group Norms for Dealing with Problem Employees

A manager with a problem employee faces two decisions: whether to do anything at all, and if action seems to be called for, what form it should take. Managers choose their strategy on the basis, first, of their diagnosis of the situation. They ask themselves: what is the nature of the problem, and what extenuating circumstances are there (Klaas and Wheeler, 1990)? The approach they take to someone whose skills are inadequate is likely to be different from the one they take to an employee suspected of substance abuse. But their choice of strategy is also affected by group norms, which may reflect values in the organization's culture. They ask their peers how they have dealt with similar problems, and they hear stories via the grapevine about what others have done and what the result was. They also talk to their superiors and to the employee relations staff in their organization. The latter play a role in imparting technical information about how to follow complex procedures, but at the same time, they convey more or less explicit messages about what range of strategies will be considered appropriate.

Some of the approaches available to the manager are quite formal; some are more informal. Of course, the popular notion is that you cannot fire a government employee. In fact, the biggest surprise in talking to managers about these cases is how many did use the formal process and how many employees left government as a result. Of the cases described, about 15 percent ended with the dismissal of the employee, and in another 17 percent the person voluntarily resigned, usually after he or she had learned that a dismissal was likely. A further 6 percent were resolved by the person's retirement. In some of these cases, the person was already eligible to retire; in several others, where physical or mental illness was involved, a negotiated settlement provided for disability retirement. When these three categories are added together, we see that in over one-third of the cases, the employee was either formally pushed out of the organization or, more informally, strongly encouraged to leave. Many of the cases that were still pending were slowly wending their way to similar outcomes. A small number of other cases (under 10 percent) were handled by formal means less punitive than dismissal, including suspensions, downgrades, or letters of reprimand. In short, the formal system may be slow and unwieldy, but a determined manager can make it work if he or she is willing to invest the time required.

In a number of cases, the manager had taken positive steps short of initiating a formal disciplinary action. About 14 percent of cases were handled by giving the person a poor performance appraisal or by providing counseling, either directly or by referral to an employee assistance program. Some of these cases were resolved successfully at that point, with no need for further action.

Of course, some managers want to avoid the trouble of taking a formal action. Among more informal means of dealing with problems, by far the most popular was a transfer (17 percent of cases). Finally, in about 7 percent of cases, the manager was simply tolerating the situation—doing nothing or putting the person on the shelf (that is, reducing the person's workload or otherwise working around the problem).

Informal strategies are particularly difficult to study, both because there is a strong social desirability factor (that is, managers know there is a "right" answer to questions about discipline) and because managers occasionally resort to tactics that are questionable or even illegal. Not surprisingly, managers in several agencies were much more likely to say others were guilty of shipping off their problems elsewhere or of ignoring problems than to admit that they had done such things themselves. In fact, they may have been more forthcoming to an outsider than they would have been in response to a more "official" inquiry, which may explain why I found somewhat higher levels of these informal approaches than did a GAO study, which reported that "eight percent [of supervisors surveyed] had poor performers that they did not assist. Rather than deal with these individuals, the supervisors indicated that they reduced the employee's workload, gave the employee easier work, hoped that the situation would work itself out, or reassigned the employee to another unit" (U.S. General Accounting Office, 1990c).

According to Gaertner and Gaertner (1984), one can interpret disciplinary action in two ways. It can be seen as instrumental action, designed to solve a problem. In that case, managers are likely to select actions that have been successful in the past. But one can also see disciplinary action as symbolic behavior expressing both individual values and organizational culture. As Gaertner and Gaertner explain, "even if a given action is shown to be generally effective, if it is not congruent with a supervisor's values, he/she will not do it" (p. 14). Looking at the different approaches managers took in the four agencies in this study gives strong support to the symbolic view of disciplinary action. Managers certainly wanted to resolve the problem, but their actions clearly reflected the need to be sensitive to organizational norms, and it was obvious that they relied on both their supervisors and the employee relations staff not only for technical support but for cues to the boundaries of acceptable behavior.

Some of the clearest norms about such limits were articulated by managers in FCS and in EPA Region Three. As we saw in Chapter One, these are both clan cultures—that is, cultures where strong emphasis is placed on the human relations quadrant in the competing values model. A personnel specialist in Region Three explained the values of the organization to me as follows: "The people who are in charge here care about the people who work here, more than people even know. A question I'm always asked is the effect it would have on their personal lives. If I wanted to fire a single parent, it would be hard, because this place has too much of a heart. When I first came here, I thought they were giving away the store here, but that's the way they do business, and I've never seen it do more harm than good."

At FCS, discussions of discipline were explicitly linked to the image of the agency as a family. Managers felt that top leadership would support them if they took action, but only within limits. As one explained, "There's a lot of family attitude at FCS, and if you have a twenty-nine- or thirty-year employee [whom you want to discipline], I don't think you're going to get a manager that's going to back you." A related norm is that managers do not rush to push people out the door if they have personal problems but try to give them support. One of the most dramatic examples in this regard was a woman who had been injured on the job. Rather than force her to leave on disability, the organization kept her position open while she went through a lengthy recovery. Further, she received extraordinary personal support from the head of her office. As she told me, "They didn't have to keep my position for me after a year. They talked to me every week and kept me going."

EPA managers told similar stories of sticking with and supporting employees who had personal problems. Managers at EPA are much more likely than those at the other agencies to report employees with drug- and alcohol-related problems. Indeed, an employee relations specialist estimated that "probably about 60 percent of the cases that come to me have some element of alcoholism or drug abuse that I can document. My suspicion is it's really higher than that." These are often tough cases for managers to deal with. One of the more moving stories I heard was from an EPA manager.

I had a secretary who was drug- and alcohol-dependent. There was lots of absenteeism. We talked, and I referred her to the rehab people here. She went into a hospital for detox, and I lost her services for three months and had to advance her leave and find someone to replace her for a while. When she graduated from her AA course, she invited me to attend, and it was good. It caused me to think about not drinking, and I quit, which was a side benefit. She's back and very productive, and she's in school now. I'm still a cheerleader for her.

As this example makes clear, supporting an employee through hard times rather than taking a hard line can pay off. However, managers in several organizations griped that their superiors would not back them when—in the managers' opinion—firm action was called for. For example, a midlevel manager who had come to FCS fairly recently (and therefore had not grown up in that culture) was very aware of the differences between FCS and his previous agency: "At [my previous agency], I got rid of three people in two and a half years, using various methods. Here, I have had occasion to discipline one person, and it went up to my boss, who's an SES, who basically told me to use kid gloves, be nice to the person. 'You know you're right, but you can't do this.' This agency is different."

In fact, FCS may not be that different. Even at EPA and the Navy, managers complained that they were discouraged from giving poor performance appraisals. For example, one supervisor at the EPA regional office told me, "There is extreme resistance to giving people poor performance appraisals. It's against the culture. It's seen as too big a hammer for personality problems that should be worked out between adults."

Informal Strategies: Transfers, Turkey Farms, and Tolerance

As we can see, strategies vary along a continuum from informal to formal. In all four organizations in this study, managers tended to rely first on informal approaches. But what they did next differed somewhat. In general, managers at the two Department of Agriculture sites were less likely to move to formal actions than managers at EPA or the Navy. Further, the meaning that managers at different agencies gave to their actions, particularly informal ones, reflected their differing values. The two most common informal actions managers took when a situation appeared unlikely to improve were transferring the employee or putting him or her on the shelf. Let us look at how each of these works in practice.

At all four agencies, there was considerable discussion of the practice of taking problem employees and sending them somewhere else. But what was most striking was the different meaning that managers gave to this action. At FCS, managers reconciled their behavior with the family culture by justifying the action as in the best interests of the employee. For example, one person told me, "I had a strangely shaped peg and didn't have a hole for him. He was a Vietnam vet with very good interpersonal skills, and we were able to find a perfect place in a field office."

Although moves may be designed to help the person with a problem, there is a strong norm that you do not pass the buck, handing off a problem employee without warning to an unsuspecting colleague. Several people told me that this was unacceptable behavior, and that you could not get away with it anyway, because FCS was such a small organization. As one person articulated the norms of appropriate behavior: "We do kind of want to look after each other. We don't do things like shift bad employees unless you let the person know that it is a bad employee. And it's like a favor, the way it's done. You look out for one another."

Navy managers, in contrast, reported a fair amount of transferring of problem employees, but there it sounded much more like buck-passing. Such transfers are not presented as being for the good of the employee. In fact, managers are fairly frank about their motives, even in front of their peers. For example, a first-line supervisor admitted in a group interview: "I have had an employee that

I would have liked to . . . take stern action against just on the work performance aspect. But again, knowing that I'm creating so much work for myself to do, I've shied away from it and given good references so that that person may move on to somebody else for a problem. You know, I shirked the responsibility off to somebody else and said, 'Hey, this is a great employee. Promote him. Take him.' "

In the extreme, this approach leads to "promoting out" one's problems, particularly at the management level. A personnel specialist at EPA commented: "We have good managers, and some are rewarded, but we also have some terrible managers who [were] promoted because it was the only way to get rid of them. . . . People are promoted out or given an IPA [sent on an exchange program under the Intergovernmental Personnel Act] and that program is seen as a dumping ground for turkeys. One person I'm thinking of was promoted and put into another organization to work on a special project. Folks will say, 'I guess the way to be promoted is to screw up.' "

Turkeys, or poor performers, are not just sent out to IPA assignments. Sometimes, they are put on "turkey farms"—units engaged in low-priority work, where problem employees cannot do too much harm. Managers at several agencies talked about turkey farms. At EPA, a discussion among first-level supervisors brought out the conflict in values over this approach. One manager told the group, "You end up working your way through the management chain [asking your superiors for assistance in] trying to find a place where you can 'turkey-farm' the person." His approach was challenged by one of his peers, who questioned the ethics of passing judgment and "sentencing that person to the turkey farm," rather than trying to find a place where the person might be productive.

At APHIS, too, creating turkey farms is controversial. As we saw, the employee relations staff serves, to some extent, as the arbiter of cultural values, and one SES member was very distressed when someone in employee relations suggested that approach: "A number of years ago, a personnelist told me that one of the best

things that could be done in a given organization, was to create a—
I can't remember the term he used for it—but it was something like
a 'dead pool.' You know, this is where you put the problem cases,
and just let them sit there and live together. That's terrible. That's
absolutely terrible, when someone from within the system tells you
this is the best way to deal with them."

A related concept is putting someone on the shelf—that is,
putting the problem employee in a corner, giving him or her minimal work to do, and hoping that the person will get the picture and
leave or retire. While the SES member quoted above was shocked
by the idea of a "dead pool" (or turkey farm), his fellow managers
at APHIS were the most likely to say that employees there were put
"on the shelf." This was one case where the "social desirability" factor clearly affected responses. What was most striking about the
interviews at APHIS was the gap between what people said they
themselves did and what they described as typical in the organization. Only one person admitted to dealing with a problem by tolerating or ignoring it. But many people in both individual and
group interviews told me that the norm at APHIS was to put people "on the shelf." This term was used consistently and frequently
to describe current practice. One manager explained it this way:
"The most famous way problem employees are dealt with is that
they are shelved. You just try to make them think that they are busy.
I see that all the time." Specific examples of "shelved" employees
were individuals whose performance was inadequate, people who
were doing personal business from their desks, and whistle-blowers
whom managers were afraid to deal with.

Further, it was clear that first-line supervisors at APHIS felt
they were getting signals from their superiors that ignoring or
shelving problem employees was a culturally acceptable solution.
The SES members in the group interview talked frankly about the
fact that problem employees are either shelved or moved. They
told me about the agency reorganization in 1989, and how it was
used to put even high-level employees on the shelf: "We ended up

with some people that we didn't know where to put, so we created some positions for them, and we have some high-level people in positions right now that are not productive. We don't know where to put them."

At EPA, shelving people was much less common, and it had a different impetus. As we saw in Chapter One, EPA is a highly politicized organization that has gone through significant political upheavals. This is reflected in several stories about people who had been put on the shelf because they fell out of political favor. In a few cases, such people were later resurrected and rose to high positions, sometimes when a new administration came in. More frequently, it is clear that they were squeezed out.

The Time and Place for Formal Action

Many performance problems get solved positively through counseling or through use of the performance appraisal system. In some sense, taking a formal disciplinary action, particularly a dismissal, can be seen as a management failure—an inability to turn the situation around. In fact, Gaertner and Gaertner (1984) report that in their study (which included EPA as a site), it was the most outstanding managers who preferred informal means of dealing with problem employees.

Nonetheless, even the best of supervisors cannot succeed with all problem employees. What determines whether, as a second step, managers ship out or tolerate their problems or initiate formal action? A critical factor appears to be the level of technical support and encouragement they receive from the employee relations office. At the two agencies where managers were most likely to take formal action, EPA and the Navy, the managers also gave the employee relations staff unequivocal high marks. Most respondents saw employee relations as helpful, service-oriented, and knowledgeable; the specialists were described as being accessible and as willing to assist managers in such tasks as drafting formal letters to employees. In almost all cases, the employee relations staff gave managers both the technical and the moral support to go through the process. They helped with informal solutions, such as arranging a transfer, but also (with only rare exceptions) did not try to dissuade managers from going through the formal process. One of their services was to share information about how similar cases had been handled in the past. This is important because if the handling of a case does not follow precedent, it is more vulnerable to reversal if the employee appeals or starts a grievance procedure (Redeker, 1989). Further, such precedents are expressions of organizational norms.

At FCS, and to a lesser extent at APHIS, managers were frustrated by the messages they got from the employee relations staff. At FCS, while several managers said they had received good support, a number felt the employee relations staff were overly cautious. One person saw them as being paralyzed by "the overwhelming fear of a lawsuit or grievance," but their caution may also reflect perceptions about the kinds of actions top-level management will support. In short, the employee relations staff at FCS appeared to be reinforcing and communicating cultural norms that said, "Take formal action rarely, and only as a last resort."

It is true that the fear of facing protracted litigation or having a case reversed on appeal is a significant deterrent for some managers and personnel staff. But how realistic is this fear? First, as we saw, in the majority of cases where formal action is initiated, the employee sees the handwriting on the wall and leaves voluntarily in order to avoid having a dismissal on his or her record. The number of cases that actually go to formal appeals or grievances is quite small, but there were, indeed, some horror stories. The only place where such stories were widespread was at the Portsmouth Naval Shipyard, which was also the only site with a significant number of blue-collar employees and with active unions. The nature of the shipyard workforce was reflected in the kinds of problems supervisors faced; the shipyard was the only site where I heard about cases of fighting or theft of equipment. It was also the only site where significant numbers of managers told me about using formal disciplinary actions short of dismissal, such as letters of reprimand or suspensions. But the fear of losing a discipline case on a technicality came up frequently. For example, a Wage Grade (blue-collar) supervisor in a group interview reported that he "once went through great pains to remove an individual, and the individual was back on the shipyard not a month later with all back pay, over a technicality in this office." When I asked for more detail, the supervisor said, "Basically, [the employee] never showed up for work. Constantly undependable. And we just went to remove him. And it was just some paperwork screwup here. I don't remember what they did. He grieved it [filed a formal grievance], went to court in Boston, I guess it was, and he came back on the shipyard. You hear of it. Every code [every part of the organization] has got one of those stories."

He was quite right. Virtually everyone in the room chimed in with a similar story. When I raised this issue with the personnel officer in charge of such cases, I got a strong response: "Those technical nightmares they talk about were back in the beginning, back in the early eighties. There hasn't been a case overturned on a technicality in eight years. When I hear that, I bristle. That's a cop-out. You have to have documentation, but you don't need the mounds of documentation for performance-based actions that you used to. It's never been easier to remove someone for poor performance."

While he may be right that it is now unlikely for an action to be overturned on appeal, the reality of recent experience may be less powerful in affecting managers' behavior than the stories and myths that circulate around the agency. It takes only one or two really difficult situations, perhaps embellished as they travel through the grapevine, to convince managers that it is better to cut a deal or to avoid facing a problem than to become embroiled in a grievance or appeal.

To summarize: Most managers would prefer to deal with problem employees informally. But when they are faced with a problem that does not improve, they are likely to go through the lengthy and complex formal process only if they have strong support both from their superiors (sometimes several layers up) and from the employee relations staff. The last thing they want is to find themselves out on a limb, facing an angry employee or a long-drawn-out appeal, without both technical and moral support.

Conclusions

Analyzing how managers deal with problem employees is particularly complex because this is one area where all the different factors we have been considering come together—where we can look simultaneously at the effects of the formal civil service rules and regulations, of the organizational environment, of the budget, and of managers' own role perceptions and skill levels. What conclusions can we draw from this analysis?

Is Changing the Rules the Answer?

First, we can say that the formal rules count, but not that much. While managers often say it is the complexity and slowness of the formal system that keeps them from acting, a little probing leads to the conclusion that the rules are only one of a number of constraints on managers and not necessarily the biggest. Would changing the rules make things easier? Perhaps, but there are some big caveats. First, it is not just the rules themselves but managers' perceptions of the rules that really count. The procedural changes made as part of the 1978 Civil Service Reform Act (CSRA) were passed amid much verbiage about getting rid of the deadwood in government, but managers did not see them as making a significant improvement, and in fact, the new procedures for performance-based actions are not used very much.

Further, changing the formal rules will not have any effect if the standards used to adjudicate appeals and grievances remain the same. In fact, one can go so far as to say that the real rules are not the ones written in the law or the Code of Federal Regulations but those that evolve through the equivalent of case law. For example, the Merit Systems Protection Board, in a landmark case, *Douglas* v. *Veterans Administration*, 5 M.S.P.R. 280 (1981) (cited in Shaw and Bransford, 1992), set forth the standards that agencies should apply in determining the penalties for specific offenses. These "Douglas factors" then became the standards that guide agency actions, and managers must be familiar with them. Training manuals or managerial guides probably devote as much or more space to standards deriving from such precedents as they do to the formal regulations (see Shaw and Bransford, 1992).

The importance of the appeals and grievance procedures in actually setting the standards is only reinforced by the role of the courts. Because the courts have set forth general standards of due process based on the view of a government job as "property" (Shafritz, Riccucci, Rosenbloom, and Hyde, 1992), any change in formal rules that jeopardizes the right to due process is likely to be overturned by the courts. In fact, the planners of the 1978 CSRA considered, in their earliest drafts, much more drastic changes in the rules for discipline but were told that their proposals would never hold up in the courts.

More recent proposals for change share the same flaw. The National Performance Review, headed by Vice President Al Gore, has talked about deregulating the government, including personnel policy. One of its goals is to "reduce by half the time required to terminate federal managers and employees for cause and improve the system for dealing with poor performers" (National Performance Review, 1993a, p. 25). Given all the complaints about how long the process takes, this sounds like an admirable idea, but let us look at the specifics. The proposal is in two parts, one a recommendation that "agencies . . . halve the length of time during which managers and employees with unsatisfactory performance ratings are allowed to demonstrate improved performance" and the other a call for legislation to change the required time for notice of termination from thirty days to fifteen. The second proposal is fairly trivial; when managers complain about how long it takes to go through the disciplinary process, they probably are griping not about giving the employee an extra two weeks in which to prepare for a hearing but rather about the months of documentation and counseling that precede that point. However, changing the length of time employees are given to demonstrate improved performance is dangerous. The problem is that the reformers cannot control those with the real power in this area. If MSPB or those hearing grievances or the courts feel that the time given to show improvement is too short, they will overturn these actions. In fact, it is the complex, overlapping appeals/grievance/EEO processes that probably need fixing. The National Performance Review report *Reinventing Human Resource Management* (1993d) makes precisely this point. It states, "While an employee's right to due process must be protected, there is a need for streamlining the current processes" (p. 40). Among the solutions it recommends is adoption of alternative methods of dispute resolution.

In truth, managers are more ambivalent about the current rules than one might initially think. After they have vented their frustration with the system, at least some go on to say that it should not be too easy to fire an employee. And their views change somewhat with their perspective. When they think about what could happen if the tables were turned and someone were taking action against them, the protections in the present system do not look too bad.

It is also clear that changing the formal rules may have little effect on the organizational culture. Currently, working within the same formal rules, managers in different organizations tend to handle problem employees in different ways. These differences reflect the cultural values dominant in the organizations, the signals managers get from top leadership, and even the agencies' budgets. Budgetary effects can cut both ways. On the one hand, managers may be less tolerant of poor performers when times are tight and there is little slack in the organization. On the other hand, as we will see in Chapter Seven, if the agency has imposed a hiring freeze or a reduction in force is threatened, managers may have a disincentive to act since they may not be able to replace the person they dismiss and may even lose the position and be unable to replace the person later when resources open up.

Depending on the organizational environment, managers may see informal responses to problem employees as appropriate. Managers are unlikely to take actions that their organizations or superiors will not back them on. In the ideal scenario—which is sometimes realized—they find win/win solutions, such as moving the employee to a job where he or she is happy and productive. But many managers will look for solutions that lower the costs to them personally, even if these solutions are not in the best interests of the organization as a whole. Shipping one's problems elsewhere is particularly attractive if it is condoned or even supported by the organization.

Managerial Avoidance

It should come as no surprise that managers avoid dealing with difficult employees. We all tend to avoid tasks that are unpleasant. But in this case, that natural tendency is exacerbated by two factors: managers' role definition and their know-how. Taking the time and energy to deal with problem employees is particularly difficult for managers whose sense of their "real" job is technical, not managerial. This is particularly true for the people I have termed worker-managers—people who, in some sense, are straddling the fence between the two roles of technical expert and supervisor of others. Which side of the fence they lean toward will depend on the incentive structures under which they work. The signals they get from their supervisors about how to set priorities and how to deal with specific problems are therefore very important. They are even more important for a pseudo-supervisor, who has only minimal supervisory responsibilities. In that case, the real authority to take action falls to the person who is officially the second-level supervisor but who may or may not have any sense of what the problem employee is doing on a day-to-day basis. This unclear division of authority is always awkward and can be disastrous.

Finally, some managers are frank in admitting that they avoid dealing with problems because they just do not know how to handle them and do not understand the formal procedures. These are not "bad" managers but individuals who lack training. Often, there is no incentive to get this training until a problem arises—at which point, unfortunately, it may be too late.

The issue of discipline figures prominently in such stereotypes of government as the impossibility of firing a government worker and the contemptuous saying, "good enough for government work." Is the government getting a bum rap? It is hard to estimate the amount of deadwood in any organization. I would argue, first, that some parts of government are doing much better than others at dealing with their problems, whether informally or formally. Second, there is some evidence that private sector managers, too, are hesitant to take disciplinary action, both because of the desire to avoid conflict and because of the fear of lawsuits (Imundo, 1985). But however we assess the severity of the problem, what is clear from this analysis is that there are no quick fixes; simply changing the formal rules will not get at the equally important organizational constraints. Genuine improvements will only come through changes in the organizational culture, in the definition of managerial roles, and in the methods of selection and training of new managers. In fact, the National Performance Review report *Reinventing Human Resource Management* (1993d) recognized the importance of improving both organizational culture and management skills in this area. In addition to calling for streamlining the formal procedures, as discussed above, the report advocated the development of a "culture of performance that supports supervisors' efforts to deal with poor performers" (p. 41), pointing out that lack of management support was seen by supervisors as an obstacle to action. Further, the report called for improving "supervisors' knowledge and skills in dealing with poor performers" (p. 41)—particularly interpersonal skills, but also skills in performance planning and performance management and knowledge of disciplinary policy and procedures. Taken as a whole, these recommendations fit well with the conclusions of the research described here: that managers' strategies for dealing with problem employees are shaped by more than the formal rules and procedures. The culture and values of their organization, their (and their organization's) definition of the supervisory role, and their background and training as supervisors are all determining elements in their choice of strategies.

Part Three

The Budgetary
Imperative

Chapter Six

The Position Classification System: A Budgetary Control System in Disguise

The last two chapters focused on the traditional personnel functions of hiring and firing. In this chapter and the next, we turn to those areas where the civil service system and the budgetary system intersect to constrain managers. These include the mechanisms for determining pay, the effects of personnel ceilings, and managerial responses to budget cuts. This chapter addresses the critical issue of pay.

Not surprisingly, managers want to have a say in deciding what their employees are paid. Pay levels affect their ability to hire new employees, and pay raises are an important means of rewarding individuals whom managers want to retain. But managers cannot set pay directly, because pay levels are determined by two separate pay-setting systems. The first is the arcane and complex *position classification system*, which determines entry-level pay and progression within a pay range. The second is the system that sets annual raises and, now, locality pay. Managers have no input into the second system, and its problems have put great pressure on the first system. Managers have some limited control over the position classification system, but this control is indirect and exercised only with great difficulty, as we shall see. It is useful to examine the ways managers attempt to affect classification and the problems that arise when they do, because we thereby see the relationship between personnel system constraints and budgetary constraints. Indeed, I would go so far as to say that the classification system is actually a budgetary control system masquerading as a personnel control system. Examination of these issues also reveals the problems created by the clash of cultures and values between personnelists and line managers, and how these problems play out in practice.

I begin by looking at the two formal pay-setting systems, starting with the position classification system's goals—both its ostensible or official goals and what I see as its actual goals. Then, I describe briefly the relationship of the classification system to the other pay-setting mechanisms in the federal government. Finally, I turn to the question of how the classification system actually works in practice. While much of this practice is standard across government, there are also significant differences between agencies, arising from the fact that the classification system is a budgetary control system in disguise. I conclude by examining two attempts to reform the classification process, both at the Navy. The first, Manage to Payroll (MTP) was implemented across the service. The second, the Navy "demonstration project," tested a simplified system based on broad pay bands in two Navy laboratories and has had a profound influence on the debate over reform.

Position Classification in Theory and Practice

What is a position classification system and what is it for? Essentially, it is an elaborate and complex way of setting pay that, like the hiring systems discussed in Chapter Four, is designed to remove discretion from managers and to substitute "scientific" methods. The system was created by the Classification Act of 1923; the last time it underwent a major reform was in 1949. According to the U.S. General Accounting Office (1984): "The objective of the Act was to provide consistency in pay, staffing, and other personnel functions across the various positions which then comprised the federal white-collar work force. . . . All positions were to be paid in accordance with the qualifications required and the responsibility and difficulty the jobs entailed" (Appendix, p. 1). In short, the stated goal of the system is to create what is usually called *internal equity*. That is, people who do the same jobs, no matter where they work in the federal government, should receive the same pay. A computer programmer in the Navy, for example, should get the same pay as a computer programmer with the same level of responsibility at EPA. As we shall see below, this goal is not often met.

The Classification System and the Pay System: Where Is the Real Problem?

There are actually three different systems that affect pay. The classification system determines the starting salary for a position (or at least the range) and also ensures periodic raises as an employee moves up the ten steps in each grade. But federal employees also receive annual raises through a complex system that was designed to ensure comparability with the private sector. Unfortunately, for many years, this system did not work. Successive presidents, moved by political considerations, refused to approve the raises that the system determined were needed. As a result, federal salaries, particularly in some occupations and geographic areas, fell far below salaries offered by employers in the private or even the public sector (Shafritz, Riccucci, Rosenbloom, and Hyde, 1992; National Commission on the Public Service, 1990).

This pay gap put increasing pressure on the classification system, since the only way to make up the difference was to reclassify an employee's position to a higher grade. The recent pay reform, the Federal Employees Pay Comparability Act (FEPCA) of 1990, was designed to reduce gradually the disparity between public and private sector pay levels and to introduce other flexibilities into the pay system, including authority to offer recruitment, relocation, and retention payments when needed. Among other things, this means that managers are now able, in some circumstances, to offer new employees salaries above the minimum rate for their position.

But FEPCA also set up two different ways to calculate annual raises. On the one hand, it attempted to institutionalize—and to protect from political pressures—a formula for calculating an across-the-board annual raise for all federal employees that is based on changes in the national average cost of labor in the private sector. On the other hand, it added a new wrinkle: locality pay. No more would all federal employees receive the same pay regardless of whether they lived in New York City or Missoula, Montana. Rather, there would be adjustments to base pay for those areas where labor costs (and presumably living costs) were higher. This was first implemented in three metropolitan areas immediately after passage of FEPCA, and went national for the first time in 1994.

But what the authors of the legislation did not anticipate was that political support for federal employee raises would remain weak, particularly in a period when the overall budget is being trimmed. In this environment, the two methods of raising pay have been seen as competing with rather than supporting each other. The result was that in 1994, federal employees received one raise but not the other: locality pay was implemented, giving raises to most workers (of varying amounts depending on the area in which they lived), but there was no annual comparability raise. Further, the comparability raise proposed for 1995 was significantly below what the terms of FEPCA would have required.

To summarize: In spite of repeated attempts at legislative reform, the system for setting annual wages is still not firmly institutionalized, and average federal wages are still below those of the private sector, which has resulted in continued pressure to manipulate employees' classifications to make up the difference.

Classification Wars

The classification process is not always a war, but it is a prime source of conflict between managers and personnel specialists. The conflict stems from differences in values and incentive structures in the two groups. As we saw, the formal classification process is designed to further the goal of internal equity. In order to meet this goal, classification has evolved into a system of daunting complexity. All jobs are first placed into job series based on the kind of work per-formed—for example, GS-830, mechanical engineer, or GS-343, management analyst. They are then classed by grade level. Grades range from 1 to 15.[1] The logic of this system is based on the values of the old "scientific management" school, which advocated break-ing down the work of an organization into narrowly defined posi-tions, each with clearly delineated responsibilities. Further, the logic embodies a central value of the classification system: that one clas-sifies the position, not the person occupying it. As we shall see, this value runs directly counter to the value systems of many managers and is a frequent source of conflict. Some critics also argue that the assumption on which traditional classification systems are grounded—that efficiency is promoted by dividing the functions of an organization into narrowly defined jobs—is now outdated and that rigid classifications make it harder to use staff flexibly or to give them opportunities to develop their skills by working at a variety of tasks. Classification systems can also hinder the implementation of some aspects of Total Quality Management, such as self-managed teams; they tie employees into narrowly defined job descriptions that make it difficult to broaden work assignments.

The people charged with administering this system, the position classifiers, are staff members in the personnel office. Typically, they have been formally trained and socialized to accept and uphold the logic of the system, which is based on the value of internal equity. This value is reinforced by the incentive structures within agencies.

It is my contention that the classification system is distorted by a not-always-hidden agenda: to keep costs down. Employee pay is a significant portion of most agencies' budgets. Not surprisingly, there is pressure to keep this share of the budget from growing too rapidly, and the pressure has only intensified in recent years. Salaries are controlled by controlling the classification process, both on a case-by-case basis and, periodically, through agencywide or even governmentwide programs to reduce grade levels (see, for example, U.S. General Accounting Office, 1986).

But there is a range of opposite pressures that push grade levels up. As Levine, Peters, and Thompson (1990) point out, "grade creep" reflects managers' desire to keep their staff happy. But it also stems from other sources, including greater use of technology, which requires more highly trained staff, and the desire to build in "skills slack . . . [that is], surplus skills as a hedge against uncertainty" (p. 342). Further, both personnel ceilings and the pressure to contract out (to be discussed in Chapter Seven) result in higher grade levels, since it is easiest to contract out routine, lower-graded work.

Most importantly, while there are overall budgetary incentives to keep salary costs, and thus classification levels, down, these incentives do not operate on managers. Most managers also have no reason to embrace the value of internal equity; maintaining the integrity of the classification system is not high on their list of priorities. Further, they are not rewarded for keeping their salary costs down, since they cannot easily reallocate any savings to cover other costs. Rather, they are rewarded for effectively carrying out their mission. And to do that, they need to be able to hire good staff, to hold on to them, and to reward their efforts. While the scholars may debate whether money is a motivator (Herzberg, 1968; National Research Council, 1991), most managers know that money counts. Thus, managers' goals differ from those of the classification and budgeting systems. Their concern is not for the consistency of the classification system or for cost containment but for their ability to compete in the market for good employees. This competition may entail internal equity issues. Managers do not want their positions to be graded lower than those in other parts of government, since that would make recruitment more difficult. Further, there is a fair amount of competition inside some agencies over resources. Those units with more resources will try to raid the best employees from other units by offering higher grade levels.

Managers are also very concerned with *external equity*—that is, comparability of pay levels between the federal government and other employers, such as state governments and the private sector.

If pay levels are not competitive, top candidates will be drawn else-where. But the current classification system is not designed to address the need for external equity, a fact that causes managers no little frustration. Further, managers want to be able to reward and hold on to individual employees whose work is outstanding, but the system is not designed to make this easy, either. Indeed, most classi-fiers would see this concern as irrelevant to the classification process.

In short, there are several actors here, each pursuing different goals. Classifiers are concerned with upholding the original goal of the system: internal equity. The signals they receive about whether to be relatively lenient or stringent in applying the classification standards originate both in the culture of the organization and in the budgetary climate. Budget officials, and often top management, are concerned with controlling overall costs. And managers want more control over what their employees are paid, both to meet the goal of external equity and to be able to reward top performers.

The net result of these conflicts is that there is often a large gap between theory and practice in how classification decisions are made. In theory, the system is objective and fair. But is this really the case? To address this question, it will help to look at the actual process of classifying a position.

The Classification Process in Theory and Practice

In theory, classification is an orderly, rational process. The supervi-sor begins by defining a specific position that fits the needs of the organization, after applying the tenets of position management and organizational design. (See Warman, 1986, for a reasonably com-prehensible discussion of some of the "principles" of organization design.) He or she then writes a detailed position description (PD) and gives it to the classifier to review and classify. The classifier compares the PD to the classification standards developed for that job series by the Office of Personnel Management (OPM). These standards are based on a number of criteria, including the nature of the job and the knowledge required to do it, the complexity of the work or the amount of originality required, the amount of supervision received, and so on.[2] The position is then classified, following which it can be advertised, with qualifications based on the classification.

In theory, this is an objective process in which the classifier simply compares the description of the position with the standards and comes up with the appropriate job series and grade level. Also in theory, there is a clear division of labor between the manager and the classifier. The reality is not so simple.

In practice, position classification is a highly politicized process and the focus of a great deal of conflict, both substantive and procedural. Let us look at each in turn.

The system is designed to be objective; every well-trained classifier should be able to look at a PD and come up with the same classification. This is the theory that OPM itself put forward in a handbook for managers that advised a manager who is explaining a job classification to an employee to "discuss the objective basis of position classification" (U.S. Office of Personnel Management, 1981, p. 52). But most studies recognize what one terms "the central importance of human judgment" in the classification process (Warman, 1986, p. 33) and acknowledge that a classifier requires considerable knowledge and skill to be able to apply general, and often outdated, standards to specific positions (Warman, 1986; U.S. Merit Systems Protection Board, 1989).

Further, OPM has been moving in recent years toward broader, "generic" standards. This only increases the amount of discretion in the classification process. As a result, the same position might indeed be classified differently by different classifiers. A particularly disturbing example was cited in an MSPB study of the classification process, which described a Department of Labor test of one of OPM's draft generic standards, which entailed applying the standard to several hundred positions. Each test classification was reviewed either by both a classifier and a manager or by several classifiers. The results were not encouraging: "Grade ratings obtained by applying the draft guide, even ratings of familiar standard position descriptions by trained classifiers, resulted in a high level of inconsistency. . . . For example, classifiers rating one position by the guide selected the most popular grade only 58 percent of the time; in the second blind test, agreement was even lower with only 46 percent selecting the most popular grade. Thus, the likelihood of two trained classifiers applying the draft guide and coming to the same conclusion was only slightly better than one chance in two" (U.S. Merit Systems Protection Board, 1989, p. 20). Small wonder, then, that managers recognize the inconsistencies in the system, and that they often disagree with the classifiers, particularly over the appropriate grade level.

However, much of the conflict is not really about substance but about process, and also about roles and role definitions. In Chapter Four, we saw how the division of labor between line managers and personnel specialists in the area of hiring varied from agency to agency. The same is true in the area of classification, where, again, different approaches reflect differences in the organizations' cultures and in the way managers and personnelists define their roles. For personnelists, the role conflict between control and service, discussed in Chapter Three, is once again central. For managers, the issue is the one discussed in Chapter Two: how broadly do they define their role? Do they see human resources functions as central to their role, and if so, are they willing to devote their own time to nitty-gritty tasks such as writing a PD, or do they want to delegate this work to others? Taken to its logical conclusion, the question becomes: do managers have to become classification experts?

Agency Approaches to Classification: Continued Battles and a Cease-Fire

The previous section gave a brief description of how the system is supposed to work in theory and of some of the conflicts that emerge in practice. I now turn to an examination of how the system is actually used in different organizational settings. In the first section, I look at the two Department of Agriculture agencies (FCS and APHIS) and at EPA. I then turn to the Navy, which has taken a different approach to classification.

Classification Wars at the Department of Agriculture and EPA

When I began this analysis, I expected to find fairly dramatic differences between the two Department of Agriculture agencies on the one hand and EPA on the other. In fact, the situation was more complex than I expected. I did find a fairly clear relationship between budget levels and classification practices. But with respect to procedures, there were few clear differences between the agencies. Rather, the practices at the two Department of Agriculture agencies and at EPA are variants on a theme, and that theme is continual conflict between managers and classifiers—conflict that few people see as serving a useful purpose.

The Link Between Grading and Budgets

I posited that there would be substantive differences in how agency personnel specialists interpreted and applied the classification standards in disputed cases, and that these differences would flow from two factors: the agency culture and its budget. In particular, if classification serves as a budgetary control system, those agencies with more money at their command would tend to be more lenient in applying classification standards, allowing grade levels to go up. This is just what managers see as happening. They talk to their peers in other agencies about classification issues, and at both the Department of Agriculture and EPA, most form the impression that Agriculture grades lower than EPA does. In fact, the difference was quite striking. At both APHIS and FCS, many interviewees spontaneously mentioned that their agency was graded lower than other agencies. No one at EPA made this claim. In fact, one person frankly stated that he was taking advantage of EPA's higher grades to raid others. In the Navy, too, no one mentioned being graded lower than other agencies.

Without going in and conducting an audit, I cannot substantiate these perceptions of agency differences, but they are deeply held. To what do people attribute the differences? They see both budgetary and cultural pressures at work. Both managers and classifiers recognize that classification is really a budgetary issue. Several people talked about the problems of secretarial grades in these terms. One spoke of managers' budgetary priorities: "There [are] competing factors here. To upgrade the secretaries is going to cost you more money. And right now, a lot of organizations are either making a lot of computer purchases so if they have money available they want to put it in that direction, or they're trying to modernize their furniture, . . . and I just have a feeling that again, the emphasis is going to be on modernizing furniture or computer capabilities and not really get down to providing a better grade level for the secretaries."

Personnelists agreed. An FCS senior personnel manager acknowledged the differences between FCS and EPA. As he explained, "When you compare across agencies, EPA secretaries get much higher grades than here, and it depends on the agency's budget and their ability to pay."

Budgetary differences help explain why grade levels are higher at EPA. By the same logic, we would expect to see a difference in perceptions between APHIS and FCS managers, since, as we saw in Chapter One, APHIS budgets have been growing of late while FCS budgets have been cut. But managers in both organizations see the classification system as being interpreted very strictly, and they attribute this to the overall culture of the Department of Agriculture. First, they see their own classifiers, as well as the department as a whole, consciously taking a hard line on classification issues.

As one APHIS supervisor said, "People at FSO tend to hold down people at the lower ranks, [even though OPM] seems to be saying some upgrading should go on. They've given agencies the authority, but they don't want to use it. They don't want to change." A personnel manager at FCS put the blame on the department and told me of an attempt to get the department to approve higher grades for employees all the way from the secretarial level to the SES. According to him: "AG [the Department of Agriculture] is not on the cutting edge, such as EPA is. . . . AG's view of regs [regulations] is not as liberal. We really stick to the letter of the law as far as classification."

From the point of view of managers, classifiers seem almost to take pride in the fact that they are hard-nosed. As one manager told me: "Pay is not equal in all agencies. We seem to have a low scale compared to other agencies. I had a secretary who was a [grade] 5. She moved to another agency to do the same type of work, and she was upgraded to a 7. I pointed it out to headquarters, and they said, 'Because some people overclassify is no reason we should.'"

People in the Department of Agriculture agencies are convinced that having lower grades harms them in a number of ways, most obviously in being able to hire and hold on to the best people. But it causes other problems as well, as an FCS supervisor explained:

> We had a lot of interaction with HHS [the Department of Health and Human Services] and a couple of other agencies, and I'd send a senior staff person to a meeting, and she would be by far the lowest-graded person there at that meeting. The others would generally be [GS-]14s, and sometimes our branch chiefs, who were 14s, would have to go along to the meeting, not because they were particularly knowledgeable but just because we had to get "grade clout." And the branch chief, who was over me, would be negotiating with 14s who were staff people in other agencies, and I think that sets up a bad position.

As this observation makes clear, in the status-conscious bureaucracy of the government, having a lower grade puts one at a disadvantage when one has to negotiate with higher-graded people. Morale is also hurt when employees see others receiving higher pay and greater recognition for doing similar work.

Conflicts Between Managers and Classifiers

These agency differences in how the classification standards are applied should not come as a surprise, given the differences between these agencies both in culture and in budget. As we saw in Chapter One, the Department of Agriculture agencies do have a more traditional, by-the-book culture than EPA. And while APHIS has grown somewhat in recent years, the FCS budget and workforce have been shrinking, so it is not surprising that FCS is trying to hold the line on costs. One might expect that the tendency in the Department of Agriculture to keep grades lower would lead to higher levels of conflict than in an agency such as EPA, where grades have been allowed to rise. The startling discovery here is that this is not the case: EPA managers describe conflict with their personnelists (and vice versa) about as much as do APHIS managers and personnelists. And FCS appears to have a somewhat lower level of conflict overall, although while I was conducting this study there was ongoing debate about one specific job title (a story I return to in more detail below).

How can we explain the fact that the level of conflict over classification does not appear to bear much relationship to the liberality with which positions get classified? To answer that, we must look in more depth at the sources of conflict. Here, I examine four of these sources:

1. The differing approaches of line managers and classifiers
2. The differing incentive structures of the two groups

3. The conflicts over role and division of labor
4. The overarching issue of power

First, as we saw in Chapters Two and Three, managers and person-nelists are very dissimilar kinds of people. They come from con-trasting backgrounds, and they have absorbed very different values. As a result, they sometimes feel they are talking across a canyon. On the one hand, personnelists keep trying to get managers to accept the principles they feel are central to good position man-agement, as an FCS personnelist explained:

> Position management tells you the best way to structure the organi-zation. You try to cut back on overlapping functions, and on over-supervision. Do you have too many layers? For example, you might have division directors at the 15 level, and under them you would have branch chiefs at the 14, and under them section heads at the 13. They are working supervisors, usually with a staff of five to seven people. That's pretty good from a position management standpoint. But some want to add a nonsupervisory 13 in that section. You end up with a 13 supervising a 13. It's not recommended, but most super-visors see nothing wrong with it. . . . They don't understand. Maybe they do, but they just want to do it, and mostly they get what they want and we advise them.

On the other hand, many managers reject the underlying logic of the classification system. As one EPA manager put it:

> I could make an argument, from an organizational standpoint, and I'm sure these arguments were made, back when they started the classification system, that you ought to be able to set up certain stan-dards for certain job categories. . . . But from a practitioner's stand-point, that just does not make sense. I have changing needs from year to year, let alone from decade to decade, and these classifica-

tion standards, a lot of the time, were written thirty years ago. And it just is a millstone around our necks that serves no useful purpose other than fighting back and forth with the classifier.

Managers and supervisors disagree over more than the philosophical underpinnings of the classification system. They also work from different incentive structures. Classifiers understand the budgetary imperatives underlying their work. From their point of view, managers would give away the store if they had half a chance. Classifiers in both APHIS and EPA used almost identical language in expressing this. As one said: "My experience is managers do not recognize in the least bit any kind of responsibility for the taxpayer's dollars. It's not a consideration. There's no regard for position management, no regard for trying to keep payroll costs at a certain level. I don't see anyone saying we only have a certain amount of money and we should use it this way. There's no accountability; it's just building a bigger empire. It's not just selfish—they are committed to the mission—but there's no recognition that the management responsibility includes trying to do more with less."

While many managers would argue that classifiers are overzealous in holding the line, some recognize that there is some truth in what the classifiers say about them. As one put it, "If every manager had his way, we'd all be upgraded and so would all of our staffs, and the budget would go through the roof." But this same manager went on to explain classifiers' resistance to upgrades in more personal terms: "You ask them to take actions that would increase a person's grade and salary structure beyond their own. They don't see it happen to them, so why should they help it happen for somebody else? They're fairly low-graded themselves. I think there's a personal bias that comes into it."

Given that grades are probably higher at EPA, one might expect that there would be less pressure for reclassification, but this does not appear to be the case, at least in part because EPA managers fighting to get higher classifications for their employees are stressing external, not internal, equity. That is, they do not really care that their employees are making more than those in other federal agencies, because they are competing for employees in a national market and often losing.

The respective roles of managers and classifiers continue to be a source of conflict in both agencies. On the surface, this is an argument about who should do what, especially who should write the position descriptions. FCS classifiers appear to take the hardest line in this regard. They state bluntly that they do not write PDs. The managers agree, with some exasperation, and they see the process—which follows closely the outline given above—as adversarial. As one explained: "They're a barrier. . . . It's not like we get real assistance. . . . The personnel office, rather than writing the PD, said, 'You write something, and we'll see if it passes.' It was judged against a standard that I couldn't see. It was like shooting at a moving target."

In both APHIS and EPA, where the personnel office has tried to focus on providing service to managers, the division of labor is less clear-cut. At APHIS, I heard a variety of stories from personnelists. Apparently, in some cases, they will write the PDs or at least consult on the process, although it is clear that they would prefer that the manager take responsibility for at least developing a first draft. At EPA, too, the personnelists sometimes take on this task. Particularly at EPA, personnelists pointed out that the task is often delegated by managers to their administrative officers (AOs) but that managers themselves needed to at least understand the system and, further, that personnelists were more likely to be forced to help write the PDs for offices that did not have AOs.

I would maintain that underlying all these arguments about approach or about who does what is the central issue of power and control. To put it baldly, the current system gives control over a key resource not to managers but to personnelists, who do not report to the managers and whom managers can influence only with difficulty. The fact that the system we are examining is, in large part, a budgetary system is pertinent here, since some would argue that "outside" control is necessary to maintain accountability for expenditures. But the consequence is that conflict is built into the structures. Both sides recognize this as an issue. As one personnelist put it, "What happens [in my agency] is managers don't understand they're just supposed to describe the job, and we set the classification. It comes in as, 'Here's a description of a grade 13' [analyst], and if it comes back different, all heck breaks loose. They see us as a rubber stamp."

Managers are all too aware that a classifier has power, and this sometimes rankles even more because they are forced to deal with someone lower than them in the bureaucratic hierarchy. As one manager put it: "They are extremely frustrating to deal with. They are people who are not high-graded, and they make it as difficult and frustrating as possible. That's how they exercise their power. This person jerks them eight ways to Sunday—he's a GS-12 classifier."

Of course, not all relationships between managers and classifiers are conflicted. But as long as classifiers have the final authority, the potential for conflict hangs over the relationship. How does this affect the strategies managers have developed to cope with their limited power? It is to this question that I turn in the next section.

Strategies in the Classification Wars

In the area of hiring, as Chapter Four showed, there were fairly consistent differences between agencies in how managers defined their roles and in the division of labor between managers and personnelists. The patterns are less clear when managers deal with classification problems. Although there are some agency differences in approach, it would appear that each individual manager makes strategic decisions about how to cope with classification. There are three main dimensions that emerge when one listens to managers explaining their approaches: an active-passive dimension; a cooperative-confrontational dimension; and a technical-political dimension. Let us look at each in turn.

First, we see in the area of classification a range of active and passive approaches similar to those we found in hiring (discussed in Chapter Four). That is, managers can choose either to get actively involved or to remain relatively passive and let others deal with classification. But whereas in hiring there were consistent agency differences, in classification there was wide variance within each agency in the amount of management involvement as well as in the reasons for different approaches. On the one hand, one FCS manager had withdrawn from involvement out of a feeling of total powerlessness. As he explained:

> I have never been successful in reclassifying an employee. . . . I've tried to upgrade positions, and trying to get personnel to understand what it is about this position that requires an upgrading of grade level, you would almost have to convince them that this person is going to walk on water, you would almost have to convince them that [this] person would do more on his job than you do as a supervisor. And I've just not had any luck at all. I don't know what accounts for that, but it's been very frustrating for me, so much so that I've basically given up.

On the other hand, another FCS manager chose carefully when to get directly involved and when to delegate: "We have an administrative assistant we have charged with our basic, routine liaison with personnel, processing 52s [forms that document personnel actions]. . . . But for the big stuff, like when I was trying to create a nonsupervisory senior job, I did it myself. I wrote the job description, I debated it with the classification specialist, and I did it that way."

At APHIS, there was a wide range, from those who had minimal involvement to the SES member who said that he involved himself in every human resources issue and who spent considerable time and energy working on upgrading staff. Some of the most active, aggressively involved managers were at EPA, but even there I saw a wide range of approaches.

Those who did get actively involved then had to make a second strategic decision: whether to adopt a cooperative or a confrontational stance in their relationship with the classifier. Some chose a cooperative approach in order to get what they needed from the classifiers. For example, an EPA regional manager described his strategy.

> Well, I find, historically—I think this is just human nature—if you go down to the personnel people and say, "I've got this problem. Can you help me?" then they are very likely to help you. If you go down to them and say, "You guys have been screwing up. This person is in the wrong place, and I demand that you do such and such," they're going to fight you. And one of the advantages of the style of most of the people in this region and most of the people in this room, is that we're more likely to do the former than the latter, and we don't try to bully or bludgeon the personnel people into doing things.

Others saw the cooperative approach as unrealistic because there was no willingness to cooperate on the side of the personnelists. For example, an FCS manager explained: "As for the personnel office, we're grateful for smaller impediments, rather than larger ones. . . . [It's] not a service organization."

Finally, approaches to classification may lean toward the technical or toward the political. Managers who chose to become involved in these issues had to decide at what level they wanted to become technical experts. The process of classification is truly arcane and complex, and managers tend to be very busy people with many other demands on their time. Their responses ran the gamut. At one end of the continuum was a noncareer SES member who told me that she made a conscious decision not to become an expert on all aspects of the personnel process but rather to use the personnel office as a resource when she needed it. At the other was the EPA manager—probably the most outspokenly aggressive manager I talked to when it came to the classification wars—who told me that he had taken a class on classification just so that he would know how to cite chapter and verse when he fought with the classifiers. The majority of managers were somewhere in the middle; they were similar to the APHIS midlevel manager who told me, "I got involved a little in classification in trying to get an upgrade for one of my employees, but not to the point of understanding why an 11 is an 11 and a 12 is a 12."

Assuming some mastery of the system by managers (or good staff support from the personnel office or from a shadow personnel office), what are the technical strategies managers use to "work" the classification system? The goal, of course, is to get a worker's classification, and thus pay, increased. The most widely used approach is to redefine the job to include a broader range of duties—a process known technically as "accretion of duties." Often, this is quite legitimate, as missions or technology change and jobs are redesigned. But there are two controversial issues here.

One important issue is whether one can legitimately upgrade a position not because its duties have changed but because the individual occupying it is a superstar who does outstanding work. The standard line of the personnelists is that classification should not reflect the amount or quality of work an individual employee performs; only if the person is doing different work at a higher level of responsibility should the position be upgraded. They would argue that the individual should get a performance award instead or that the organization should hire more people at the lower grade level. This is intensely frustrating to managers. The topic came up for extended discussion in my group interview with EPA managers at the regional office. As one explained: "When they take the skills that that person is using and apply them against the manual, they say . . . , 'This job rates out as a 7. It doesn't matter if she is doing the work of three people. You should just get two more people.' And I don't know whether I buy that. You know, if the person is doing the work of three people, it seems like we ought to be able to promote [him or her] for doing that kind of work, and yet that doesn't fit into the personnel view. I mean, that's just not in their thinking."

The other issue is even more controversial: the fact that some managers try to game the system by padding positions. I discussed one dysfunctional aspect of this in Chapter Two. The creation of pseudo-supervisors is a direct outgrowth of the need to move people into supervisory positions to justify a grade increase. As we saw, some of them are actually supervisors in name only or are given only a small part of what would normally be considered supervisory responsibilities. I cited an example from the Navy, but the phenomenon occurs in other agencies, too. For example, at EPA, a first-line supervisor told me: "Unfortunately, we have to compete with the outside, and the only way to compete and try to keep people, and this is a massive thing, is to pay them more. And how can we pay them more? We make them supervisors. Or we have to give them additional duties which they're not qualified [to perform] or we don't expect them to perform."

Creating dual tracks for promotion alleviates some of this problem. By increasing the top grade for technical positions, several agencies have reduced the need to create pseudo-supervisors or to promote good technical people into supervisory positions they do not really want. For example, managers in a group interview at FCS told me that they used to move people into supervisory positions to justify a higher grade, but that this was happening much less frequently because there were now some nonsupervisory positions at higher grade levels. But justifying higher nonsupervisory grades under the classification standards is sometimes difficult, and the success rate is uneven both within and across agencies.

The classification standards are also dysfunctional in their requirement that a supervisory classification be based on the number of people supervised, not on the actual work performed. This has the effect of distorting organizational structures. It is particularly problematic in agencies that are trying to cut back or to streamline operations but are afraid that if they do so they may be forced to downgrade supervisors whose actual work has not changed or who may even be doing more work because of the loss of staff. Here, the issue is not padding staff to increase grades, but justifying the retention of grades as staff are cut. For example, a group of SES members at APHIS told me that they were directly involved in this issue because staffs in state offices had been reduced. As the managers cut back the size of offices headed by area veterinarians, they ran up against the standards that linked grades to numbers supervised. As one put it, "We're really in danger of losing ability there to supervise. . . . How do you come up with a justification to get the grade based on technical needs? We're spending a lot of time on that right now."

Accretion of duties was the most frequently mentioned method for upgrading a position. A close second was simply changing the job title of a position. In this case, the manager argues that the person's duties actually are better reflected by a new title rather than by the old title. Of course, the new title will bring a higher grade and may also have greater promotion potential.

I most frequently found this approach used in dealing with secretarial positions. Because the pay differential between public and private sector positions is especially acute at the secretarial level, managers find it particularly hard to get and to hold on to good secretaries. Further, the work of secretaries has changed significantly over the past twenty years. Increasingly, professional employees are doing their own word processing, and secretaries are called on to do more demanding administrative work or to learn quite complex computer programs.

At APHIS, several people told me that they had dealt with this problem by reclassifying their secretarial positions to program assistant or budget assistant. As one of them explained it: "The majority of our secretaries have gone from the 318 series to budget assistants as a reclassification because there was a career ladder in program assistants. . . . So all of them have budgetary responsibilities now that they're reclassified. Some of them got some remarkably substantial jumps in grade because of their responsibilities under that new classification."

Personnel offices may even encourage use of this technique when faced with intense pressure from managers to upgrade such positions, but not all managers are willing to go along with it. One APHIS SES member recognized that this strategy, which the personnel office was pushing, might have a downside: it might actually distort what his secretary did. "When they did the job audit of my secretary, they said it was clear she merits a 9. They said, 'If you change her job series to program assistant, you have no problem.' But why do we have to change her series? It just doesn't make any sense. That's one I'm not relenting on, because she's not a program assistant, and she should be rewarded for what she does, and she likes what she does."

Most attempts to change job titles are microbattles concerning an individual employee. However, while I was conducting my interviews at the Food and Consumer Service, the last stages of a protracted macrobattle were being played out, involving the agency, the Department of Agriculture, and the Office of Personnel Management. The dispute concerned a classification that covered more than half of FCS employees: the food assistance program specialist (usually shortened to food program specialist [FPS], or 120 series). The length of this battle, which began soon after the series was created in 1972, and the energy devoted to it are testimony to the importance of the labels placed on employees by the classification system. They also underline how complex change becomes when a personnel system does double duty as a budget control system.

It was FCS itself, shortly after it was created, that asked for a new, specific classification to cover the majority of its employees. Stories about the genesis of the classification have passed into the folklore of the agency. The official line is that it fit the kinds of work the agency did initially, such as outreach and actual delivery of services, but that shortly after it was created, the work of the agency shifted more toward administering and evaluating programs (Food and Nutrition Service, 1992). But the story told by one informant is that an early personnel director thought he could protect people from a reduction in force (RIF) by creating a unique series; he made such a good case for the separate series that it became hard to undo.

Most people I talked to agreed either that the series was a problem for them personally or that it was generally perceived to be a problem by many employees. Both managers and staffing specialists told me about how it affected hiring. One person told me: "As a staffing specialist, I never liked the use of 'food' in the title. People would walk by our booth at job fairs and say, 'Oh, that's not for me.' And I've taken a million calls from people who work in kitchens or supervise cooks and think they qualify." The reactions of many employees attested to the power of labels; they disliked the title because they felt they were not taken seriously when they applied for jobs elsewhere. Although one manager asked whether the agency should be concerned about making it easier for employees to leave, most acknowledged that the lack of prestige associated with the title was a problem.

But many managers were skeptical about the possibility of change, some because so many previous attempts had failed and others because they saw the underlying issue as grade level and, hence, money. As we saw, FCS employees tend to see themselves as lower-graded in comparison with people at other agencies. If they are given more common titles, such as 343 (management and program analysis series) or 301 (miscellaneous administration and program series), it will be easier to compare their grade levels with those in other agencies (such as the Department of Health and Human Services) and to make the argument that they should be upgraded. This is why some people felt that any change in the series title would have to be cost-neutral, and why a senior manager shared with me his anxieties about the budget ramifications of a series change and his fear that it might lead to cutting the number of employees in order to cover higher salary costs.

In this case, strong leadership by the administrator, who was committed to resolving this problem, finally led to approval of a change by both the department and by OPM. But meanwhile, enormous energy had been wasted over a period of many years. This was due in part to the sheer inertia built into the system but also to concerns that the hidden agenda was a desire for a pay raise.

Both upgrading an individual via accretion of duties and changing job titles (for an individual or a whole group) can be seen as technical strategies in the classification wars, but the line between technical and political strategies is not clear-cut. Each of these technical strategies shades into politics to the extent that people are gaming the system—for example, by exaggerating an employee's duties. This process of manipulating the system requires technical knowledge of the classification standards, but the astute manager may be able to delegate the technical work (that is, the actual PD writing) to an administrative assistant or even to a cooperative personnelist. All he or she needs to understand is the broad outlines of the process. Or the line manager may know enough to ask to see the relevant class standard and may then use it as a model for writing a new PD. One APHIS manager told me, "I decided early on that if I wanted anything done, I would have to do it myself. I do research on the standards so I can write PDs." Of course, this irritates some classifiers, but as one personnel supervisor explained: "We don't lock the classification standards away. If we give [them] to [managers], the next day we may see a benchmark in the PD, and it drives the classifiers crazy. But it's the manager who has to sign attesting that it's accurate."

A somewhat more explicitly political strategy is to throw the claims to "scientific" accuracy back at personnelists by playing what I call the "PD comparison game." This entails finding a PD for a position that is similar to, but graded higher than, one in your own office (perhaps from another regional office in your agency), taking the PD to your personnel office, and asking for it to be classified. An FCS manager in a regional office described precisely how the game is played (and why personnel staff often refuse to cooperate):

> I've got a PD from another region—a GS-12. And I had our classi-fier look at it, and [that person] classified it as an 11. So there's dif-ferences. I put three others in from different regions, and they were 12, and they looked at them, and they were all classified as 11s. They tell me every other classifier will look at it differently. But they have a hidden agenda there. If they were to tell you that any one of those three [was a 12], then you come back in and say, "I want to classify my position." What are they going to do, tell you now you can't do it? So it's the safe thing to do, to always classify low. You can't get in any trouble that way. . . . They play it safe. And again, given their mission, they are probably doing what they are supposed to do.

The point at which the politics can become heavy is when a classifier does not support what a manager wants. In those agen-cies where the personnel office stresses customer service, person-nelists feel under intense pressure not to say no. They will work hard to find a solution to the problem. As one explained: "At the point where there is real conflict, or the step before that, before you utter the 'N' word, you go back to be sure there isn't some-thing missing. If you need something substantive, you talk to the manager. When it doesn't look like you can do it, you go back and give them another chance. So you aren't hearing, 'They never came to me.'" But classifiers make it clear how hard it is to be responsive to managers, particularly when they face demands they consider unreasonable.

The seriousness of the classification wars is clearly indicated by the willingness of managers to escalate the battle when necessary. At both of the Department of Agriculture agencies and at the EPA, managers told me that they had sometimes gone over the person-nel specialist's head in order to get a higher grade. They may start by going to the supervisor immediately over the classifier or to the director of personnel, but there were several cases where they went all the way to the deputy director of the agency. In regional offices, appeals are made to the headquarters personnel office. In the Agriculture agencies, managers appeal, on occasion, to the departmental personnel office. And on rare occasions, they go all the way to OPM. Classifiers know that this may happen, and they worry whether their bosses will back them up.

This frequent conflict takes its toll. Classifiers feel caught between the pressure to be creative and the need to follow the regulations. As a result, they were by far the most embittered and unhappy of the personnelists I spoke to. One was quite honest about her feelings: "I've already decided I can't do this [work in classification] until I retire. It's too stressful." Managers are often critical of classifiers, whom they frequently describe as narrow and unhelpful. What is clear is that this system takes up enormous amounts of time and energy, that it adds significantly to the costs of managing people, and that many managers question how much value is added by this whole complex system. Both managers and classifiers wonder if there is not a better way. In the next section, I look at one agency that is trying a different approach.

Two Navy Attempts at a Cease-Fire

At both the Department of Agriculture and EPA, the frequent conflicts over classification stemmed primarily from two sources: the reality that power over a significant resource was held not by line managers but by personnelists and the fact that cost control was being exercised indirectly, via the personnel process, rather than directly. One result of this traditional system is that managers are not held directly responsible for controlling personnel costs; the incentive structure rewards them for increasing rather than decreasing their staffs. In fact, the Navy found that, under the old system, it had trouble staying within its payroll budget. According to the

U.S. General Accounting Office (1990b), in fiscal year 1985, the Navy exceeded its payroll budget of $9.9 billion by $500 million. These budget issues are only exacerbated by the complexity and the rigidity of the traditional classification system. The Navy has taken two different approaches to solving this problem: a navywide change in budgeting and classification authority and an influential demonstration project testing out a greatly simplified classification system along with other reforms. Let us look at each in turn.

Manage to Payroll: Changing the Balance of Power. Changing the dysfunctional incentive structure of the traditional budgeting and classification systems requires several interlocking reforms. Managers must be given authority to allocate resources and to make classification decisions, and they must be held responsible for managing within their budget. In the Navy, these changes are linked to a new method of internal budgeting: Manage to Payroll. MTP, as it is called, was designed to free managers of rigid constraints by giving them a budget amount and letting them have more authority over how to allocate it. As one manager explained it, "Basically, MTP is a way of management where they give you the funds and you go and do the job." In theory, this gives managers more flexibility in times of growth but also more control over where and how to take cuts. MTP can have a significant effect on management of people, as it allows managers much more leeway in deciding how many people to hire and at what grades, how to handle training and travel funds, and so on.

Along with MTP authority, line managers have been given authority to classify the positions in their units. The combination has made a noticeable positive difference. Several managers told stories about the games they used to have to play around classification, and said how glad they were not to have to go through that anymore. As one described the change: "The personnel office has relinquished classification standards to the directorates [that is, the large operating units]. The scrutinization and the adherence to standards without good interpretation by the personnel office are no longer there. The game you'd play was to write the words to that standard to satisfy them. It was a paper game. Now, you don't need to play the game."

In short, MTP, combined with classification authority, caused a shift in power from personnelists to line managers, forcing the personnel office to redefine its role away from emphasis on compliance with the rules and toward a more cooperative stance in providing technical help to managers. As a result, many managers saw a significant improvement in their relationships with the Consolidated Civilian Personnel Office (CCPO). An SES member said, "I think [CCPO] views themselves as a service. I can't overemphasize how much difference MTP and the ability to classify our jobs make. They realized we didn't need them."

Changing incentive structures by giving managers a set budget to manage has also clearly made a difference in managers' behavior. According to the General Accounting Office (GAO), "The Navy believes that because responsibility for the budget has been delegated to lower-level managers rather than being centrally managed at the command level, there is a greater awareness of personnel costs" (U.S. General Accounting Office, 1990b, p. 3). The GAO also pointed out that since the introduction of MTP, the Navy has done much better at staying under or at least close to its civilian payroll budget.

However, this approach is no panacea; it solves some but far from all the problems that the current classification system creates for managers. Managers told me about several drawbacks to the Navy's approach. First, most first- and second-level managers, and even some SES members, felt that authority over both classification and MTP was held at too high a level. The theory of MTP was that each manager would be given a budget to manage. The practice is quite different. Both classification authority and especially MTP authority are held at such a high level (usually, the directorate—or admiral—level) that even some SES members complain that they have little control over their resources. The GAO corroborated this finding; it found quite uneven levels of delegation. What this means in practice is explained by one frustrated SES member: "It's managed at the directorate level. That is one level below the commander. I'm at group level, second level below the commander. And I don't manage my MTP. If I did, I would probably be able to replace [staff members who have left]. Now, someone else is overstaffed, so I can't hire."

Frustration over the high level at which MTP authority is held was a common complaint. One of the sources of the problem appears to be the formal hierarchical culture of the Navy, which may make it difficult for top-level managers to delegate away their own control of resources. But this is not just a Navy problem: higher-level managers' reluctance to delegate authority has been identified as an issue in a number of other organizations implementing similar reforms (U.S. Office of Personnel Management, 1989).

Further, even though classification authority has been delegated to line managers, these managers are still forced to work within the complex and restrictive classification system. Some of the dysfunctions that have developed in the effort to get around this system are still in evidence—for example, the creation of pseudo-supervisors and the inflation of position descriptions (PDs). Most managers do not want to become experts in the ins and outs of classification, so in some cases, the organizational level that has classification authority has hired consultants to handle the technical aspects. It is not clear that these people are better qualified as classification experts than CCPO staff, and they appear to play some of the traditional classification control function.

One particularly disturbing issue is the unwillingness of some managers to accept classification authority. A classifier at the CCPO told me that most of those at NAVSEA have delegated it back, and a senior personnel person at Portsmouth said that none of the managers there had wanted the authority. According to him, a couple of shipyards have delegated classification authority, but "you end up setting up phantom personnel offices, and the whole organization gets out of control." This may reflect the fact that managers are already overloaded and find the complexity of the system daunting. But it also may be true, as some personnelists believe, that certain managers are unwilling to take responsibility for making hard decisions or for giving bad news to their staff; they would rather demonize the personnelists and blame them for denying someone an upgrade.

Further, some managers themselves fear that, absent thorough training and consistent oversight, managers will abuse classification authority. This was a subject of some discussion in my group interview with SES members, one of whom explained: "When you have the ability to classify, especially when you get that suddenly, when you haven't had it before, it's like putting a hungry person in a candy store. You can be disciplined and have a piece of candy, or you can make yourself very sick. To demonstrate the point at a field activity like a naval shipyard, when I first went to a shipyard in 1969, there were two or three GM-15s in the entire shipyard. When I left, you probably couldn't count them. Everybody, almost, was a 15." It is this threat of pressure for grade inflation that makes linking classification authority to budget authority so important. Managers themselves will then be faced with making the trade-offs between fewer higher-graded employees and more lower-graded staff members.

While the Navy's MTP has not solved all the problems we saw in the traditional classification system, it is probably a move in the right direction. First, it controls payroll budgets directly rather than doing so indirectly by using the classification system as a budgetary control system. Second, it give managers (albeit at a high level) direct control over classification decisions. As a result, the need for elaborate game-playing or protracted conflict with personnelists is much reduced. According to the GAO report: "Officials said that lengthy justifications and rebuttals did not have to be prepared to justify position classifications. Also, one classification officer said that the average turnaround time for a classification action had decreased from 30 to 45 days before MTP to 18 days or less after MTP" (U.S. General Accounting Office, 1990b, pp. 4–5).

The Navy Demonstration Project. While MTP is a significant reform, it does not address many of the worst aspects of the classification system, particularly its complexity and rigidity. But the Navy has a model for addressing these problems and has tested it extensively in a formal demonstration project at two Navy laboratories. This was the first demonstration project authorized under Title VI of the Civil Service Reform Act, which allowed agencies to suspend civil service law under specific conditions in order to test out new approaches to personnel management. Among the goals of the Navy demonstration were increasing the labs' ability to hire and retain scientists in competition with the private sector, giving managers more control over personnel decisions, and making the personnel system less cumbersome and more flexible (Ban, 1991a). Changes were made in procedures for entry-level recruiting and performance appraisal; in addition, the Navy demonstration tested a streamlined flexible classification system—a method generally referred to as *broad-banding.* Instead of dividing jobs into hundreds of separate titles, this system used job banding, which grouped all "like" positions into five career paths (U.S. Office of Personnel Management, 1984):

1. Professional (includes scientists, engineers, and other professionals)
2. Technical (includes technical support, photographer, quality inspection, and other technician positions)
3. Administrative (includes professional administrative and program analyst occupations)
4. Technical specialist (includes specialized positions in the areas of intelligence, communications, computers, facility management, and quality assurance)

5. Clerical/assistant (includes secretarial, assistant, and clerical positions)

Further, the demonstration implemented *grade banding*, which combined GS grades 1 through 15 into broad pay bands. Each career path has different pay bands associated with it, each pay band typically encompassing at least two traditional pay grades. Thus, each path has four to six pay levels.

The net result is a greatly simplified system, in which the line manager can handle classification by using basic descriptions of positions within each career path. Further, the broad pay bands permit linking pay to performance appraisals by making it easy to move employees' salaries up within the broad band.

Two other agencies have conducted demonstration projects of simplified classification systems. The National Institute of Standards and Technology demonstration used a system quite similar to the Navy's, while the Air Force, in a project called Pacer Share Demonstration, combined blue- and white-collar supervisors into one pay schedule. An OPM report summarizing results of these three demonstrations concluded that: "under all broad-banding systems, satisfaction with classification has increased significantly, and the Navy data, in particular, indicate that the classification process has become much less contentious. Demonstration managers became more satisfied with the services received from their personnel offices when the focus of attention shifted from a process to a service orientation" (U.S. Office of Personnel Management, 1992a, p. 88).

To summarize: Both Navy reforms—Manage to Payroll and the Navy demonstration—point the way to significant improvements in classification from the perspective of managers. The Navy demonstration and its progeny have shaped the debate over classification reform. Their influence is clear, for example, in a 1991 report by the National Academy of Public Administration, which supports broad-banding and simplified classification systems.

Conclusions

As we have seen, the traditional classification process is a significant constraint on managers—one that is made more complicated because of the complex relationship between budgetary and personnel controls. Classification serves as a method to control costs. It is designed and controlled by personnelists, who justify it on grounds of rational personnel management. This leads to an elaborate game in which personnelists and managers face off in tests of wills and of technical knowledge. The net results are reduced authority for managers to manage their staffs, an enormous waste of resources spent on long classification processes and conflicts, and budgetary control that is neither efficient nor effective.

The fact that the current rigid classification system has dysfunctional effects, leading to gaming and other bureaupathic behaviors, is certainly not news. Shafritz detailed many of these problems in his research over twenty years ago (1973). What is surprising is how resistant the system has been to change. Indeed, many classifiers and senior personnel managers support only marginal adjustments and resist the notion of radical classification reform. For example, at a meeting in 1991, ninety federal directors of personnel "recommended that the current position classification system should remain" (Ross, 1992).

Classification reform is high on the list of the National Performance Review's proposals for reforming human resources in the federal government. In fact, the NPR diagnosis of the problems created by the current system echoes many of the issues that this research raises. The NPR report on human resources (1993d) lists a number of problems with the current system. For example, it faults the system for a lack of mission focus; it sees the value of internal equity as having become an end in itself, driving the system to ever greater levels of precision that have no payoff in more effective government. The report describes a system with low credibility, where "despite all the attempts to build precision into the system through central control and rules, the fairness of the system appears to be questioned by the vast majority of the people whose opinion is perhaps most important," namely, the employees (p. 20). It criticizes the system's complexity and inflexibility and the fact that it fragments responsibility; managers have no obligation to consider the cost consequences of classification actions, while personnelists "do not have to face the consequences that classification actions have on program missions" (p. 21). Finally, the report makes clear how classification reinforces a hierarchical orientation in government, particularly because it provides higher grades for supervisory work.

The specific reforms called for by the NPR flow from this analysis. The report recommends the removal from federal law of the technical details of the system—particularly the classification criteria associated with specific grade levels—so that they can be revised as needed without going through a lengthy legislative process. It proposes that agencies be permitted to move to a broad-banding system on a voluntary basis, with guidance from OPM. And it encourages agencies to experiment with unique approaches to broad-banding under a revised and expanded demonstration project authority. At the same time, the report makes clear that broad-banding is not a panacea and that it can increase salary costs if not linked to appropriate budget controls. For those agencies that choose to remain in the current fifteen-grade system, the NPR calls for delegating final classification authority to the agencies and eliminating OPM's authority to review and reverse agency decisions. Within agencies, classification authority would be given to line managers, who would be provided with appropriate training and decision support systems. Classification decisions would be made "at a level of management that operates under a fixed budget that includes all pay-related costs" (p. 24). Finally, agencies would be given additional flexibility in setting pay rates, such as entry pay or within-grade pay increases.

All the changes proposed by the NPR would tend to reduce complexity and increase flexibility, while at the same time increasing fiscal accountability for line managers. These changes make very good sense in light of the research presented here. They would reduce, if not eliminate, the conflict between managers and personnelists over classification. They would also reduce dramatically the enormous waste of resources on long classification processes and conflicts.

The NPR proposals echo another conclusion that flows from the research. Acknowledging that classification is really about budgetary control makes it clear that any classification authority has to be linked to financial accountability. Otherwise, there will be no incentive for managers to keep pay, and costs, down. Further, the complexity of the current system is a deterrent to managers, even when they have the necessary authority. Moving to a more simplified system is essential if managers are to be able to exercise their classification authority. Even if the system is simplified, managers will require thorough training in order to do classification well. While personnel staff can provide technical support, managers need to learn how to use classification and pay as a management tool—something that will be a novel idea to many of them.

The experience with MTP in the Navy also has potential lessons. Most importantly, broad-banding will not work well if authority is held at too high a level. While it makes sense to link classification and budget authority, if both are held three or four levels up, first-line supervisors and even midlevel managers will hardly be empowered. Further problems are caused by the existence of pseudo-supervisors, which, ironically, is a result of attempts to game the old system. If real managerial authority is held at a level higher than the pseudo-supervisor's level, who will make classification decisions? The most likely scenario is that supervisors who verge on the pseudo—that is, who are uncertain how much authority they really have—will feel that they need to review all classification decisions one or more levels up the chain of command, thereby slowing down the process yet again.

Finally, our being aware of how many managers are really "worker-managers" sensitizes us to workload concerns. Managers cannot be overburdened with responsibilities and discharge all of them well. If they are asked to take on classification responsibility, they may resist—even though they see the change as desirable—simply because of the burden involved. Another reform proposed by the NPR is the broadening of managers' span of control and a reduction in the number of managers. Asking worker-managers to take on responsibility for more people at the same time as their other functions are expanded may be a recipe for disaster.

Chapter Seven

Coping with Ceilings, Freezes, and Reductions in Force

As we saw in the last chapter, what appear to be civil service constraints can actually be budgetary constraints in disguise. In this chapter, we examine an area where civil service and budgetary systems converge even more closely: the procedures used to control the number of federal employees. These fall into two categories: processes that limit hiring (termed *ceilings* or *freezes*) and the complex procedures for conducting layoffs (known as *reductions in force*, or RIFs). These procedures are a significant source of constraint on federal managers. And as with position classification, their effects are particularly dysfunctional because they are indirect methods of budget control. That is, costs are kept constant or reduced not only by directly controlling the budgets that managers are given but by also controlling the number of people they can hire or by requiring them to lay off staff. Here, too, use of indirect controls leads individual managers to apply a variety of coping mechanisms, some of which are dysfunctional for the organization as a whole. These coping strategies vary according to the severity of the cuts required and are also influenced by both organizational culture and individual management styles.

This chapter is divided into two sections. The first looks at restrictions on hiring—that is, ceilings and freezes—while the second examines the much more drastic effects of RIFs.

Ceilings and Freezes

Both ceilings and freezes are methods of controlling the number of people hired, but they differ somewhat in how they are imposed and in their effects. Ceilings are simply caps on the number of people an organization can hire. Formerly, they were based on the number of people employed at the end of the year, but that method encouraged managers to game the system by laying people off for the last pay period of the year, in order to get below the ceiling, and then rehiring them. So current ceilings are based on average number of full-time equivalent (FTE) employees on payroll throughout the year, a method that is harder to game but which gives the agency some flexibility in determining the mix of part-time or full-time employees (National Performance Review, 1993d). Departments or agencies submit budget requests to the Office of Management and Budget (OMB) in terms of both dollars and FTE. OMB then notifies them of their FTE ceilings. The internal budget staff then divides the ceiling among the main components of the organization, which may then additionally subdivide it among subcomponents. The same process is simultaneously taking place for the dollar budget, but the critical fact, from our perspective, is that the two are not necessarily linked. That is, an organization may receive an increased budget but not an increase in FTE.

Most organizations labor under ceiling restrictions. However, it should be pointed out that Congress, reacting against OMB-imposed ceilings, has actually mandated floors for some programs. Minimum staffing levels have been established for major organizations, such as the Food and Drug Administration, as well as for specific installations such as an individual Coast Guard yard (National Performance Review, 1993d). Floors, like ceilings, limit the discretion of management in allocating resources.

Ceilings are used to control the size of the federal workforce as a whole, and the size of the workforce in individual organizations, independently of the budget. Why the need for two accounting systems? The foremost reason is political. In an electoral environment where candidates run against "big government," there is political capital to be made from reducing the size of the federal workforce as well as from cutting the budget deficit. In addition, letting the workforce grow, even when adding new programs, is politically difficult.

Freezes are closely related to ceilings but somewhat more drastic in their effects. When an organization is at or over ceiling, it cannot (at least in theory) hire new staff until there is a vacancy. This may result in a temporary hiring freeze. When a freeze is imposed, all hiring stops. Such freezes may be specific to an agency or to a part of an agency. Freezes can also be imposed across the entire government, as a way to reduce the size of the federal workforce as a whole. For example, President Reagan's first act immediately after his inauguration was to impose a governmentwide hiring freeze. In such cases, agencies are prevented from hiring even if they have both FTE and budget available.

Freezes can vary in a number of ways. In a "hard" freeze, for example, absolutely no hiring will take place for some period of time, whereas in a "soft" freeze, there may be leeway to hire, say, one person for every three who leave. Freezes may also be interrupted by thaws of varying duration, which provide a window in which managers can hire. Both ceilings and freezes can have a number of dysfunctional effects, and both elicit a range of coping mechanisms by individual managers. We look at each in turn below.

Effects of Ceilings

The problems with ceilings derive from the fact that they have a somewhat arbitrary quality and are divorced from both the organization's mission and from its budget. An early critique of the use of ceilings by the National Academy of Public Administration (1983) termed them effective in keeping down the total number of federal employees but concluded that they have, "over many years, created serious managerial problems within government, because [they have] contributed to the abdication of effective work force planning" (p. 22). The National Performance Review (1993a) takes a similar view: "FTE ceilings are usually imposed independently of—and often in conflict with—budget allocations. They are frequently arbitrary, rarely account for changing circumstances, and are normally imposed as across-the-board percentage cuts in FTEs for all of an agency's units—regardless of changing circumstances" (p. 19).

But as we have seen with personnel systems, ceilings are actually administered somewhat differently from agency to agency, which led to some lively debates about what really constrains managers more, the budget or the ceiling. Some argued that ceilings were irrelevant because there never was enough money to hire up to the ceiling. Others felt that a ceiling was actually no barrier— that if they had the dollars, they could hire. They would game the system in a variety of ways. As one put it: "We don't tell people we are going to hire over ceiling, but we recruit aggressively and make pessimistic assumptions about the number of people who will leave. And at the end of the year, if we are over ceiling, as long as we have the money to pay them, it's not a problem."

But there were also large numbers of managers who found ceiling constraints a real problem; the ceilings, they said, put pressures on them and their staffs that forced them to do the work of the organization in less than ideal ways.

The organizational differences were striking in this regard. At APHIS, where resources have not been particularly tight, there was almost an even split between the two sides (with a handful of people saying neither ceilings nor budgets were major constraints), and considerable disagreement about how stringently ceilings were enforced. At the other agriculture agency, FCS, the situation was somewhat different because the agency had taken large budget cuts in recent years. But there, too, concerns were expressed both about the size of the budget and about ceiling limits. In the Navy, the whole issue was transformed through the introduction of the Manage to Payroll (MTP) system. In theory, MTP gave managers the flexibility to manage their budgets, but the reality is that they, too, operate within personnel ceilings.

The place where this issue triggered the strongest reaction was

EPA, where frustration was at a high level. There, interviewees who named ceilings as the primary problem outnumbered those who blamed budget restrictions by three to one, with a significant group identifying both as equally problematic. As we shall see, these agency differences affect the ways individual managers cope with ceilings.

Coping with Ceiling Constraints

How do managers cope with the constraint of ceilings? There are two main approaches: one focuses on attempting to ease the strain by internal means, and the other entails going outside the organization for help, primarily to contractors. Internally, managers use a variety of strategies. First, they try to fill in, where possible, by using people who do not count against ceiling. These include co-ops (students who are working while going to school) and retired people working part-time through a program organized by the American Association of Retired Persons (AARP). Programs such as these are still quite small, but some organizations have come to rely more heavily on them. For example, a personnel manager at the EPA region told me that they have a Senior Environmental Employee Program (a part-time program for retirees, similar to the programs run by AARP) employing over eighty people, which was expected to continue to grow.

A discussion of the co-op program at EPA makes it clear how much ceilings affect managerial behavior:

> One of the new programs that was just established about six months ago . . . is the co-op program, where you can get people out of colleges. They don't count against your ceiling. . . . Back about ten or twelve years ago, we had this program, . . . and we found about six good people, some of whom are still with the agency. But then the agency changed the rules, and they required that [these people] be charged to your ceiling. But now that they no longer count against

ceiling, that's a great opportunity for us to bring people in, train them and test them and cultivate an understanding between them and the agency and their schools.

Unfortunately, OMB has reduced even this small area of flexibility, changing the rules once again so that even co-ops are now counted against ceiling.

While a few managers have been able to bring in people who do not count against ceiling, most managers are forced to rely on their existing resources. Several responded to the pressure of ceilings by only hiring at what is known as the *full performance level*. In other words, if your staff size is limited, you want individuals who are already up to speed, not people who will take several years of training. Further, you may want to hire more professional employees and fewer clerical or support staff. This may be functional from the point of view of the individual manager, but it increases the problem of grade creep (discussed in Chapter Six) and may also have long-term consequences if the agency is not hiring entry-level staff to be trained for the future.

A related phenomenon is the tendency to replace people with machines, especially at the lower levels. Overall, the number of secretaries and assistants in government has gone down. The tendency is increasingly to hire only at the professional level and to let professionals do their own clerical work. Phone answering machines sit on many desks, and most professionals have (with varying degrees of willingness) learned to do their own word processing. But many professionals complain that their time (and the government's money) is wasted when they have to spend hours doing such routine tasks as copying or filing because there are no support staff available.

Another internal approach is to retrain the existing employees to move up into more demanding positions. Most frequently, this takes the form of *upward mobility* programs for secretarial and clerical employees. A Navy personnel specialist described the advantages and disadvantages of one such program, in which five people were being trained for higher-level positions: "The training coordinator and myself worked with the supervisor and the individual to give guidance on the training these people needed. We look at the total background. Whatever they need, we cut in half. So if they normally would need two years of experience, they would get one year of intensive training, and then be promoted into the position. It's unfortunate that we had to be in a freeze for managers to start turning to upward mobility. And unfortunately, they feed off that area they are shortest of—the secretaries."

Some agencies have also used ceilings to encourage minority recruitment, by holding out the carrot of positions that do not count against ceiling. For example, several people at EPA told me of divisions that had held back positions and told people, "You may exceed your ceiling and get one of these positions if you bring on a minority person."

In short, ceilings do matter to most managers, and there are not very many good ways around them. Programs for hiring part-time employees who do not count against ceiling are quite small, and managers have only limited ability to move people around or to replace them with machines. The most extensively used (and most controversial) way around personnel ceilings is to contract the work out. In the next section, we look at the pros and cons of that approach.

Contracting Out

While some managers have found inside strategies that help deal with ceilings, by far the greatest effect of the imposition of ceilings is to increase the use of outside contractors. This is a complex subject and the source of considerable controversy in public administration. Here, I want to explore both how the rigidity of the budget process increases reliance on contractors and how this reliance affects managers' ability to get the job done.

First, it is important to understand that some managers make a voluntary choice to contract out because it makes good management sense. For example, several told me that they prefer to contract out one-time studies, particularly those that require large, short-term staff efforts. Others choose to contract out in order to obtain access to technical skills they do not have on staff. Those who used contractors for specific projects had fewest problems with the people they hired, particularly when they narrowly and clearly defined the task to be performed.

But for many managers, the choice to contract out is completely involuntary. Needless to say, such managers are much less happy about relying on contractors. Many managers contract out because they have more money than ceiling—that is, while they are prevented by ceilings from hiring the people they need to get the job done, they have enough resources to pay contractors. In the extreme (but not uncommon) situation, managers have no choice; they receive their money in specific categories: one for hiring inside and another for hiring contractors (referred to at EPA as "extramural" funding). One major difference between the agencies studied here was in the amount of their funding that had been earmarked for contractors by policy makers outside the agency, particularly in Congress. The amounts were particularly high at EPA and, to a somewhat lesser extent, in the Navy.

Why would Congress designate large sums of money to be used for contractors? Certainly, one reason is the political pressure to limit the size of the federal workforce. But the net result is two federal workforces—the official one, covered by civil service rules and pay scales, and an unofficial one, often working side by side with the first and doing the same work, but technically employed by a private firm.

In some cases, there are program-specific reasons for stipulating that work will be carried out by contractors. One such program was the Superfund, created within EPA to clean up hazardous waste sites. As DiIulio, Garvey, and Kettl (1993) explain: "In creating the Superfund program . . . Congress set a ceiling for the share of the program's funds to ensure that they were not creating an agency that would acquire a permanent life to manage what they considered a temporary program. As a result, EPA has delegated most Superfund operations and many policy decisions to contractors" (p. 1).

The agencies in this study differed dramatically in their reliance on contractors. At the Department of Agriculture agencies, it was quite limited. Of the four agencies, FCS relied least on contractors. APHIS increasingly used a variant of contracting out: cooperative agreements with states. Managers frankly described this as a way to get around ceilings by, in essence, contracting with a state to hire the people and do the work. In contrast, both the Navy and EPA have relied heavily on contractors—so heavily that both have been criticized for it. Managers in both agencies spoke frankly about the pluses and minuses of working through contractors. Many recognized that they had no choice and that given their current staff levels they simply could not get the work done without contractors. But many others resented the fact that they were forced by Congress to rely on contractors and found the experience to be difficult and frustrating.

As Levine, Peters, and Thompson (1990) point out, "Whether administration by proxy is a boon or barrier to the pursuit of excellence in government is still a matter of debate." Advocates push contracting out as a route to more efficient government (Savas, 1982; Osborne and Gaebler, 1992), while critics see it as at least potentially harmful to efficiency, responsiveness, and democratic accountability (Goodsell, 1985; Kettl, 1988). But the managers are far less conflicted; a strong majority who have worked with contractors are quite critical. They see them as, on balance, less efficient than government employees, and they are concerned by the problems of supervising contractors. Let us look briefly at these concerns, and at how managers attempt to cope with them.

As far as efficiency is concerned, managers see contractors as less efficient because they increase costs, lower quality, and take too long. In spite of the image of the private sector as more efficient than government, an APHIS manager explained, "contracts almost never save you money, because you have to do so much oversight and give them the information base." Or as an EPA regional manager put it, "A contractor is someone who borrows your watch to tell you what time it is." Quality was an even bigger issue than cost. Several managers complained that the quality of work they received was only minimally adequate, but that they had little leverage since it was very difficult either to withhold payment for mediocre work or to reward excellent work. Further, the complexity of the procurement process, which entails lengthy competitive bidding procedures, means that work cannot be done quickly unless the contractor is already on board. Indeed, a recent MSPB study reported that "the vast majority of SES respondents said that the Federal procurement process takes too long (91 percent) and involves too much 'red tape' (89 percent)" (U.S. Merit Systems Protection Board, 1992c, p. 40).

Managers also see reliance on contractors as raising a series of other, more far-reaching issues. These include managers' ability adequately to supervise the work of contractors, ethical issues, and long-term capacity problems. First, managing contracts requires expertise different from that used in directly managing a staff; this includes knowledge of the complex set of rules governing the contracting process. But as we have seen, managers' training is primarily technical, and many are still worker-managers, continuing to do technical work while managing a staff. Few managers, and even fewer of their staff members, have had formal training in the management of contracts. Yet they are frequently faced with the dilemma of how to get work done when the staff doing the work do not report directly to them. One person I talked to at EPA told me he had not had a problem managing contracts, but explained: "The one thing that got impressed on me early was that you couldn't act like a supervisor. You couldn't say, 'I have this task. Assign this person to it.' You could say, 'Assign a person with these qualifications.'"

Some managers are seriously concerned about their ability to provide adequate oversight of contractors. In the extreme cases, their in-house staff is simply too small and stretched too thin to keep track of what the contractors are up to. In other cases, limits on travel make on-site visits impossible. One EPA first-line supervisor (who moved to EPA from a position with a contractor) articulated these oversight problems: "We have no resources. The level is ridiculously low for the breadth of the program. It's so low that it's dangerous [to our ability] to control the resources in the program. We have intramural and extramural and grants. We don't have enough intramural resources to oversee the extramural work. There is no travel money to go to the states to see what they are doing. We don't have the minimum amount of people time to oversee and operate this program. We are really not sure what they're doing with that money."

Managers also raise ethical concerns about working with contractors, ranging from potential conflicts of interest (for example, when a contractor to a regulatory agency is also working for industries the agency regulates) to an agency's being ripped off by the contractor. Of course, lack of adequate oversight increases the risk. Managers warned about possible scams, such as "billing you for something they already did for someone else. . . . [Another unit] may ask them to do the same thing they're doing for you, and they never tell you and bill the agency twice for the same work."

But some of managers' concerns transcend day-to-day management issues. They fear that overreliance on contractors will mean that their agencies will lose the technical capacity to do the work themselves. As an EPA midlevel manager described it: "I attended a meeting here on EPA guidelines . . . and the spokesperson in this meeting who did all the talking was the contractor. [That person] knew more—[that person] developed the guidelines, [that person was the expert], and if that person died, you'd be out of luck.

Because we don't have the expertise here. So I think we've given up a lot to contractors, especially in the technical areas."

While the contractor builds expertise, the technically trained staff members become contract managers, often with a loss of morale and of their own technical skills. Further, the boundaries of the kinds of work that may appropriately be contracted out are unclear. Both EPA and the Navy have been faulted by the General Accounting Office (GAO) for excessive reliance on contractors and for inappropriately contracting out such functions as policy development, representation of the agency, and even some procurement functions (U.S. General Accounting Office, 1991). As a result both of these criticisms and of some very visible procurement scandals, the Navy launched an ambitious initiative to identify positions that could be moved back from contractors to in-house staff. According to the GAO report, three commands in the Navy planned "to convert about 2,000 staff-years of contractor support to in-house positions over the next 5 years" (p. 56).

But managers tell a different story. From their perspective, this has been a classic no-win process, where they lose their contractors but then cannot hire the needed in-house staff to replace them because of hiring freezes. A Navy SES member described this quandary:

> In the past two to three years, there's been a concerted effort to continue to reduce [use of contractors]. In our area, there's been significant reduction. There was a scheme that was approved, I think it went all the way to Congress, where you were to convert contract support services to government employees, and the idea was that for every two you cut off, you get one in replacement, or some formula like that, where the deal was that you make money that way, or the government did. In reality, what happened is, they've cut your budget and you can't hire either. They got you both ways.

The above story makes two important points. First, many managers feel so strongly that in-house staff are more efficient that they are willing to exchange a given number of contractor staff for a smaller number of in-house replacements. Second, the story makes clear how hard it is to reduce reliance on contractors when, at the same time, pressure to limit the size of the federal workforce is pushing in the opposite direction.

How do managers cope with the dilemmas posed by the use of contractors? First, the more astute managers try to exert as much direct managerial control over the work of the contractors as possible, in an attempt to keep costs down and quality up. As an EPA manager who worked extensively with contractors explained:

> You can't direct the individuals doing the work on a contract; you can only go through their management. And you are supposed to go through the prime [the lead contractor] to direct a subcontractor. We're normally pretty good at pressuring the prime to let us go directly to the sub. We talk to other EPA people about how to get to a specific contractor. The contractors learn that if they want more work, and if they don't want to tarnish their reputation, they have to play ball. When you're in the field, you've got to be able to direct the work, and that's all.

Other managers described trying to develop an ongoing relationship with contractors who had developed needed expertise. But the procurement process, at least at the time of this research, actually impeded good management of contractors. As we saw above, managers had few positive or negative incentives with which to affect consultant performance, particularly since, amazingly enough, managers were not allowed to consider consultants' past performance in awarding new contracts (Kelman, 1990). In fact, Kelman, one of the more outspoken academic critics of the procurement process, was brought into the Clinton administration to spearhead procurement reform. The Federal Acquisition Improvement Act, passed in late 1994, streamlines and simplifies the procurement process and also permits managers to consider contractors' past performance.

Another coping mechanism poses some interesting dilemmas for organizational culture. The relationship between use of contractors and organizational culture is complex. On the one hand, one might expect organizations with tight, close-knit cultures to avoid use of contractors (although they might not be able to avoid it if it is mandated by Congress or forced by the pressure of ceilings). On the other hand, reliance on contractors may change the culture, leading, for example, to an organization with rather permeable boundaries. Not only do contractors frequently work side by side with civil service employees, often doing the same work, but considerable raiding goes on in both directions. The proverbial "revolving door" includes recruitment of contractor staff into the agency as well as movement out from the civil service to contractors. Movement out of the agency may pose potential conflict-of-interest problems for the departing staff. Movement in from contractors may also be problematic. Recruiting from contractors may be shrewd, since such staff may already be up to speed and managers may already have had a chance to see the individuals in action. But there is potential for abuse. For example, as we saw in Chapter Four, there have been cases at EPA where a manager trying to hire someone dealt with the long delays of the civil service hiring process by asking a contractor to bring the person on temporarily until the civil service position came through. That meets the manager's need to ensure that he or she does not lose a valuable employee, but it goes well over the line of what is legal and ethical. In general, fuzzy organizational boundaries and staff instability may also make it difficult to develop a consistent organizational culture.

But while managers can work at the margin to improve their ability to manage via contractors, it is clear that for many of the managers in this study, the externally imposed requirement that they must use contractors rather than hire in-house staff is a significant constraint. The fact that several said they would be glad to make do with fewer people if they could hire internally shows the effectiveness of ceilings as a way to control the size of the federal workforce, if that is the goal. There is no doubt that, given the opportunity, many of these managers would move funds in order to hire more staff. But this fact also points up the inefficiency of controlling the budget indirectly via personnel ceilings. In many cases, managers are convinced that they could get the work done more cheaply if they had more flexibility to decide when to contract out and when to hire.

Dysfunctional Effects of Freezes and Attrition

While ceilings are used to maintain an organization's workforce at a given level, lowered ceilings may cause an organization to impose a freeze. In that case, either there is no external hiring to fill vacant positions or replace staff who have left or hiring is severely limited. This is still a case of indirect budget management. If managers had control over their budgets and faced a budget reduction, they could choose where to take cuts. But in a freeze, they have no discretion; cuts in the size of the workforce are mandated externally. While gradual reduction of the workforce via attrition is less disruptive than laying staff off (as we shall see in more detail later), freezes create a number of problems for organizations and individual managers. Foremost among them are misallocation of staff resources and chronic pressure on staff and managers to fill the gaps created by personnel shortages. Let us look in more detail at how managers cope with each of these problems.

Freezes and the Luck of the Draw

The biggest problem with relying on attrition is that because the effects will be uneven across the organization the process is not easily controlled. There is an element of chance here. Some parts of the organization will lose few staff members over time and will remain in good shape, while others, for reasons that managers cannot control, will lose many staff members and be in serious trouble.

A Navy manager described the uneven impact of attrition on his organization: "We've had hard turnover. People who couldn't stand the pressure, and people raiding us. There's great pressure to let the office of high attrition take the hits. If you're arguing RIFs versus letting those with high attrition take the cuts, attrition will win every time. The command was to reduce 4 percent a year. We took a 20 percent loss in fifteen months. It was unfair."

These problems are likely to be exacerbated if the organization encourages people to leave by providing incentives, such as a chance to take early retirement or a bonus for leaving. At the time of the study, while the Navy was in a freeze and FCS had experienced periodic freezes, no agency in the study was offering incentives, but in 1993 and 1994, agencies were authorized to give early retirement and "buyout" bonuses if they determined these incentives were necessary in order to meet the workforce reduction goals set by the Clinton administration. Incentives may encourage staff with valuable skills and institutional memory to leave; such people will be particularly hard to replace.

Organizations can cope with this staff allocation problem in several ways. First, they can carefully target the employees that are to be offered incentives. Second, they can make the freeze a soft freeze, allowing limited replacement hiring but controlling approval to hire at a high level in order to meet the personnel needs of those parts of the organization with the most pressing shortages. The tendency to manage attrition at a high organizational level is typical in most organizations (Rubin, 1980). High-level control is necessary if top management wants actively to manage the process by setting clear priorities and making conscious decisions about how to reallocate resources.

While this is good management from an overall agency perspective, from the viewpoint of lower-level managers, it is one more frustrating constraint. In practice, when a position becomes vacant, the organization with the vacancy does not have an automatic approval to fill it. Rather, top management controls the resource, and managers have to demonstrate their great need in order to get permission to replace lost staff. The net effect, for managers, is to increase competition for resources and to slow down any hiring dramatically. Although the formal civil service system for hiring can be quite slow, managers at every agency made it clear that getting budget approval to hire was often an even bigger roadblock. This was particularly true in the Navy and FCS, the organizations under the most consistent budget pressure. Managers told of losing prospective staff because of the long delays and because unexpected freezes were imposed while attempts to hire were under way.

One result of these problems is strategic behavior on the part of managers who know that having a vacant position is dangerous; in a freeze, they not only may be forced to keep the position vacant but may lose it permanently. Strategic behaviors range from the relatively benign to those that are clearly dysfunctional in the long term. One fairly simple strategy is to recruit for positions that are not currently vacant, in anticipation of future needs, or to continue to recruit even though there is currently a freeze. Managers want to have good candidates identified in advance so that if a vacancy opens up or if there is a thaw they can hire quickly. But there are obvious costs to this approach. First, managers and personnel staff waste a great deal of time in the lengthy recruitment and interview process for openings that may never appear. Second, applicants' time is wasted, and they are given false hope of a position that is, in fact, ephemeral. Sometimes, people are kept dangling for months and may even turn down other job offers in the hope that they will eventually be hired. This raises clear ethical questions.

Similarly, managers in agencies where freezes are likely, or where there are brief thaws, have a strong incentive to hire as quickly as possible—even to hire a barely qualified person just to hold on to the position. Several managers raised concerns about this tendency. For example, one EPA manager described the reaction to an impending freeze: "They instituted a hiring freeze at the end of the fiscal year, but they gave a little warning to the program offices. They said, 'If you want to hire, do it now.' People went out and made offers to people on the phone without ever interviewing them or being able to conduct a proper recruitment process. It's how a personnel process can be destroyed, and you can be dealing with grievances for years."

In the same vein, managers dealing with problem employees will be even more likely than usual to overlook problems and to tolerate marginal performers. They ask themselves whether it is worth going through the lengthy, time-consuming, and sometimes stressful process of taking action to get rid of a marginal employee if the end result is that they lose the position. One Navy manager faced this dilemma. She described "inheriting" a problem employee and going through the formal process of reprimanding and counseling him. When the employee's performance improved, at least to the minimally satisfactory level, she was unsure what to do. As she put it, "I'm not sure I want to cut him loose now, given the hiring situation. Would I be able to replace him? Maybe not."

Coping with Low Ceilings and Freezes: Doing Less with Less

When a ceiling does not increase but the work responsibilities do or when a freeze has been in place for a while and the organization has lost critical staff members, managers face difficult challenges. They are required to balance two distinct roles, which can be described in terms of the competing values model. On the one hand, they need to emphasize the rational goal quadrant, making sure that the necessary work gets done. On the other hand, they must operate in the human relations quadrant, maintaining morale and helping employees deal with the stress created by being short-handed, since the last thing they want is to lose any more staff members. As a Navy manager described the problem: "The lack of human resources [that is, of adequate staff] is the biggest issue. It brings morale down. . . . Because we can't hire, the work gets put on others." At the same time, managers recognize that it is harder to motivate or reward their staffs because resources are tight all across the board. Training money has frequently dried up, and even expected promotions are often put on hold.

Managers recognized the paradox of piling more work on remaining staff and asking them to take on assignments that were not in their job descriptions while at the same time trying to prevent burnout. In some cases, the way managers dealt with this problem reflected their organization's culture. This was particularly the case at the Food and Consumer Service. FCS has taken severe cuts in recent years, so freezes and gradual attrition have been a fact of life for a long time in this small, clan culture organization that people describe as being like a family. FCS managers were particularly likely to express concern about the personal effects of stress and burnout on their staffs and to look for ways to reduce the pressure on people. But FCS managers are not alone in trying to find creative ways to get the work done without totally burning out their staff.

Conscientious managers often pick up the extra workload themselves. Chronic staff shortages are one of the prime forces leading managers to continue to take on technical work; this merely reinforces the tendency at some agencies for first-line supervisors to be worker-managers. As an FCS first-line supervisor described it: "I feel like each person has a few more programs than they can manage well. There's a lot of doing, hands-on, and too little managing. I have to jump in and do routine work on occasion if a person is out."

Managers who take on more than they should under these circumstances face a high risk of burnout. One FCS manager vividly described how this feels: "Yes, it has an impact. About seven years ago, I was . . . close to having a nervous breakdown. I was working overtime all the time. And I finally woke up one day and said, 'You're going to have to learn to live with not doing your job a hundred percent. You're going to work with what you have, even though it's very frustrating, but there's not a damn thing you can do about it.' I refuse to be responsible for the budget deficit. What's worrisome is the pressure on staff. They don't always cope with it well, and I have to counsel them."

Inevitably, as the work piles up, managers face the difficult task of setting priorities. While the rhetoric calls for doing more with less, there comes a time when that simply is not possible and managers face the prospect of doing the same amount of work more slowly or of neglecting certain tasks and doing less with less. A frequent argument in the literature on cutback management is that organizational retrenchment is harder to manage in the public sector because management lacks the authority to make such decisions as cutting programs or closing offices (Levine, Rubin, and Wolohojian, 1982). It is the legislature that both sets the budget and defines the organization's mission. Midlevel and lower-level managers have even less power. They may recommend that a program be cut or eliminated, but the decision must be made at higher levels, inside or outside the organization.

While it is true that lower-level managers lack formal authority to drop functions, in reality, all managers who have lost staff have to adjust the workload. Managers described having to fight fires while letting routine work slide, and having to cut corners on how the work was done. For example, an FCS manager described how cuts have affected the agency's procedures:

> We do our best with the resources we have, with the result that some people are overworked, some people less so, but we are running late on a lot of things. . . . The agency is way down in total resources from where it was twenty years ago. We used to send staff out to visit a store before it was approved to join the [food stamp] program. Now, that effort is down from a thousand to a hundred and fifty staff years. They rarely go out to stores for preapproval visits, and if there's a problem they just request an external compliance investigation.

Facing the Challenges of Cutback Management

Having looked at the problems caused by ceilings and freezes and the ways managers cope with them, we can make some general observations. First, it is surprising that managers never mentioned any role for the personnel or human resources staff in this process. They saw it as strictly a budget process, with the budget staff setting ceilings or reallocating positions in a freeze. There was no indication that the personnel staff was playing an advisory role or providing analytical assistance—for example, by using workforce planning models to make rational decisions based on likely turnover rates. Thus, while budget decisions were having a major effect on personnel issues, it did not appear that the budget and personnel staffs were working together or that human resources staff were actively helping managers cope with the dilemmas created by ceilings or cuts.

Second, with the exception of the use of contractors, there were no clear-cut differences across organizations in the ways managers coped with cutback problems. There was some indication that APHIS and EPA experienced higher than average competition between units in response to ceiling restrictions and that ceilings were enforced more or less rigidly in different organizations, but overall coping mechanisms did not differ significantly.

In fact, managers had a somewhat limited range of approaches for dealing with ceilings and freezes. It is hard to see contracting out as a creative coping mechanism when, in fact, managers are often given no choice over whether to use contractors. Further, the approaches they used often had dysfunctional, even paradoxical effects, leading to higher grade levels, reduced staff quality, and even larger staffs (since managers will pad in anticipation of future cuts).

Many of these problems stem from the incentives created when cuts are managed indirectly—that is, when managers are forced to limit hiring or to cut staff rather than given resources over which they have direct control. The incentive to game the system would be reduced if managers had more direct authority to make decisions about where to take cuts, although if control of budget authority were held at too high a level, there might still be some incentive for gaming by lower-level managers.

Coping with Reductions in Force

The challenges for managers when staff are actually being laid off are, of course, far greater than when cuts are taken via attrition. But there are times when a reduction in force, or RIF, is necessary, particularly when the agency is facing large cuts that must be taken quickly and that are likely to be permanent. When an organization is in a condition of severe scarcity,[1] there is not enough time to take staff cuts gradually, via attrition, and recourse to a RIF is likely. Of course, like ceilings, RIFs can be politically motivated; they may be used, for example, to project an image of a "bloated bureaucracy" being reined in. This was clearly the case with some RIFs taken in the early years of the Reagan administration. Further, while agency managers will generally make RIF decisions based on budget projections, the values embodied in the organizational culture may also have an influence. FCS is an example of an agency that absorbed large cuts gradually via attrition; a RIF would have been particularly damaging in this clan culture.

Running a RIF: A Technical Nightmare

The operation of a RIF differs significantly from that of a ceiling or freeze. First, the actual process is managed by the personnel office—within targets set by the budget office. Second, the process is one of mind-numbing complexity. Third, the process is designed in a way that gives managers very little say in the decisions about who is actually laid off. As a result, it feels at times like an operation conducted not with a scalpel but with a meat-ax—or even a meat-grinder. Managers identify specific positions to be abolished. Who actually leaves is decided by a complex process based on four factors: seniority, veterans preference (veterans are almost always protected), performance appraisals, and competitive level. The last is an important term. A *competitive level* is a group of jobs that are roughly the same in grade level, classification, and duties, so that people in those jobs can be moved from one to another without harming productivity. In other words, employees at the same competitive level are considered roughly interchangeable.

Senior managers who are planning a RIF divide the organization's workforce into both competitive levels and competitive areas (geographical areas within which people can be relocated). That is, if the RIF is imposed across the entire agency, or at more than one installation, the managers determine how broadly people can be moved around. They then target specific competitive levels for cuts.

What then ensues roughly resembles a Rube Goldberg machine—with people as the components. There is a complex process of bumping and retreating as people in the jobs that are eliminated move into other jobs, forcing those people to move who then take the jobs of yet other people in a complex chain reaction. *Bumping* means displacing someone else at your competitive level who has lower seniority (including credits for performance appraisal) or is a nonveteran if you are a veteran. *Retreating* means moving back to a job you used to occupy at a lower level (or to one that is very similar). However, in common parlance, *bumping* is often used to mean both bumping and retreating. This means that for every person who leaves the agency, several are moved, often into jobs they do not want to be in and that they are not able to perform without at least some training.

The RIF rules were revised in 1986 to reduce somewhat the disruption a RIF inevitably causes. First, the weight of performance appraisal ratings relative to seniority was increased (the basis being average ratings in the three years prior to the RIF). Second, the new rules limited bumping and retreating to three grades or three grade intervals (for jobs where people normally move up two grades at a time).[2] Prior to this change, there were no limits on the number of levels a person could be reduced, leading in the 1982 federal RIF to such extreme cases as a Ph.D. psychologist who was demoted to mailroom clerk. At the same time, the rules broadened retreat rights somewhat; a person can now retreat to a position that is essentially identical to one the individual held previously, not just to the actual position through which he or she had been promoted. In spite of these changes, the process is still enormously disruptive.

If this all sounds confusing to those who are outside government, it is at least equally confusing to the people involved. The task of managing a RIF, particularly in a large installation and when a sizable number of people are being cut, is mind-boggling in its complexity. And the psychological trauma caused both by separations and by the displacement of people from their jobs is hard to exaggerate.

How, if at all, can the traumatic effects of a RIF be mitigated? To some extent, this is a challenge for the personnel staff, but much of the burden falls on line managers. Let us look at each in turn in the context of an actual RIF. The Portsmouth Naval Shipyard was selected as a site for this study precisely because it had recently conducted a RIF. Further, senior Navy personnel staff held up the shipyard as a model of RIF management. Thus, this is an example of "best case" site selection; one might expect RIFs at other locations to have more technical problems as well as more impact on operations than the one at Portsmouth. But even there, the process was not easy to manage. Many of the problems are created by the rigidity and complexity of the formal procedures.

Role of the Personnel Office in a RIF

The personnel office (at Portsmouth, the industrial relations office) plays a central role in managing a RIF. It is up to personnel to make sure that the process runs smoothly, and at the same time, the office needs to be sensitive to the resulting human trauma. On the basis of my interviews with line managers and with staff of the Portsmouth industrial relations office (IRO), I would say that there were four key elements in the approach taken by the personnel staff to the technical aspects of the RIF: use of a computer program to manage the process; use of conservative ground rules to reduce disruption; training of supervisors; and sharing of information with workers and unions. Let us look briefly at each.

First, the Portsmouth IRO staff designed complex computer software to keep track of the process of bumping and retreating. They entered data on seniority, performance appraisal ratings, veteran status, and past work history, after checking in each case for accuracy. This all took over a year. In general, the process worked well, but there were a few inevitable glitches when employees were given inaccurate information. Most of the errors were caught, because the IRO staff offered counseling to individuals who received letters and, when requested, checked data for accuracy. It is clear that while other organizations might attempt to speed up the process, by borrowing IRO software for example, running a RIF is not something that can be done well on the spur of the moment. Months of advance planning are needed, and even then, no amount of preparation can prevent at least a few errors.

A second element of the organization's approach was to try to keep retreating to a minimum. To the extent that retreating and bumping could be limited, the disruption to organizations and individuals would be reduced. As a senior member of the IRO staff explained: "We were very conservative on retreats. It had to be your actual old job, not just the title, and we were very conservative on bumps, because you had to be fully qualified. Some activities would open it wide open [permitting more extensive bumping] and cause more disruption. One goal was to reduce disruption."

Finally, the IRO staff provided training to supervisors and to departmental personnel staff (shadow personnel offices) of organizations to make sure they understood what was happening, and IRO staff tried to share information frequently with both workers and unions. Both efforts were well-meaning, but probably neither went quite far enough. Supervisors, particularly Wage Grade supervisors, told me that in some cases they still did not fully understand the process. Even those who felt they did often had trouble explaining it to their staff. One informant in the IRO told me that if they had to do it again, they would give even more training to supervisors and managers. As for the sharing of information with employees, this became difficult because the picture kept changing. Incorrect information had to be amended, and there were also unscheduled departures. Some people, expecting to be cut or anticipating that this RIF would not be the last, found other jobs and left voluntarily. Thus, the initial list showing who would be separated changed considerably over time. One manager told me a painful story of an employee who uprooted his family and moved to another shipyard on the basis of the initial list, only to find out later that he would not have been terminated after all.

Role of the Manager in a RIF

Even when well-run, the RIF process will have a number of damaging effects. First, of course, many organizations will lose well-trained staff as a result of bumping and retreating and, for the same reason, will gain others who are rusty or who have never done their new jobs before. Second, the people who actually lose their jobs in a RIF are generally those with low seniority, particularly nonveterans. At Portsmouth, this meant that the entire current crop of apprentices, who had recently completed or were going through extensive training at considerable expense to the organization, went out the door. Further, managers bemoaned the fact that it is typically the best workers who choose to leave voluntarily during a RIF. But the personal effects are also dramatic. For those with strong loyalty to the organization, the loss of trust can be devastating. Some who remain show the symptoms of survivor's guilt. And it is extremely difficult to keep employees focused on the task at hand when a RIF is in progress. Managers respond in two ways: they try to manipulate the system to the advantage of their staff, and they attempt directly to address the morale and productivity issues.

Gaming the RIF Process

While the complex set of RIF rules and procedures is designed to treat all employees fairly, its underlying values are particularly supportive of seniority and veterans preference. In spite of the increased weight attached to performance, there will be many cases where a good employee is lost and someone less productive keeps his or her job. Further, on its face, the process gives little discretion to managers. But needless to say, many managers do all they can to manipulate the system to protect those individuals or parts of the organization they deem least dispensable. The tools at their disposal are limited and vary depending on managerial rank.

Senior managers have the greatest opportunity to affect the process if they play a role in the initial determination of competitive levels from which cuts will be taken. In theory, these decisions should be based on an analysis of current and future workloads and on a rational determination of the functions that could be eliminated (or have staff trimmed) with the least impact on organizational mission. The newly reconfigured organization should then have the needed skill mix for the future. In practice, competitive levels can be manipulated to some extent if the personnel office will cooperate. The most extreme story I have heard in this respect came from the National Aeronautics and Space Administration (NASA). According to my source, NASA once tried to define each secretary to top management as a separate competitive area, arguing that since the agency did highly scientific work, secretaries who were familiar with that work were not interchangeable. While most organizations would not go so far to manipulate the system, there is some evidence (in the other direction) of RIFs targeted to eliminate a specific individual. An APHIS personnel staff member at the Field Servicing Office in Minneapolis who had worked on a RIF for another Department of Agriculture agency told me of one such case: "Sometimes they do RIFs to get rid of somebody. If it doesn't get the right person, it's back to the drawing board."

A second strategy, which is most available to upper-level or midlevel managers, is to move staff from one unit or position to another prior to the RIF in order to protect them. Several interviewees mentioned such actions at Portsmouth. For example, a senior manager told me, "I moved people from one code [that is, one part of the organization] to another because we had more funding there, basically to protect them and because it was good financial management. At the same time, it gave them training in another area, which is good but which people resist."

Managers at all levels, and especially first-line supervisors, have one potentially powerful tool at their disposal: the performance appraisal rating. When I asked a group of Wage Grade supervisors if they could manipulate the system, one responded that the workers can, by improving their performance and thus earning a higher rating. There is no doubt that having been through a RIF, workers will be much more conscious of the importance of performance appraisals in the future. This can be positive if it leads to actual changes in performance. But it can also lead to heavy pressure on supervisors to inflate the ratings. A common argument is, "Well, everyone else does it, so I have to, in order to protect my people." It is to their credit that I did not hear this argument from Portsmouth managers. What I did hear was, first, a recognition that they could use the performance rating to protect people if they chose. As a Wage Grade supervisor pointed out: "They're very useful. . . . You can give the non-vet an 'O' [outstanding]; you can give the vet a 'sat' [satisfactory]. Kind of balance them out. Great for RIF purposes. The non-vet is still going to go out the gate before the vet. Yeah, but it makes him feel better. Gives him a chance."

However, some supervisors recognized that their peers might use the performance appraisal for the less benign purpose of protecting friends and cronies. There is no doubt that for the RIF process to be perceived as fair, the performance appraisal process must also be seen as fair. This concern was raised by spokespersons for several agencies commenting on the new RIF rules. An MSPB study of the changes in RIF procedures reported the following: "Sixteen departments and agencies called attention to the critical need for the performance appraisal system to be fair, and to be perceived by employees as fair, because of the increased weight on performance ratings in deciding retention during RIF. . . . A common thread ran through most of [their comments]: there are still problems in the administration of their performance appraisal systems that could cause difficulties in the event of a RIF" (U.S. Merit Systems Protection Board, 1987b, pp. 9–10).

To summarize: Faced with an enormously complex and unwieldy process, managers have some limited play; they can sometimes—but only sometimes—protect those they want to retain and push others out the door. But the extent to which I saw such manipulation of the process at Portsmouth was quite limited. Mostly, managers have no choice but to take the process as it comes and cope with the results.

Coping with the Emotional Consequences of a RIF

As we saw above, the cumulative effects of attrition over time can be quite severe. But the impact of a RIF is immediate and traumatic. There is no way to convey how it feels to receive a RIF notice, particularly for people who have worked their whole lives for an organization and who have a sense of loyalty to that organization. And there is no way to convey the challenges of trying to manage an organization while this dramatic upheaval is going on all around. Further, managers must try to support their staffs and keep the work going even when they, too, may be affected by the RIF. Employee reactions to the stress will vary, but RIFs typically engender strong feelings. Often, there is anger and hostility in those leaving. At Portsmouth, managers told me that problems with people who were affected by the RIF were infrequent, but there were a few cases of individuals "acting out." One told me of a meeting where feelings were expressed very directly:

> Your good workers, they stay productive. Then you have your not-so-good workers. . . . We have an office conference room, and [in one case] the white-hat [foreman] . . . had all the people in there who had gotten their letters [RIF notices], and he was explaining to them about the job fairs and different things, and after the meeting, guys got right up and walked across a nice table, you know, down the side, and doing one of these numbers [rude gesture]. You just mentally remembered who the person was, because his chances of ever coming back were really slim to none.

There are also emotional costs for those who remain; they may feel frustrated by the additional workload or distressed by being bumped down to a lower level that they had worked for years to rise above. Not everyone copes well with taking on additional work. One manager told me that he had warned his staff a couple of weeks ahead of time that "we are going to have to take on more work, . . . but one person got all upset and started flinging things."

The complex process of bumping also has obvious costs in morale and productivity. Several of the Wage Grade supervisors agreed with the person who told me: "If you take the person who is used to the white-collar work and put the tools in that person's hands, he'll tend to think he's been degraded. Absolutely. Coming from a nice clean job all day to a dirty job all day. It is degrading. I'm sure there's a big ego-type problem."

But the dominant mood during a RIF is one of uncertainty. As a Wage Grade supervisor phrased it, "Am I going to have a job after it's done, or am I going to be bumped back further down? How far can I be bumped back before I go out the gate? I could go from a $55,000-a-year job to out the gate for minimum wage." At Portsmouth, the uncertainty persisted even after the RIF was complete because of widespread speculation about the need for another RIF the following year. In fact, one of the typical characteristics of a RIF environment is the constant churning of the rumor mill, with stories that change from day to day or even from hour to hour.

Not surprisingly, some organizations have reported terrible morale and plummeting productivity during and following RIFs. It is to the credit of the management at Portsmouth that this was not the case there. In fact, managers were divided in their reports of the impact of the RIF, with a few reporting major effects but most saying that there was no appreciable effect or that effects were relatively minor. Many described trying to balance the need to be understanding and the imperative that the work continue to move forward. One thing that helped in some cases was guidance and support from higher levels of leadership.

> When we first heard about it, the general foreman got together with us, with the foremen, and told us exactly what he knew about the RIF and tried to clear up any rumors. He gave us all the facts that he could tell us, and he told us that there's people working for us at the time that may get RIFfed, and they may not be themselves every day. So he told us to look out for that and try to keep the senior people, that knew that they weren't going to get RIFfed, from picking on them or making statements. And actually, that was kind of a warning, and the morale wasn't too bad, really.

This story reflects two aspects of the managerial role during a RIF: looking out for the emotional well-being of the affected employees but also sharing information. Because of the negative effects of uncertainty, sharing as much information as possible is vitally important. It also serves to reduce the reliance on the rumor mill, with its misinformation and half-truths. Meeting regularly with staff and sharing information were two of the most frequently mentioned coping strategies.

The IRO also played an important role, not just in the technical aspects of conducting the RIF but in providing services to those affected. The office counseled individuals to make sure the RIF notices had been properly issued, and consulted frequently with the unions so that they knew what was being done and why. IRO also arranged for extensive outplacement services for people likely to lose their jobs. These included job fairs, letters to 3,500 companies, and the establishment of a worker assistance center in nearby Kittery, Maine, for which a grant was obtained from the Department of Labor. In addition, IRO provided training in such subjects as financial management, stress management, and job search skills. Managers recognized the symbolic importance of providing these services. As a Wage Grade supervisor put it: "I think this job fair showed the people that we were trying. When I say 'we,' [I mean] the government, the shipyard was trying to do something to get them a good job, [we] cared about them and worried about them. We just weren't going to say, 'Yeah, you got your letter, sixty days you're out of here. Too bad.' And I think a lot of people appreciated that. And that was very positive."

While managers, with IRO help, were providing support both to those leaving and to remaining staff, they still had to keep things running. Not only had they lost staff, but they were forced to absorb new staff who had been bumped or retreated. Some of these employees had moved up years ago and others had never done the work they were now assigned to. These staff movements meant that there was a high initial need for training, but this was hard to provide when training resources were scarce and when every person was needed in order to get the work out on time.

As we saw, even with gradual cuts, managers faced the dilemma of how to set work priorities with fewer staff. This was a source of great frustration to some Portsmouth managers, who felt that senior management had been unwilling to adjust functions and workloads or to set clear priorities. In an atmosphere of tremendous pressure to meet tight deadlines on complex jobs, serious conflicts arose, as one manager told me: "[The work's] getting harder to handle. People are having to wait longer for us to get to their problem. We have to handle all the boats. It's as if you went into a garage and demanded a car be taken off the lift and yours put on now. People aren't happy if they aren't first priority. They hire people on purpose that are demanding like that to get the job done, but there are a lot of ugly feelings in the process."

In short, managers face several dilemmas when a RIF is being implemented: how to mitigate the effects of the RIF by protecting their best employees; how to keep up morale in the face of uncertainty and emotional distress; how to support and train new employees who have been bumped into their units; and at the same time, how to keep the work flowing. While managers at Portsmouth were on the whole quite impressive in the way they faced these multiple challenges, the formal system did not lighten their burdens. When we compare the RIF process to the procedures used to administer ceilings and freezes, we find some differences but also some significant similarities. Handling the technical aspects of a RIF is clearly the responsibility of the personnel office. While the budget office may make the calculations that determine the size of the RIF, it is the personnel staff that have to manage the complex procedures for determining who is affected—who actually goes out the door and who can be bumped or retreat to a lower-level job. Even with high-tech software and ample lead time, this is hard to do without glitches. The personnel office's ability to communicate with both managers and individual employees who are affected is critical to reducing anxiety and keeping the inevitable rumor mill under control. Further, assistance to terminated employees, in such forms as outplacement services, helps directly but also indirectly by making it clear that the organization cares about the people affected.

Technical training in RIF procedures is therefore important for the personnel staff managing the process. But formal training in advance of a RIF may also be very useful for managers faced with new and difficult management tasks.

Since only one of the organizations in this study was actually conducting a RIF, it is impossible to make comparisons that would reveal how different organizations, with different cultures, would handle the process. But there is likely to be a circular relationship here. The way organizations manage this painful process will be reflective of their culture, but the experience of a RIF will leave its marks on the culture; stories and myths will be handed down that communicate the values of the organization as they were reflected in management's actions and employees' responses at such a highly charged time. Management needs to be very sensitive to the messages that its actions convey.

Finally, as with ceilings and freezes, RIFs are an indirect way of managing budget cuts. The decision on whether to conduct a RIF is generally taken at the very top of an organization, although senior managers are consulted on which positions to abolish. Lower-level managers have very little power here, and few tools with which to affect the outcomes of the process. As we shall see, there are proposals to eliminate use of FTE ceilings, but there are no sweeping proposals to deregulate or simplify the complex RIF process. It is clear that the rigidity of the RIF process seriously limits managers' ability to exercise control as the process unfolds, but giving them more power would raise difficult questions about how to balance efficiency and managerial control with safeguards against abuse.

Conclusions

At the time of this study, RIFs were fairly unusual. This may change, since one of the recommendations of the National Performance Review (NPR) on which Congress acted with alacrity was the proposal to make cuts in the federal workforce of over a quarter of a million employees. (The final figure was 272,900. See Kettl, 1994, n. 18.) The NPR proposals for cutbacks reflect two of the issues raised in this chapter: the political impetus for cuts and the difficulties posed by indirect measures of budget control.

As Kettl (1994) makes clear, there were several different groups at work in designing the NPR. The NPR staff, primarily career civil servants, focused on management reform and deregulation. Staff in agencies, whom Kettl characterized as "an army of reinventers" (p. 5), developed specific recommendations on streamlining operations and improving customer service. But the group that dominated in the end was the senior political strategists who argued that what would sell politically was cuts in government. As Kettl summarizes it, "They have focused single-mindedly on the NPR's cost savings and personnel reductions as critical elements in the Clinton Administration's reelection strategy" (p. 5). Once again, given the stereotype of a bloated bureaucracy, the political issue is not just cutting the budget but being seen as tough enough to cut the number of federal workers.

This fact meant that the NPR, too, had to manage cuts in the federal budget indirectly, by adjusting the size of the workforce. Further, the process of taking the cuts was, from a rational-management perspective, illogical. The NPR based the justification of staff cuts on the logic of deregulation, arguing that simplifying and streamlining civil service, budgeting, and procurement procedures meant that organizations could reduce the large staffs needed to administer the current "arcane rules" (National Performance Review, 1993a, p. 13).

But Congress approved the cuts and agencies were required to begin taking them before there had been any change in the rules. In fact, the political nature of this process and the internal conflict within the NPR are highlighted by perhaps the most dramatic inconsistency in the report. On the one hand, the NPR advocates deregulating the budget process as a way to improve government efficiency and save money. The supporting report on budgeting (1993b) criticizes in some detail "restrictions on spending money that are not needed for policy control [and that] take away the manager's capacity to perform." Linked to this general argument for deregulation is a recommendation to eliminate full-time equivalent ceilings, which, the NPR report claims, are often cited by managers as "the single most oppressive restriction on their ability to manage"

(1993a, p. 19). The budget report makes this argument at some length, detailing many of the problems discussed above, including the mismatch between ceilings and dollars and between ceilings and workload, and the tendency to take across-the-board cuts in ceiling. It further points out how ceilings increase pressure to contract out work that could be done less expensively or more appropriately in-house, as well as how ceilings contribute to grade creep.

While the NPR reports make a convincing argument for eliminating the use of ceilings, the actual recommendation that resulted was to eliminate them—but not quite yet. As the NPR report puts it, "FTE controls are the only way to make good on the President's commitment to reduce the federal bureaucracy" (National Performance Review, 1993a, p. 19). The report therefore calls for the Office of Management and Budget and agency heads to stop using FTE ceilings, but not until fiscal year 1995 (a deadline that is unlikely to be met).

The NPR cuts may also put greater pressure on agencies to contract out work previously done by the people who are leaving. As we saw above, relying on contractors may actually raise rather than reduce costs. Fear of what D.C. Delegate Eleanor Holmes Norton calls an "unregulated shadow government of contract employees" is prompting legislative proposals to "prohibit agencies from contracting work previously performed by employees who accepted buyouts" (Harris, Oct. 3, 1994).

Whatever the final outcome of the NPR reforms, it is certain that, given the size of the budget deficit and the current political environment, federal managers will be coping with cutback management for the foreseeable future. One thing that is clear from this research is that federal managers in cutback situations need help. They need training specifically focused on the technical and the human relations aspects both of gradual cutbacks and, particularly, of RIFs. Further, reforms that would allow them to manage their budgets more directly would greatly enhance their ability to make rational adjustments to deal with scarce resources.

Conclusion

Loosening Constraints
and Changing Culture:
The Potential for Reform

This concluding chapter briefly recaps the major findings of the research reported here and then draws some conclusions from them, both for individual managers and for those attempting to reform the whole system of bureaucratic constraints described in these pages.

It should come as no surprise to any observer of the federal government that managers' complaints about the excessive level of constraint are pervasive. This research has documented many of these constraints, particularly in the area of personnel management. Further, it has shown how interaction between the civil service system and the budget process sharply limits managerial discretion in such areas as hiring and setting pay.

We have also looked at the techniques managers use to cope with these constraints. In some cases, managers have been creative and aggressive, and have successfully navigated the system to meet their goals. In the Introduction to this work, we looked at three responses to bureaucratic constraint. Using the terms employed there, we have found that significant numbers of managers are, indeed, "creative copers." But even these managers found that their success came with a cost; the time and energy required to work within or around the system were significant, and most managers would be quite happy not to have to pay these transaction costs.

It is also true that some managers fit the image of "the manager as Gulliver," hemmed in and limited by a system they do not quite understand. In certain cases, their problems stem not just from the complexity of a rulebound system but also from their lack of knowledge and their narrow definition of their managerial role. But in other cases, managers have made considerable efforts to push against the system and have failed. Some of these people have crossed the line and become what I termed "demoralized managers," going through the motions and waiting for the day they can retire.

This research also demonstrates the power of organizational culture. Agency cultures differ, sometimes sharply, and these differences affect management style and managerial strategies for coping with constraints. It is clear that managers at EPA and, to some extent, in the Navy are more likely to fit into the creative coper category than those in the two Department of Agriculture sites. This does not necessarily mean that they are better managers but rather that the level of tolerance, or even encouragement, of such a management style is greater in their agencies. Similarly, differences in the cultures and role definitions of agency personnel offices affect managers' ability to navigate the complexities of the civil service system, both through the level of technical support given and via the cues personnelists provide about organizational norms of behavior.

Finally, we have looked at the practice of managing the budget indirectly, through use of the position classification system to keep pay levels down and through use of ceilings and freezes to regulate the size of the workforce. It is clear from these findings that indirect budget controls cause a number of problems: they limit managers' discretion and cause dysfunctional distortions that may actually raise costs as managers attempt to game the system to get around the controls.

We look now at some of the implications of these findings—for managers, for agency leadership, and for those attempting to reduce the level of bureaucratic constraint throughout the system.

Improving Management: Changing the Rules or Changing the Managers?

The results of the research presented here have a direct bearing on how we think about the quality of management in the public sector. The implication is not that managers who do not cope with constraints creatively are incompetent. In fact, the majority of managers interviewed for this study were outstanding in their jobs, caring and thoughtful in their approaches to the challenges they faced. In the term used by Norma Riccucci (1995), many of these individuals are "unsung heroes." But there is certainly room for improvement in some areas. This study was not intended to be an assessment of the quality of managers, either individually or by agency. As we saw in Chapter Two, other studies have concluded that, overall, the quality of first-line supervisors in the federal government is relatively high. The typical recommendations for improvement of management quality focus on modifying the selection criteria for new managers and on providing more training, particularly training tailored to managers' needs (U.S. Merit Systems Protection Board, 1992a). These changes would be an important first step. This research has documented the continuing tendency to promote the best technicians into supervisor jobs without much effort to determine their supervisory potential; it has also revealed inadequacies in training, particularly training for new supervisors and specific training in the complexities of the civil service system. This research therefore supports the conclusions of the Merit Systems Protection Board (1992a) that "perhaps because of time or budget constraints, many first-line supervisors are placed in situations without the necessary skills to perform the tasks required of them" (p. 30).

Attention to both selection criteria and training will be even more important if significant deregulation of the system occurs. As the director of human resources management for one federal agency put it: "The requirement [in the future] will not be as much to know the rules of the system, how to apply them, or how to beat them, but rather the ability to work in a more ambiguous, unstructured situation. . . . We will need to select managers who are not so control-oriented, but are . . . more comfortable with change, flexibility, and accountability for results in fluid situations" (Stroud,

1994, p. 5). Current managers will also need retraining. As Stroud acknowledged, "It would be a mistake to assume that managers who have been working effectively in the more structured, regulated situation of the past will naturally make the transition to a situation that provides more choices" (p. 5).

But changing selection criteria and training is the responsibility of the agency, not of individual managers. What are the lessons here for managers themselves? Should they all take the more extreme creative coper as role models and aggressively challenge the system, going around it whenever it gets in their way? What are the practical and ethical boundaries of appropriate behavior?

First, it is evident from this research that managers are limited not just by formal rules and regulations but by the norms of acceptable behavior in their organizations. These norms often reflect the deepest values inherent in the organizational culture and have evolved over years. People joining the organization—and insiders, too—typically find out about norms when they unwittingly violate them, a phenomenon that was evident in this research. In Chapter Five, for example, we encountered a manager, relatively new to his organization, who ran up against an organizational norm to "use kid gloves, be nice to the person." Managers who overstep organizational norms are likely to fail or, at least, to be perceived as troublemakers.

Some of the strategies used by creative copers also present ethical dilemmas for individual managers. Certainly, some managers appear Machiavellian, taking actions that are clearly illegal or at least in a gray area of legality. They would argue that pursuit of legitimate goals justifies bending (if not breaking) the law. Individual managers need to decide not only what their agencies will tolerate but how far they, as ethically responsible individuals, should go in violating the spirit if not the letter of the merit system through such strategies as "wiring" searches or creating turkey farms.

This research also makes clear that the way individual managers define their role makes a difference in their response to constraints. Role definitions differed somewhat across agency lines; nevertheless, most managers would be well-advised to consider how they choose to balance the different aspects of the job of management. The version of the competing values model presented in Chapter Two is helpful in this regard, presenting in graphic form the key functions of management. It has been used to structure management texts (Quinn, Faerman, Thompson and McGrath, 1990; Faerman, Quinn, Thompson, and McGrath, 1990) and has also been incorporated in management training programs (Giek and Lees, 1993; Thompson, 1993; Sendelbach, 1993). Some agencies have even linked the model to their systems of performance appraisal, with strengths and areas for improvement identified in terms of the competing values roles and linked to training and development (Giek and Lees, 1993). As an individual diagnostic tool, it can help managers gain a better understanding of their own strengths and weaknesses, and also of the fit or lack of fit between their management style and their organization's culture. But whatever formal tool they use, many managers would benefit from a better understanding of how to balance all the conflicting demands of the management role.

Prospects for Deregulation

The findings reported in this book also bear directly on the desirability of reforming the system of controls within which managers work. There is strong support among managers for deregulation and simplification of the systems for hiring, firing, and paying their employees and for giving managers a more direct voice in all these operations. It is clear that all these systems both add to the frustration level of managers and increase the costs of government operation. Further, the linkage between the civil service system and the budget process—in particular, the indirect control of budget levels via staffing levels—adds another layer of inefficiency to the system and may actually increase rather than decrease costs.

As we have seen throughout this book, many of the specific

reforms proposed by the National Performance Review directly address managers' concerns. These reforms include streamlining and decentralizing the hiring process, shortening the period needed to fire poor performers, simplifying the classification process and giving line managers classification authority, and abandoning the use of FTE ceilings. But these reform proposals raise questions in three areas: the political prospects of reform, ethical implications, and the linkage of reform of the formal systems to culture changes. Let us look briefly at each.

Political Issues in the Reform Process

While the National Performance Review (NPR) report set forth an ambitious reform agenda, this was only the first step. The more difficult steps will be selling these reforms both to Congress and to the American people, getting legislation passed, and then implementing the provisions of the new law. Each of these steps is problematic. To understand why, we need to return to an issue raised in the Introduction: why these formal rules and regulations were developed in the first place and what purpose they serve. As we saw, in the cases of both the civil service system and the procurement process, the complex system of formal controls has evolved primarily as a way to prevent abuse—that is, manipulation of the system for political or personal gain. While these controls have worked imperfectly, as the occasional scandals attest, they nonetheless provide some protection and, at the same time, serve the important symbolic functions of articulating clear standards of behavior and assuring the American people that their government will treat them fairly. Other controls, particularly within the budget process, are designed for a different purpose—as a mechanism of policy control. Both Congress and the president—through the Office of Management and Budget (OMB)—allocate resources in accordance with their policy priorities. Here, too, controls sometimes serve symbolic functions; as we have seen, use of FTE controls on the federal workforce is a response to the political need to stand up to "big government."

Finally, external controls are imposed to enforce what Wilson (1989) terms "contextual goals"—that is, goals that are secondary to the central function of the organization. Often, these relate to process. In the personnel area, they include the values of fairness and openness in hiring, fairness and due process in dealing with problem employees, and affirmative-action goals, among others. As Wilson points out, "Equity is more important than efficiency in the management of many government agencies" (p. 132).

The political environment within which reform is being considered is complex. On the one hand, the pervasive negative views of government and antibureaucratic sentiment that fueled the Perot movement in 1992 would appear to lend support to "good government" reform proposals. Indeed, polls showed that the "Reinventing Government" initiative was very popular and that voters favor making government more efficient, not just cutting its size (Osborne, 1995). On the other hand, those who mistrust government officials may not be so supportive of deregulation that gives those officials more discretion.

The stunning Republican electoral victory in 1994 changed the political environment for reform in several ways. First, it increased the emphasis on reducing the size of government and the number of federal workers. Initial proposals were breathtaking. Senator William Roth, the chair of the Government Operations Committee, was quoted as saying that the federal workforce and overhead expenses could be cut by as much as 40 percent and the number of agencies could be reduced by half (Harris, 1995). Rather than resisting cuts, the administration made identifying further cuts the main focus of a new phase of reinvention, which began with a request to agencies to answer such questions as what would happen if their agency were eliminated (Rivenbark, 1995a). In short, because it sharply intensified the focus on cutting, the election may have further deflected attention away from deregulation.

Second, the election changed the political equation and, probably, the administration's reform strategy. Prior to the election, the administration had apparently made a strategic decision to combine the main reform issues into a single comprehensive legislative package and to rely heavily on union support for passage. It is clear that the unions were among the big losers in the election. The loss of a Democratic majority in both houses meant that the unions' congressional allies could no longer block legislation that the unions opposed. The effects were immediate. Unions were reported to be incensed because a draft version of civil service reform legislation circulated by the administration immediately after the election left out labor-management partnership and other labor issues (Harris, Dec. 26, 1994).

Overall, the prognosis for passage of legislation significantly deregulating the civil service system remains unclear. Republicans have traditionally been supportive of reform efforts that apply private sector models to government with the goal of improving efficiency (Romzek and Dubnick, 1994). But recent years have seen an increase in micromanagement by Congress, both of substantive issues and of process. Divided government, with the Republicans controlling Congress and Democrats the administrative branch, may reduce support for deregulation. Congress may not have incentives for permitting deregulation that gives greater discretion to a Democratic administration and results in a net loss of congressional power, even if the result is likely to be increased efficiency.

But not all changes require congressional action. Some steps to deregulate the personnel process have already been taken. In 1994, the Office of Personnel Management (OPM) abolished the old 10,000-page *Federal Personnel Manual* (FPM) and replaced it with a streamlined 1,000-page version. OPM also eliminated mandatory use of the SF-171 for job applicants and allowed agencies to accept résumés, agency-specific forms, or new short forms developed by OPM. And OPM was actively considering other changes it could implement without legislation (Rivenbark, 1995b). Indeed, some have faulted the administration for moving too quickly. Problems may be encountered in implementing deregulation if agencies choose to reregulate—for example, by moving pertinent sections of the FPM into agency regulations.

Ethical Issues in Reform

As we have seen, one of the reasons deregulation may be a hard sell politically is the fear that managers will misuse the broader authority they are given. The issues here go to the heart of a debate within the field of public administration, going back more than fifty years, over the efficacy of internal versus external controls. The civil service system was built on the belief that external controls, in the form of laws and regulations, and the attendant fear of punishment for violators, were necessary to keep people in line. In contrast, those advocating internal controls stress "values and ethical standards cultivated within each public servant . . . [which] encourage ethical conduct in the absence of rules and monitoring systems" (Cooper, 1990, p. 125). The success of deregulation, then, rests on the assumption that if external controls are lifted, internal controls will be successful in regulating behavior and preventing widespread abuse.

What is the likely outcome if the system is significantly deregulated? Reactions will undoubtedly be different from one organization to another. As we have seen above, previous research shows dramatically different levels of abuse even under the heavy hand of the current system. Clear signals from top agency management will be important in establishing behavioral norms in a newly deregulated environment (Luke, 1991).

Widespread political abuse is unlikely. But as we saw earlier, one of the purposes of the current rigid constraints is to enforce "contextual goals." Whether managers will buy into these goals and act to support them is a much more problematic question, particularly since most of the incentives for managers are based on their ability to get the core work of the organization done. Certainly, one advantage of deregulation is that it would reduce the hypocrisy rampant in the current system, which espouses noble contextual goals but tolerates manipulative strategies that undermine those goals. This situation produces widespread cynicism about the fairness of the system. But will a deregulated system meet the fairness test? And will it expose newly "empowered" managers to lawsuits from employees who feel they have been treated unfairly? Indeed, Romzek and Dubnick (1994) question whether significant deregulation can succeed over the long term because distrust of government is so pervasive that perceived abuses will lead to calls for reintroduction of controls.

In short, one danger here is moving too far in the direction of deregulation—tossing out useful regulations along with those that are unnecessary, because there are no clear standards indicating which are which. Taking an extreme antibureaucratic and antiregulatory stance, as the NPR does, may make it difficult to strike a healthy balance between flexibility and control, leaving both managers and employees adrift without adequate guidance on appropriate behavior.

Impediments to Cultural Change

One of the central themes of this work is that constraints on managers lie not only in the formal structures and systems of rules and regulations but also in the culture of the organization and within managers themselves. The issue of culture, then, is central to any reform effort. Many managers have been socialized into what I referred to in the Introduction as a "culture of control," where their freedom of action is circumscribed both by formal regulations and by hierarchical control (Lane and Wolf, 1990). Simply loosening the formal controls will not turn them into "Gulliver unchained," springing into action to make use of newfound authority. Unlearning years of habits will probably be a gradual process for many—one that will need to be supported by change in the whole underlying culture.

Because of the differences in existing cultures that this research has documented, organizations are not all starting from the same place in implementing reforms. Therefore, structural and regulatory reforms need to give agencies considerable flexibility in deciding how to restructure control systems to fit the particular organization's needs. Just as one-size-fits-all regulations were unresponsive to organizational differences, so standardized reforms may also miss the point.

Many of the calls for culture change are based on the assumption that reformers outside the organization or top leaders within it can shape an organization's culture at will. In fact, this would be strongly contested by many experts on organizational culture, who see culture as something that grows organically from within over a long period of time and is thus, at best, only minimally subject to conscious manipulation by top leadership (Trice and Beyer, 1993). While others (Deal and Kennedy, 1982) see culture as much more malleable, most scholars would agree with Sathe's assertion (1985) that "a radical change in the content of a culture is more difficult to accomplish than is an incremental change, and cultural resistance to change is greater in a strong culture than in a weak culture" (p. 243).

Let us look at the specific content of the culture changes proposed for the federal government and at the strategies proposed for managing the process of culture change. The reforms proposed by the NPR are quite eclectic, influenced by a range of sources, including the work of Osborne and Gaebler (1992) and government reforms abroad, particularly in Great Britain, Australia, and New Zealand (Kettl, 1994). Many of the changes proposed have their origins in recent reform efforts in the private sector, particularly Total Quality Management (TQM), participative management, and labor-management relations. The language used emphasizes private sector values, such as entrepreneurial behavior and customer service. And the values are strongly antibureaucratic, with a heavy emphasis on "empowerment" of lower-level managers and rank-and-file employees.

There are obvious connections between the efforts to delegate and deregulate and the process of culture change. Both call for opening up rigid, encrusted bureaucracies and moving toward more flexible organizations that foster creativity and reward innovation. But the key to both aspects of reform is managers. And what is missing is a clear vision of the role of managers in the future. On the one hand, they are being given more authority in personnel and budgeting. On the other hand, they are being asked to share authority with their employees via the quality and labor-management partnership processes—a major culture change for traditional hierarchical bureaucracies (Ban, 1994b). It is not surprising that many managers are confused about what this will all mean in practice. The stress and confusion will be even greater for first-line supervisors who are worker-managers or pseudo-supervisors. These changes may require major rethinking of the managerial role and of whether it is still possible to ask people to continue to be technical specialists while taking on supervisory responsibilities.

To what extent are managers likely to accept or support the new culture? A central aspect of the proposed changes is the quality movement. Certainly, some parts of government are successfully implementing TQM programs, but other agencies are struggling to get off the ground (Radin and Coffee, 1993). Still others, including some in this study, began the quality process with enthusiasm but have since faltered (Ban, 1992). In fact, one manager told me that his agency's total quality effort had been superseded by the push to reinvent government, so the relationship between the two is far from clear. While the proponents of TQM make sweeping claims for what it will accomplish, to date there is little hard data about its actual impact on efficiency, effectiveness, or staff morale. And managers who have survived the planning-programming-budgeting system (PPBS), zero-based budgeting (ZBB), and quality circles are cynical about yet another management reform (Radin and Coffee, 1993).

But TQM sends very mixed messages to managers about how they are valued and what role they are to play. At the extreme, it is based on a value system that sees most people as wanting to do good work but as being hampered by poor management. Indeed, W. Edwards Deming, originator of TQM, has been quoted as saying that 80 percent of employee problems are actually caused by poor management. But this assumes that people stop being smart and motivated when they cross the line into management—a strange assumption indeed. Further, the thesis may also be based on an overly rosy view of employees. While many will thrive on the challenges of a more participative workplace, others will continue to be problem employees. How will a manager identify and deal with them in the new environment if there are no individual performance appraisal systems and if decision making is participative? Again, it is critical that the responsibility and authority of managers be clear.

Many of the values espoused by the proponents of culture change are directly antithetical to some agencies' traditional values. Organizations that already have some elements of an adhocracy culture will find it easier to move to the fluid, decentralized entrepreneurial style advocated by the NPR. But those with the most traditional hierarchy culture are likely to find this a very difficult process. Further, managers used to defining their roles as largely or entirely internal will have trouble taking on the entrepreneurial role envisioned by the reforms. But the NPR does not have a very sophisticated model for changing organizational culture. The approach appears to rely on heavy doses of exhortation and symbolism (such as Vice President Gore's "hammer awards" to "reinvention heroes") combined with training designed centrally and delivered through a training of trainers model (Ban, 1994b). But this is only a first step. Most works on culture change see that change as a multistep process involving considerable effort over a long period of time and with a considerable risk of failure (Wilkins and Patterson, 1985). Simply offering training on new approaches is unlikely to change behavior or underlying cultural values; it must be accompanied by changes in the organization's reward system or incentive structure (Sethia and Von Glinow, 1985). The National Performance Review envisions a reward system based on measurable outcomes, but many organizations will find this very difficult to implement (Franklin and Ban, 1994).

Conflicts between the different strands of reform may also cause implementation problems. One of the most obvious of such conflicts, as we saw in Chapter Seven, is between the call for budgetary deregulation, including the abolition of personnel ceilings, and the promise to cut over a quarter of a million federal employees. Whether or not ceiling controls are actually lifted at some time in the future, the NPR reformers face the dilemma of how to change organizational culture while simultaneously shrinking the size of the organization. One of the central themes of the NPR is the need to empower employees and lower-level managers and to encourage creativity, risk-taking, and innovation. But, as we have found, cutback management puts great strains on managers, particularly first-line supervisors, who are stretched thin, forced to pick up more of the hands-on work, and at serious risk of burnout. At the same time, rank-and-file employees are uncertain and fearful of the future. These are hardly ideal conditions in which to encourage people to stick their necks out by taking greater risks. Nor do managers in these conditions have the time and energy to be creative. Further, RIFs can put great strain on the existing culture, undermining employees' trust in and loyalty to the organization.

The strains of dealing with NPR cutbacks are particularly severe for managers, since they are a primary target of the cuts. The NPR called for a "delayering" of the government by means of reductions in excess levels of middle management; however, it did not specify which levels were unnecessary. As a result, most managers felt threatened, and many became cynical or downright hostile to the reforms (Ban, 1994b; Kettl, 1994).

The process of delayering now under way, in which agencies are being asked to reduce both the total number of managers and the number of managerial levels could, in theory, provoke some careful thought about how many managers are really needed, what functions they should perform, and what skills they require. But the process thus far is being managed in haste, with agencies pressed to meet arbitrary numerical targets, and has not provided a vehicle for such careful analysis (Kettl, 1994).

Delayering could also help agencies deal with the sometimes serious problem of worker-managers and pseudo-supervisors by leading to a clarification of the line between supervisor and non-supervisor—particularly if it is accompanied by clearer delegations of authority down to lower levels of management. But again, a number of agencies are doing the opposite. Rather than clarifying roles, they are further confusing them by retitling first-line supervisors "team leaders," though without any substantive change of duties. Consequently, people who are no longer classed as supervisors are still directing work and conducting performance appraisals (Ban, 1994b).

There are also serious conflicts between the threat of cutbacks and the implementation of TQM, which requires a culture of trust. It is tough to change the organizational culture at a time when there are major changes going on in the regulatory environment and even the agency structure, but it is particularly tough when people fear that if they do too well in implementing the cultural change, they might eliminate their own jobs. In short, cutbacks targeted at managers, not surprisingly, make them insecure and leave them wondering how long they will continue to be needed.

Further, as we saw, the NPR recommendations for movement toward a quality culture call for managers to be held responsible for results. This raises a number of difficult questions. How will results be measured, and who will establish the criteria? It is important to remember here that one reason government managers have relied so heavily on process controls and measurement is that much of what government does is difficult or impossible to measure or monitor (Wilson, 1989; Swiss, 1992). And who will actually be measuring results and holding managers responsible if the ranks of midlevel managers are reduced and the traditional oversight offices are shrunk? Will evaluation offices need to be set up or expanded to monitor individual or programmatic outcomes?

Finally, a narrow focus on outcomes has some risks for a changing organizational culture. As some businesses have found to their sorrow, rewarding people for results alone may foster a culture that, in effect, says, "I don't care how you do it (or the ethical corners you cut). Just get it done."

As we have seen above, while cuts in government were included in the NPR at least partly for political reasons, they were justified on the basis of deregulation and restructuring, which would reduce the need for both managers and oversight staff. But Congress has been all too willing to adopt the politically palatable half of this program—namely, the cuts—without making the regulatory changes on which they were based. This is potentially disastrous. As the National Academy of Public Administration (1994) said in an appraisal of the NPR, "To take the personnel cuts and not make the systems changes could result in a reduced, and perhaps altogether inadequate, capacity to operate those frail and complex systems, let alone successfully reinvent them" (p. 37).

In short, the future for federal managers is unlikely to look quite like the current picture presented in this research. There is a potential for dramatic change that would solve many of the problems caused by the constraints described here—change that would really unchain Gulliver. Managers could be freed from the web of formal controls; at the same time, positive organizational cultures could be developed and the traditional bureaucratic culture of control could be sloughed off. But there is a real danger of reform going awry, either because reform efforts fail to win political support or because

loosening constraints in an environment that is hypercritical of government results in a loss of legitimacy and a perception of abuse.
Under these circumstances, the pendulum could swing back to a
reliance on external controls, and Gulliver could find himself back
in chains.

Notes

Introduction

1. At the Food and Consumer Service, only two group interviews were conducted. The number of SES members there was
so small that I interviewed most of them individually rather
than conduct a group interview. At all other headquarters
units, three group interviews were conducted.
2. At the Portsmouth Naval Shipyard, which is enormous, two
interviews with Wage Grade (blue-collar) supervisors were
conducted, and white-collar supervisors were interviewed
individually.

Chapter One

1. A word about terminology: the component parts of the
department are technically "services," such as the Food and
Consumer Service, but they are often referred to as "agencies."
The term "department" refers to the Department of Agriculture as a whole.

Chapter Three

1. Currently, an applicant for an entry-level position in personnel at grade GS-5 can qualify either with a bachelor's degree
or with three years of general work experience that includes
at least a year of personnel work at the equivalent of GS-4. In
contrast, most private sector employers require a bachelor's
degree (U.S. Merit Systems Protection Board, 1993).

2. These figures are unpublished data from the study reported in U.S. Merit Systems Protection Board (1993). The trend toward requiring a college degree for personnel work is much more advanced in the private sector. One study stated that "today some 95 percent of HRM professionals have some collegiate training" (Hoyt and Lewis, 1980, p. 53).

Chapter Four

1. ACWA groups the same one hundred-plus positions covered by the Professional and Administrative Career Examination (PACE) into six job families, each covered by a separate test. The groupings are: Group 1: health, safety, and environmental; Group 2: writing and public information; Group 3: business, finance, and management; Group 4: personnel, administration, and computers; Group 5: benefits review, tax, and legal; and Group 6: law enforcement and investigation.

2. Recently, at least in the D.C. area, OPM has begun to delegate to agencies the responsibility for hiring in some of these occupations, including management analyst and personnel specialist.

3. The only exception to the requirement to rate and rank the candidates is if there are three or fewer applicants identified and either none is a veteran or all are veterans.

4. Schedule B was designed originally for other purposes, but was expanded temporarily to cover PACE occupations. For a fuller discussion, see Ban and Ingraham (1988) and U.S. Merit Systems Protection Board (1987a).

Chapter Six

1. There are a handful of jobs at GS-16 to GS-18, but most such positions were folded into the Senior Executive Service when it was created in 1979.

2. There are currently two different systems being used to develop the standards. One is the Factor Evaluation System (FES), which assigns points to nine specific factors. Many published standards have not yet been converted to the FES; they use narrative descriptions of the work at each grade level, based on similar factors (see Shafritz, Riccucci, Rosenbloom, and Hyde, 1992; Warman, 1986).

Chapter Seven

1. Some years ago, Allen Schick developed a typology of four types of resource scarcity (Schick, 1980). Severe scarcity, as I am defining it, is similar to his worst case category.
2. The one exception is for veterans with a 30 percent or greater "service-connected compensable disability," who can retreat as many as five grades or grade levels (U.S. Merit Systems Protection Board, 1987b).

References

Aberbach, J. D., Putnam, R. D., and Rockman, B. A. *Bureaucrats and Politicians in Western Democracies*. Cambridge, Mass.: Harvard University Press, 1981.

Allison, G. T., Jr. "Public and Private Management: Are They Fundamentally Alike in All Unimportant Respects?" In *Setting Public Management Research Agendas*. Proceedings of the Public Management Research Conference. Washington, D.C.: Office of Personnel Management, 1980. Reprinted in F. S. Lane, *Current Issues in Public Administration*. (5th ed.) New York: St. Martin's Press, 1994.

Animal and Plant Health Inspection Service, U.S. Department of Agriculture. *Strategic Plan: Meeting Producer and Public Needs*. Washington, D.C.: Animal and Plant Health Inspection Service, U.S. Department of Agriculture, 1989.

Anthony, W. P., Perrewe, P. L., and Kacmar, K. M. *Strategic Human Resource Management*. Fort Worth, Tex.: Dryden Press, 1993.

Ban, C. "The Navy Demonstration Project: An 'Experiment in Experimentation.'" In C. Ban and N. M. Riccucci (eds.), *Public Personnel Management: Current Concerns, Future Challenges*. White Plains, N.Y.: Longman, 1991a.

Ban, C. "The Realities of the Merit System." In C. Ban and N. M. Riccucci (eds.), *Public Personnel Management: Current Concerns, Future Challenges*. White Plains, N.Y.: Longman, 1991b.

Ban, C. "Can Total Quality Management Work in the Federal Government? The Politics of Implementation." Paper presented at the American Political Science Association annual meeting, Sept. 1992.

Ban, C. "Twenty-Five Years of Human Resources Management: *Plus Ça Change?*" Remarks prepared for a roundtable at the annual meeting of the American Society for Public Administration, 1994a.

Ban, C. "Unions, Management, and the NPR: Forging a New Partnership?" In D. F. Kettl and J. J. DiIulio, Jr. (eds.), *Inside the Reinvention Machine: Appraising Government Reform*. Washington, D.C.: Brookings Institution, 1994b.

Ban, C., Goldenberg, E., and Marzotto, T. "Controlling the U.S. Federal Bureaucracy: Will the SES Make a Difference?" In G. E. Caiden and H. Seidentopf (eds.), *Strategies for Administrative Reform*. Boston: Lexington Books, 1982a.

Ban, C., Goldenberg, E., and Marzotto, T. "Firing the Unproductive Employee: Will Civil Service Reform Make a Difference?" *Review of Public Personnel Administration*, 1982b, 2(2), 87–100.

Ban, C., and Ingraham, P. W. "Retaining Quality Federal Employees: Life After PACE." *Public Administration Review*, 1988, 48(3), 708–718.

Ban, C., and Marzotto, T. "Delegations of Examining: Objectives and Implementation." In P. W. Ingraham and C. Ban (eds.), *Legislating Bureaucratic Change: The Civil Service Reform Act of 1978*. Albany: State University of New York Press, 1984.

Ban, C., and Redd, H. C., III. "The State of the Merit System: Perceptions of Abuse in the Federal Civil Service." *Review of Public Personnel Administration*, 1990, 10(3), 55–72.

Ban, C., and Riccucci, N. M. (eds.). *Public Personnel Management: Current Concerns, Future Challenges*. White Plains, N.Y.: Longman, 1991.

Ban, C., and Riccucci, N. M. "Personnel Systems and Labor Relations: Steps Toward a Quiet Revitalization." In F. J. Thompson (ed.), *Revitalizing State and Local Public Service: Strengthening Performance, Accountability, and Citizen Confidence*. San Francisco: Jossey-Bass, 1993.

Brower, R. S., and Abolafia, M. Y. "Bureaucratic Entrepreneurship: Enacting Alternative Channels to Administrative Effectiveness." Unpublished paper, 1994.

Bruce, W. M. *Problem Employee Management: Proactive Strategies for Human Resource Managers*. New York: Quorum Books, 1990.

Budget of the United States, Fiscal Year 1992. Washington, D.C.: U.S. Government Printing Office, 1991.

Cameron, K. S., and Quinn, R. E., *Changing Organizational Cultures*, Part I (Prism 4, an assessment instrument, and Prism 5, a change workbook). Ann Arbor, Mich.: School of Business, University of Michigan, n.d.

Campbell, A. K. "Revitalizing the Federal Personnel System." *Public Personnel Management*, 1978, 7(6), 58–63.

Campbell, A. K. "Civil Service Reform as a Remedy for Bureaucratic Ills." In C. Weiss and A. Barton (eds.), *Making Bureaucracies Work*. Newbury Park, Calif.: Sage, 1980.

Carr, D. K., and Littman, I. G. *Excellence in Government: Total Quality Management in the 1990s*. Arlington, Va.: Coopers & Lybrand, 1990.

Coalition for Effective Change. *Comments on NPC Report: Create a Flexible and Responsive Hiring System*. Washington, D.C.: Coalition for Effective Change, 1994.

Cohen, S., and Brand, R. *Total Quality Management in Government: A Practical Guide for the Real World.* San Francisco: Jossey-Bass, 1993.

Cooper, T. L. *The Responsible Administrator: An Approach to Ethics for the Administrative Role.* (3rd ed.) San Francisco: Jossey-Bass, 1990.

Deal, T. E., and Kennedy, A. A. *Corporate Cultures: The Rites and Rituals of Corporate Life.* Reading, Mass.: Addison-Wesley, 1982.

Dean, J. W., Jr., and Bowen, D. E. "Management Theory and Total Quality: Improving Research and Practice Through Theory Development." *Academy of Management Review,* 1994, *19*(3), 392–418.

DiIulio, J. J., Jr. (ed.). *Deregulating the Public Service.* Washington, D.C.: Brookings Institution, 1994.

DiIulio, J. J., Jr., Garvey, G., and Kettl, D. F. *Improving Government Performance: An Owner's Manual.* Washington, D.C.: Brookings Institution, 1993.

DiPadova, L. N., and Faerman, S. R. "Using the Competing Values Framework to Facilitate Managerial Understanding Across Levels of Organizational Hierarchy." *Human Resource Management,* Spring 1993, *32*(1), 143–174.

Faerman, S. R., and Peters, T. D. "A Conceptual Framework for Examining Managerial Roles and Transitions Across Levels of Organizational Hierarchy." Paper presented at the National Public Management Research Conference, 1991.

Faerman, S. R., Quinn, R. E., Thompson, M. P., and McGrath, M. R. *Supervising New York State: A Framework For Excellence.* Albany, N.Y.: Governor's Office of Employee Relations, 1990.

Foulkes, F. K. (ed.). *Strategic Human Resources Management: A Guide for Effective Practice.* Englewood Cliffs, N.J.: Prentice-Hall, 1986.

Franklin, A., and Ban, C. "The Performance Measurement Movement: Learning from the Experiences Of Program Evaluation." Paper presented at the annual meeting of the American Evaluation Association, 1994.

Frost, P. J., and others (eds.). *Reframing Organizational Culture.* Newbury Park, Calif.: Sage, 1991.

Gaertner, G. H., and Gaertner, K. N. "Formal Disciplinary Action in Two Federal Agencies." *Review of Public Personnel Administration,* 1984, *5*(1), 12–24.

Giek, D. G., and Lees, P. L. "On Massive Change: Using the Competing Values Framework to Organize the Education Efforts of the Human Resource Function in New York State Government." *Human Resource Management,* 1993, *32*(1), 9–28.

Goodsell, C. T. *The Case for Bureaucracy.* Chatham, N.J.: Chatham House, 1985.

Gormley, W. *Taming the Bureaucracy: Muscles, Prayers, and Other Strategies.* Princeton, N.J.: Princeton University Press, 1989.

Gruber, J. E. *Controlling Bureaucracies: Dilemmas in Democratic Governance.* Berkeley: University of California Press, 1987.

Gulick, L., and Urwick, L. (eds.). *Papers on the Science of Administration*. Augustus M. Kelley, 1973. (Originally published 1937.)

Harris, C. "Limits Opposed on Contracting After Buyouts." *Federal Times*. Oct. 3, 1994, p. 3.

Harris, C. "Unions Left Out of Reform." *Federal Times*, Dec. 26, 1994, p. 5.

Harris, C. "Congress Plans Fast, Deep Cuts." *Federal Times*, Jan. 16, 1995, pp. 1, 5.

Herzberg, F. "One More Time: How Do You Motivate Employees?" *Harvard Business Review*, Jan./Feb. 1968, 46, 53–62.

Hoogenboom, A. *Outlawing the Spoils: A History of the Civil Service Reform Movement, 1865–1883*. Urbana: University of Illinois Press, 1961.

Hooijberg, R., and Petrock, F. "On Cultural Change: Using the Competing Values Framework to Help Leaders Execute a Transformational Strategy." *Human Resource Management*, Spring 1993, *32*(1), 29–50.

Hoyt, D. R., and Lewis, J. "What Students Need to Enter the Personnel Field." *Personnel Administrator*, Oct. 1980, pp. 53–68.

Huddleston, M. W. "To the Threshold of Reform: The Senior Executive Service and America's Search for a Higher Civil Service." In P. W. Ingraham and D. H. Rosenbloom (eds.), *The Promise and Paradox of Civil Service Reform*. Pittsburgh: University of Pittsburgh, 1992.

Imundo, L. V. *Employee Discipline*. Belmont, Calif.: Wadsworth, 1985.

Ingraham, P. W., and Ban, C. *Legislating Bureaucratic Change: The Civil Service Reform Act of 1978*. Albany: State University of New York Press, 1984.

Ingraham, P. W., and Ban, C. "Models of Public Management: Are They Useful to Federal Managers in the 1980s?" *Public Administration Review*, 1986, 46(2), 152–160.

Katz, R. L. "Skills of an Effective Administrator." *Harvard Business Review*, Jan./Feb. 1955.

Kelman, S. *Procurement and Public Management: The Fear of Discretion and the Quality of Government Performance*. Washington, D.C.: American Enterprise Institute Press, 1990.

Kelman, S. "Deregulating Federal Procurement: Nothing to Fear but Discretion Itself?" In J. J. DiIulio, Jr. (ed.), *Deregulating the Public Service*. Washington, D.C.: Brookings Institution, 1994.

Kennedy, M. M. "Generalizing from Single Case Studies." *Evaluation Quarterly*, 1979, *3*(4), 661–687.

Kettl, D. F. *Government by Proxy: (Mis?)Managing Federal Programs*. Washington, D.C.: Congressional Quarterly, 1988.

Kettl, D. F. *Reinventing Government? Appraising the National Performance Review*, Washington, D.C.: Brookings Institution, 1994.

Klaas, B. S., and Wheeler, H. "Managerial Decision Making About Employee

Discipline: A Policy-Capturing Approach." *Personnel Psychology*, 1990, *43*, 117–134.

Klitgaard, R. *Controlling Corruption*. Berkeley: University of California Press, 1988.

Krause, R. D. "Public Personnel in a Changing World." *Public Personnel Management*, 1979, *8*(5), 340–343.

Lane, L. M., and Wolf, J. F. *The Human Resource Crisis in the Public Sector*. New York: Quorum Books, 1990.

Levine, C. H., and Kleeman, R. S. *The Quiet Crisis of the Civil Service: The Federal Personnel System at the Crossroads*. Washington, D.C.: National Academy of Public Administration, 1986.

Levine, C. H., Peters, B. G., and Thompson, F. J. *Public Administration: Challenges, Choices, Consequences*. Glenview, Ill.: Scott, Foresman, 1990.

Levine, C. H., Rubin, I., and Wolohojian, G. "Managing Organizational Retrenchment: Preconditions, Deficiencies, and Adaptations in the Public Sector." *Administration and Society*, 1982, *14*(1), 101–136.

Luke, J. S. "New Leadership Requirements for Public Administrators: From Managerial to Policy Ethics." In J. S. Bowman (ed.), *Ethical Frontiers in Public Management: Seeking New Strategies for Resolving Ethical Dilemmas*. San Francisco: Jossey-Bass, 1991.

Maranto, R., and Schultz, D. *A Short History of the United States Civil Service*. Lanham, Md.: University Press of America, 1991.

Martin, J. *Cultures in Organizations: Three Perspectives*. New York: Oxford University Press, 1992.

Miles, R. E., and Snow, C. C. "Designing Strategic Human Resources Systems." *Organizational Dynamics*, 1984, *12*, 36–51.

Mintzberg, H. *The Nature of Managerial Work*. New York: HarperCollins, 1973.

Mosher, F. C. (ed.). *Basic Documents of American Public Administration, 1776–1950*. New York: Holmes and Meier, 1976.

Nalbandian, J. "From Compliance to Consultation: The Changing Role of the Public Personnel Administrator." *Review of Public Personnel Administration*, 1981, *1*(2), 37–51.

National Academy of Public Administration. *Revitalizing Federal Management: Managers and Their Overburdened Systems*. Washington, D.C.: National Academy of Public Administration, 1983.

National Academy of Public Administration. *Steps Toward a Stable Future: An Assessment of the Budget and Personnel Processes of the Environmental Protection Agency*. Washington, D.C.: National Academy of Public Administration, 1984.

National Academy of Public Administration. *Modernizing Federal Classification: An Opportunity for Excellence*. Washington, D.C.: National Academy of Public Administration, 1991.

National Academy of Public Administration. *Helping Government Change: An Appraisal of the National Performance Review.* Draft report. Washington, D.C.: National Academy of Public Administration, 1994.

National Commission on the Public Service (Volcker Commission). *Leadership for America: Rebuilding the Public Service.* Lexington, Mass.: Lexington Books, 1990.

National Commission on the State and Local Public Service (Winter Commission). *Hard Truths/Tough Choices: An Agenda for State and Local Reform.* Albany, N.Y.: Nelson A. Rockefeller Institute of Government, 1993.

National Performance Review. *From Red Tape to Results: Creating a Government That Works Better and Costs Less.* Washington, D.C.: U.S. Government Printing Office, 1993a.

National Performance Review. *Mission-Driven, Results-Oriented Budgeting.* Washington, D.C.: U.S. Government Printing Office, 1993b.

National Performance Review. *Office of Personnel Management.* Washington, D.C.: U.S. Government Printing Office, 1993c.

National Performance Review. *Reinventing Human Resource Management.* Washington, D.C.: U.S. Government Printing Office, 1993d.

National Research Council. *Pay for Performance: Evaluating Performance Appraisal and Merit Pay.* Washington, D.C.: National Academy Press, 1991.

Osborne, D. "Can This President Be Saved?" *Washington Post Magazine*, Jan. 8, 1995, pp. 13–16, 28–32.

Osborne, D., and Gaebler, T. *Reinventing Government.* Reading, Mass.: Addison-Wesley, 1992.

Ott, J. S. *The Organizational Culture Perspective.* Pacific Grove, Calif.: Brooks/Cole, 1989.

Perry, J. L. "Strategic Human Resource Management." *Review of Public Personnel Administration*, 1993, *13*(4), 59–71.

Peters, T. J., and Waterman, R. H., Jr. *In Search of Excellence: Lessons from America's Best-Run Companies.* New York: HarperCollins, 1982.

Quinn, R. E. "Applying the Competing Values Approach to Leadership: Toward an Integrative Framework." In J. Hunt, R. Stewart, C. Schriesheim, and D. Hosking (eds.), *Managerial Work and Leadership: International Perspectives.* Elmsford, N.Y.: Pergamon Press, 1984.

Quinn, R. E. *Beyond Rational Management: Mastering the Paradoxes and Competing Demands of High Performance.* San Francisco: Jossey-Bass, 1988.

Quinn, R. E., Faerman, S. R., Thompson, M. P., and McGrath, M. R. *Becoming a Master Manager: A Competency Framework.* New York: Wiley, 1990.

Quinn, R. E., and Rohrbaugh, J. "A Spatial Model of Effectiveness Criteria: Towards a Competing Values Approach to Organizational Effectiveness," *Management Science*, 1983, *29*, 363–377.

Radin, B. A., and Coffee, J. N. "A Critique of TQM: Problems of Implementation in the Public Sector." *Public Administration Quarterly*, Spring 1993, 42–54.

Redeker, J. R. *Employee Discipline: Policies and Practices*. Washington, D.C.: Bureau of National Affairs, 1989.

Riccucci, N. M. *Unsung Heroes: Federal Execucrats Making a Difference*. Washington, D.C.: Georgetown University Press, 1995.

Rivas, R. F. "Dismissing Problem Employees." In R. L. Edwards and J. A. Yankey (eds.), *Skills for Effective Human Services Management*. Silver Spring, Md.: National Association of Social Workers Press, 1991.

Rivenbark, L. "Agencies to Ask: Are We Needed?" *Federal Times*, Jan. 16, 1995a, pp. 1, 3.

Rivenbark, L. "Rules Governing Work Life Loosen," *Federal Times*, Jan. 2, 1995b, pp. 6–7.

Romzek, B. S., and Dubnick, M. J. "Issues of Accountability in Flexible Personnel Systems." In P. W. Ingraham and B. S. Romzek (eds.), *New Paradigms for Government: Issues for the Changing Public Service*. San Francisco: Jossey-Bass, 1994.

Rosenbloom, D. "Politics and Public Personnel Administration: The Legacy of 1883." In D. Rosenbloom (ed.), *Centenary Issues of the Pendleton Act of 1883*. New York: Marcel Dekker, 1982.

Ross, L. "Facing the Tough Issues: Federal Personnel Directors Conference." *Periscope*, 1992, *13*, 2, 7.

Rubin, I. "Retrenchment and Flexibility in Public Organizations." In C. H. Levine and I. Rubin (eds.), *Fiscal Stress and Public Policy*. Newbury Park, Calif.: Sage, 1980.

Sathe, V. "How to Decipher and Change Corporate Culture." In R. H. Kilmann, M. J. Saxton, R. Serpa, and Associates, *Gaining Control of the Corporate Culture*. San Francisco: Jossey-Bass, 1985.

Savas, E. S. *Privatizing the Public Sector*. Chatham, N.J.: Chatham House, 1982.

Schick, A. "Budgetary Adaptations to Resource Scarcity." In C. H. Levine and I. Rubin (eds.), *Fiscal Stress and Public Policy*. Newbury Park, Calif.: Sage, 1980.

Sendelbach, N. B. "The Competing Values Framework for Management Training and Development: A Tool for Understanding Complex Issues and Tasks." *Human Resource Management*, 1993, *32*(1), 75–100.

Sethia, N. K., and Von Glinow, M. A. "Arriving at Four Cultures by Managing the Reward System." In R. H. Kilmann, M. J. Saxton, R. Serpa, and Associates, *Gaining Control of the Corporate Culture*. San Francisco: Jossey-Bass, 1985.

Shafritz, J. *Position Classification: A Behavioral Analysis for the Public Service*. New York: Praeger, 1973.

Shafritz, J. Remarks at a panel on "Implications of the Forces for Change on Public Personnel Administration." *Public Personnel Administration: The Next Hundred Years.* Conference proceedings summary. Albany, N.Y.: New York State Civil Service Commission, 1982.

Shafritz, J., Riccucci, N. M., Rosenbloom, D., and Hyde, A. *Personnel Management in Government.* (4th ed.) New York: Marcel Dekker, 1992.

Shaw, G. J., and Bransford, W. L. *The Federal Manager's Handbook: A Guide to Rehabilitating or Removing the Problem Employee.* Washington, D.C.: MPC Publications, 1992.

Straus, S. "Multiple Constituencies, Activities, and Standards: A Framework for Evaluating the Effectiveness of Public Personnel Departments." *Review of Public Personnel Administration,* 1991, *11,* 55–70.

Stroud, E. W. "FPM Sunset and You." *OPM Message to the Senior Executive Service,* Aug. 1994, pp. 4–5.

Swiss, J. E. "Adapting Total Quality Management (TQM) to Government." *Public Administration Review,* 1992, *52*(4), 356–362.

Thompson, M. P. "Using the Competing Values Framework in the Classroom." *Human Resource Management,* 1993, *32*(1), 101–120.

Trice, H. M., and Beyer, J. M. *The Cultures of Work Organizations.* Englewood Cliffs, N.J.: Prentice-Hall, 1993.

U.S. Army, Office of the Deputy Chief of Staff for Personnel, Department of Civilian Personnel, Planning and Evaluation Office. "Report of FY 85 Army-Wide Questionnaire Survey of Civilian Personnel." Washington, D.C.: U.S. Army, Office of the Deputy Chief of Staff for Personnel, Department of Civilian Personnel, Planning and Evaluation Office, 1985.

U.S. Environmental Protection Agency. *1988 Organizational Culture Study of the United States Environmental Protection Agency, Region III.* Philadelphia: U.S. Environmental Protection Agency, 1988.

U.S. Food and Nutrition Service (currently U.S. Food and Consumer Service). *Request to Abolish Food Assistance Program Specialist Series, GS-120.* Alexandria, Va.: U.S. Food and Consumer Service, 1992.

U.S. General Accounting Office. *Description of Selected Systems for Classifying Federal Civilian Positions and Personnel.* GGD-84–90. Washington, D.C.: U.S. General Accounting Office, 1984.

U.S. General Accounting Office. *Federal Work Force: How Certain Agencies Are Implementing the Grade Reduction Program.* GGD-86–33. Washington, D.C.: U.S. General Accounting Office, 1986.

U.S. General Accounting Office. *Federal Recruiting and Hiring: Making Government Jobs Attractive to Prospective Employees.* GAO/GGD-90–105. Washington, D.C.: U.S. General Accounting Office, 1990a.

U.S. General Accounting Office. *Observations on the Navy's Managing to Payroll Program.* GGD-90–47. Washington, D.C.: U.S. General Accounting Office, 1990b.

U.S. General Accounting Office. *Performance Management: How Well Is the Government Dealing with Poor Performers?* GAO/GGD-91–7. Washington, D.C.: U.S. General Accounting Office, 1990c.

U.S. General Accounting Office. *Government Contractors: Are Service Contractors Performing Inherently Governmental Functions?* GAO/GGD-92–11. Washington, D.C.: U.S. General Accounting Office, 1991.

U.S. Merit Systems Protection Board. *In Search of Merit: Hiring Entry-Level Federal Employees.* Washington, D.C.: U.S. Merit Systems Protection Board, 1987a.

U.S. Merit Systems Protection Board. *Reduction in Force: The Evolving Ground Rules.* Washington, D.C.: U.S. Merit Systems Protection Board, 1987b.

U.S. Merit Systems Protection Board. *OPM's Classification and Qualification Systems: A Renewed Emphasis, a Changing Perspective.* Washington, D.C.: U.S. Merit Systems Protection Board, 1989.

U.S. Merit Systems Protection Board. *Federal First-Line Supervisors: How Good Are They?* Washington, D.C.: U.S. Merit Systems Protection Board, 1992a.

U.S. Merit Systems Protection Board. *To Meet the Needs of the Nations: Staffing the U.S. Civil Service and the Public Service of Canada.* Washington, D.C.: U.S. Merit Systems Protection Board, 1992b.

U.S. Merit Systems Protection Board. *Workforce Quality and Federal Procurement: An Assessment.* Washington, D.C.: U.S. Merit Systems Protection Board, 1992c.

U.S. Merit Systems Protection Board. *Federal Personnel Officers: Time for Change?* Washington, D.C.: U.S. Merit Systems Protection Board, 1993.

U.S. Merit Systems Protection Board. *Entering Professional Positions in the Federal Government.* Washington, D.C.: U.S. Merit Systems Protection Board, 1994.

U.S. Office of Personnel Management. *Manager's Handbook.* Washington, D.C.: U.S. Office of Personnel Management, 1981.

U.S. Office of Personnel Management. *Status of the Evaluation of the Navy Personnel Management Demonstration Project: Management Report I.* Washington, D.C.: U.S. Office of Personnel Management, 1984.

U.S. Office of Personnel Management. *Civil Service 2000.* Washington, D.C.: U.S. Office of Personnel Management, 1988.

U.S. Office of Personnel Management. *Manage to Budget Programs: Guidelines for Success.* PSOG-203. Washington, D.C.: U.S. Government Printing Office, 1989.

U.S. Office of Personnel Management. *Broad-Banding in the Federal Government: Technical Report.* Washington, D.C.: U.S. Office of Personnel Management, 1992a.

U.S. Office of Personnel Management. *Delegation of Personnel Management*

Authority. Washington, D.C.: U.S. Office of Personnel Management, 1992b.

Van Riper, P. *History of the United States Civil Service.* Evanston, Ill.: Row, Peterson, 1958.

Warman, J. S. *Federal Manager's Guide to Organization Design and Position Classification.* Arlington, Va.: Dewey, 1986.

Weber, M. *Economy and Society.* Berkeley: University of California Press, 1978.

White House Personnel Office. "The Malek Manual." In F. Thompson (ed.), *Classics of Public Personnel Policy.* (2nd ed.) Pacific Grove, Calif.: Brooks/Cole, 1991.

Wildavsky, A. *The New Politics of the Budgetary Process.* Glenview, Ill.: Scott, Foresman, 1988.

Wilkins, A. L., and Patterson, K. J. "You Can't Get There from Here: What Will Make Culture-Change Projects Fail." In R. H. Kilmann, M. J. Saxton, R. Serpa, and Associates, *Gaining Control of the Corporate Culture.* San Francisco: Jossey-Bass, 1985.

Wilson, J. Q. *Bureaucracy.* New York: Basic Books, 1989.

Yin, R. K. *Case Study Research: Design and Methods.* Newbury Park, Calif.: Sage, 1984.

Yukl, G. A. *Leadership in Organizations.* Englewood Cliffs, N.J.: Prentice-Hall, 1981.

Index

A

Aberbach, J. D., 33
Abolafia, M. Y., 154
Abuse: of civil service system, 6; with deregulation, 271–272; of hiring system, 153–156; of procurement system, 6–7
Actions: adverse, 159; performance-based, 160–161
Adhocracy culture, 25–26; EPA as, 39–41
Administrative Careers with America (ACWA) exams, 125, 126, 129, 130, 133, 145, 146–147, 150, 282n1
Affirmative action, 143
American Association of Retired Persons (AARP), 231
Animal and Plant Health Inspection Service (APHIS), 15, 43–44, 145; budget of, 29, 44; ceilings at, 230, 247; classification system at, 198–201, 203, 204, 206–207, 210–211, 213; contracting out by, 235, 236; employment in, 27; managerial roles at, 75, 77–78, 84; managers at, 54, 57–58, 60, 62, 64; organizational culture of, 48–51; personnel office at, 106–109, 114, 115–116, 117; problem employees in, 169, 176–178, 179; recruiting by, 131–132, 134–138; TQM in, 50, 106–108
Anthony, W. P., 119
Appeals, legal, by problem employees, 161–162, 179–181, 182–183
Attrition, 241–242
Authority: direct hire, 126; hiring, 124–125; with problem employees, 164–165; of pseudo-supervisors, 65–68; special appointing, 127

B

Ban, C., 6, 9, 33, 36, 39, 50, 55, 85, 90, 91, 125, 129, 154, 158, 159, 220, 274, 275, 276, 277
Banding: broad, 220–221; grade, 221
Beyer, J. M., 22, 273
Bowen, D. E., 36
Brand, R., 11, 39
Bransford, W. L., 160, 161, 168, 182
Brower, R. S., 154
Bruce, W. M., 160
Budget and Accounting Act of 1921, 4
Budget system: classification system as, 189, 193, 198–201; as constraint, 2, 3–5; reform of, 12
Budgets: of Department of Agriculture, 29, 44; of EPA, 29, 37; of Navy, 28, 29
Bumping, 249, 251, 256
Bureau of the Budget, 4
Burford, A. G., 41

C

Cameron, K. S., 24
Campbell, A. K., 8, 91
Carr, D. K., 11
Carter administration, 6, 129
Carter, J., 159
Case examining, 125
Case studies, 14–15
Ceilings, 227–229; coping with, 231–233; effects of, 229–231; and managers, 244–247; NPR opposition to, 262

Centralization, of personnel offices, 114–116

Civil Service Commission (CSC), 91

Civil Service Reform Act (CSRA), 6, 7–8, 125; Navy demonstration project under, 220–221; on role of personnel staff, 91; on problem employees, 159–160, 181, 182

Civil service system: abuse of, 6; as constraint, 2, 3, 89, 123–124, 152–153; hiring policies of, 124–128. See also Deregulation

Clan culture, 24–25; of EPA Region Three, 42

Classification Act of 1923, 190

Classification system, 84, 189, 190–191; at Department of Agriculture and EPA, 198–215; in Navy, 112–113, 215–221; and pay system, 191–192; reform of, 222–225; as source of conflict, 192–195; in theory and practice, 195–197

Classifiers, 192–195, 201–205, 207, 211, 214–215. See also Personnel staff

Clinton administration, 11, 85–86, 239, 242

Co-op hiring programs, 145, 231–232

Coffee, J. N., 274, 275

Cohen, S., 11, 39

Competing values model: of managerial role, 70–79; of organizational culture, 23–26

Conflict: with classification system, 192–195, 201–205; managers' avoidance of, 166–170, 184–186

Consolidated Civilian Personnnel Office (CCPO), of Navy, 110–113, 115–116, 142, 143, 217, 218

Constraints: civil service system as, 2, 3, 89, 123–124, 152–153; on hiring and firing, 227; management types with, 8, 12–14; on managers, 2–5, 83

Contextual goals, 269, 271–272

Contractors, outside, 233–241

Cooper, T. L., 271

Culture: adhocracy, 25–26, 39–41; clan, 24–25, 42; hierarchy, 24, 25, 30, 31, 34; market, 24, 25; military, 31–34. See also Organizational culture

D

Deal, T. E., 273

Dean, J. W., Jr., 36

Decentralization, 11–12

Delayering, 85–86, 276–277

Deming, W. E., 275

Department of Agriculture, 15, 75, 281n1; budget of, 29; classification system at, 198–215; employment in, 27; hiring system at, 144, 145; organizational culture of, 42–51; problem employees at, 175; recruiting by, 131–132; RIF in, 253–254. See also Animal and Plant Health Inspection Service (APHIS); Food and Consumer Service (FCS)

Department of the Army, 63, 154

Department of Defense (DOD), 26, 39–40, 149

Department of Education, 154

Department of Labor, 196

Deregulation: arguments for, 7–11; proposed by NPR, 11–12, 119, 120; prospects for, 267–272

Diluliu, J. J., Jr., 234

DiPadova, L. N., 71–72, 74, 79

Direct hire authority, 126

Diversity, of personnel staff, 94–95

Douglas v. Veterans Administration, 182

Dubnick, M. J., 272

E

Efficiency, argument for deregulation, 9–10

Employees: in Department of Agriculture, 27, 43–44; in EPA, 27, 37; full-time equivalent (FTE), 228, 229–230, 262; in Navy, 26, 27. See also Personnel staff; Problem employees; Workforce

Engineer in Training (EIT) program, 142–143

Environmental Protection Agency (EPA), 15, 38, 39; budget of, 29, 37; ceilings in, 231–232, 233, 247; classification system at, 198–215; contracting out by, 234–235, 236–238, 239, 240; employment in, 27, 37; freezes in, 243–244; hiring by, 145–146, 148–149, 151; managerial role in, 75, 78–79, 81, 82, 84; managers at, 54, 56, 58, 60, 62–63, 64–65; organizational culture of, 37–42; personnel office at, 95, 100–106, 114, 117; problem employees in, 163–164, 169,

173–174, 175, 176, 178; recruiting by, 132, 138–141; Region Three, 42, 78, 105–106, 173

Equal Employment Opportunity (EEO), 161–162

Equity: external, 194–195; internal, 190–191, 194, 195

F

Factor Evaluation System (FES), 283n2

Faerman, S. R., 23, 71, 72, 74, 79, 267

Federal Acquisition Improvement Act, 239

Federal Acquisition Regulations (FAR), 5

Federal Employees Pay Comparability Act (FEPCA), 191–192

Federal Personnel Manual (FPM), 11, 119, 168, 270

Field Servicing Office (FSO), of APHIS, 106–109, 115–116, 136, 137–138

Firing, 170–171. *See also* Problem employees

Food and Consumer Service (FCS), 15, 43, 212, 281n1; budget of, 29, 44; ceilings at, 230; classification system at, 198–202, 204, 206, 207, 209, 211–212, 214; contracting out by, 235; employment in, 27, 43; freezes in, 242, 243, 245–246, 248; hiring by, 145; managerial roles at, 75, 78–79, 81, 84; managers at, 54, 56–57, 58, 61, 63, 64, 65; organizational culture of, 44–48; personnel office at, 93, 95, 97–100, 117; problem employees in, 159, 163, 166, 173, 174, 175, 179; recruiting by, 131, 132–134

Foulkes, F. K., 114–115

Franklin, A., 276

Freezes, 229, 241–244; and managers, 244–247

Frost, P. J., 22

Full-time equivalent (FTE), 228, 229–230, 262

G

Gaebler, T., 11, 23, 24, 235, 273

Gaertner, G. H., 172, 178

Gaertner, K. N., 172, 178

Garvey, G., 234

Giek, D. G., 71, 267

Goldenberg, E., 55, 158, 159

Goodsell, C. T., 235

Gore, A., 11, 182, 275

Gormley, W., 6

Gorsuch, A., 41

Group norms, 170–174, 183–184. *See also* Organizational culture

Gruber, J. E., 9

Gulick, L., 70

H

Habitch, H., 50

Harris, C., 262, 269, 270

Herzberg, F., 194

Hierarchy culture, 24, 25; Navy as, 30, 31, 34

Hiring authorities, 124–125

Hiring system: abuse of, 153–156; coping with, 1, 144–151; formal, 124–128; reform of, 152–156. *See also* Ceilings; Freezes; Recruiting

Hoogenboom, A., 3

Hooijberg, R., 24, 25

Hoover Commission, 7

Huddleston, M. W., 56

Hyde, A., 157, 182, 191

I

Imundo, L. V., 185

Ingraham, P. W., 6, 33, 129, 270

K

Kacmar, K. M., 119

Katz, R. L., 70

Kelman, S., 2, 5, 9, 239

Kennedy, A. A., 273

Kennedy, M. M., 15

Kettl, D. F., 85–86, 234, 235, 260–261, 273, 277

Klaas, B. S., 170

Kleeman, R. S., 129

Klitgaard, R., 155

Krause, R. D., 90

L

Lane, L. M., 272

Lees, P. L., 71, 267

Levine, C. H., 4, 129, 194, 235, 246

Littman, I. G., 11

Luke, J. S., 271

M

McGrath, M. R., 23, 71, 267
Manage to Payroll (MTP), 142, 190, 216–220, 221, 230
Management: improving, 83–86, 264–267; strategic human resources, 119–120
Managerial roles, 266–267; and organizational culture, 74–79; scope of, 72–74; and supervisory levels, 79–82
Managers: background of, 53–59, 62–63; and ceilings and freezes, 231–233, 244–247; and civil service system, 89, 123–124; and classification system, 192–195, 201–215; conflict avoidance by, 166–170, 184–186; constraints on, 2–5, 83; hiring by, 1, 144–151; interviews with, 16–17; and pay levels, 189, 191; and personnel offices, 98–100, 102–106, 108–109, 111–113, 118–121; problems in transition to, 59–69; recruiting by, 130–132, 138–143; and reductions in force, 252–259; training of, 60–62, 83–84, 168–169, 265–266; types of constrained, 8, 12–14; within military culture, 31–34. *See also* Pseudo-supervisors; Worker-managers
Maranto, R., 6
Market culture, 24, 25
Martin, J., 22
Marzotto, T., 55, 125, 158, 159
Merit Systems Protection Board (MSPB). *See* U.S. Merit Systems Protection Board (MSPB)
Miles, R. E., 119
Mintzberg, H., 70
Mosher, F. C., 7

N

Nalbandian, J., 90, 91
National Academy of Public Administration (NAPA), 8, 84, 102, 152, 221, 229, 278
National Aeronautics and Space Administration (NASA), 253
National Commission on the Public Service, 8, 84, 129, 191
National Commission on the State and Local Public Service, 8–9
National Performance Review (NPR), 11–12, 24, 155, 268; on budgeting, 12, 261–262; on ceilings, 228, 229–230, 262; on changing organizational culture, 273, 275–278; on classification system, 222–225; on delayering, 85–86; on deregulation of personnel, 11–12, 90, 92, 119, 120; on hiring, 152–153; on problem employees, 182–183, 185–186; workforce cutbacks recommended by, 12, 85–86, 260–262
National Research Council, 194
Naval Sea Systems Command (NAVSEA), 27, 34, 117, 143, 218
Navy, 15; budget of, 28, 29; ceilings in, 230, 232–233; classification system in, 215–221; contracting out by, 234, 238; employment in, 27; and freezes, 242, 243, 244; hiring in, 146, 150; leadership style, 31–34; managerial role in, 75, 78, 79, 81–82; managers at, 54, 57, 58, 61, 64, 65; organizational culture of, 26–29; personnel office for, 93, 94, 109–113, 115, 117; problem employees in, 166, 174, 175–176, 178; recruiting by, 141–144; TQM in, 36
Nixon administration, 6
Norton, E. H., 262

O

Office of Management and Budget (OMB), 4, 268; and ceilings, 228, 232, 262
Office of Personnel Management (OPM). *See* U.S. Office of Personnel Management (OPM)
Operation Jump Start, 135
Organizational culture, 16, 21–23, 51–52; of APHIS, 48–51; changing, 272–279; competing values model of, 23–26; and contractors, 240; of Department of Agriculture, 42–44; of EPA, 37–42; of FCS, 44–48; and managerial roles, 74–79; of Navy, 26–36; of personnel offices, 96–97, 100, 105–108, 109–111, 113–114; and problem employees, 170–174, 183–184, 185–186. *See also* Culture
Osborne, D., 11, 23, 24, 235, 269, 273
Ott, J. S., 16
Outstanding Scholars Program, 127, 133

P

Patterson, K. J., 276
Pay levels: and classification system, 192–195; determinants of, 189; systems affecting, 191–192
Peace Corps alumni, hiring of, 127, 145
Performance appraisal ratings, 254–255
Performance problems. *See* Problem employees
Perrewe, P. L., 119
Perry, J. L., 120
Personnel office: of APHIS, 106–109, 134–138; centralization of, 114–116; culture and structure of, 113–114; of EPA, 100–106; of FCS, 97–100; of Navy, 109–113, 141–143; of Portsmouth Naval Shipyard, 111, 113; recruiting by, 134–138, 141–143; and reduction in force, 250–252; shadow, 116–118, 121
Personnel staff: background and demographics of, 93–96, 281n1; and ceilings and freezes, 247; and classification system, 192–195, 204–205, 207, 211, 214–215; and managers, 118–121; on problem employees, 161; recruiting by, 130–132; roles of, 90–92. *See also* Classifiers
Peters, B. G., 4, 194, 235
Peters, T. D., 79
Peters, T. J., 10
Petrock, F., 24, 25
Political leadership: at APHIS, 50–51; at EPA, 40–41; at FCS, 45–48; and reforms, 268–271
Portsmouth Naval Shipyard, 15, 281n2; employees at, 27; managerial roles at, 75, 77, 82; managers' background at, 54, 61; personnel office at, 111, 113, 117; pressure for change at, 34–36; problem employees at, 179–180; reduction in force at, 250–252, 256–259
Position classification system. *See* Classification system
Presidential Management Internship (PMI), 127–128
Problem employees, 1, 158; changing rules for, 181–184; and conflict avoidance by managers, 166–170, 184–186; formal system with, 159–163,

178–184; group norms with, 170–174; informal strategies with, 174–178; legal appeals by, 161–162, 179–181, 182–183; and pseudo-supervisors, 164–166; and worker-managers, 163–164
Procurement system, 236; abuse of, 6–7; as constraint, 5, 9; reform of, 239. *See also* Deregulation
Professional and Administrative Career Examination (PACE), 129, 282n1
Program description (PD), 195, 196, 197, 213–214
Pseudo-supervisors, 65–68, 69, 224; and problem employees, 164–166. *See also* Managers
Public managers. *See* Managers
Public Veterinary Practice Careers (PVPC), 135–136
Putnam, R. D., 33

Q

Quinn, R. E., 23, 24, 71, 72, 267

R

Radin, B. A., 274, 275
Reagan administration, 28, 44, 248
Recruiting, 128–130; by APHIS, 134–138; by EPA, 138–141; by FCS, 132–134; by Navy, 141–144; perceptions of, 130–132, 134
Redd, H. C., III, 6, 154
Redeker, J. R., 179
Reductions in force (RIF), 227, 248, 248–250; at Portsmouth, 35; and managers, 252–259; and personnel office, 250–252
Reilly, W., 50
Reinventing government, 11, 269
Research, approach to, 14–17
Retreating, 249, 251
Riccucci, N. M., 9, 157, 182, 191, 265
Rivas, R. F., 166
Rivenbark, L., 269, 271
Rockman, B. A., 33
Rohrbaugh, J., 23
Romzek, B. S., 270, 272
Rosenbloom, D., 3, 157, 182, 191
Ross, L., 222
Roth, W., 269
Rubin, I., 242, 246
Rule of three, 126

S

Sathe, V., 273
Savas, E. S., 23, 235
Schultz, D. A., 6
Sendelbach, N. B., 267
Senior Executive Service (SES), 16, 55–56, 60, 282n1
Sethia, N. K., 276
Shafritz, J., 153, 157, 182, 191, 222
Shaw, G. J., 160, 161, 168, 182
Shelving, of problem employees, 177–178
Snow, C. C., 119
Space and Naval Warfare Command (SPAWAR), 27, 34, 117
Spoils system, 3
Straus, S., 90
Stroud, E. W., 265–266
Subcultures, 21–22
Supervision, adversarial, 166–167
Supervisors, 79–82. See also Pseudo-supervisors; Worker-managers
Swiss, J. E., 278

T

Thompson, F. J., 4, 194, 235
Thompson, M. P., 23, 71, 267
Total Quality Leadership (TQL), 36
Total Quality Management (TQM), 10–11, 15, 273–275, 277; in APHIS, 50, 106–108; and classification system, 193; in EPA, 39, 101; in Navy, 36, 110, 111
Training, of managers, 60–62, 83–84, 168–169, 265–266
Transfers, of problem employees, 175–176
Trice, H. M., 22, 273
"Turkey farms," 176–177

U

Upward mobility programs, 232–233
Urwick, L., 70
U.S. Army, 63
U.S. General Accounting Office (GAO), 126, 172, 190, 193, 238; on Navy classification system, 216, 217, 219–220
U.S. Merit Systems Protection Board (MSPB), 67–68, 83, 84, 89, 236, 255, 265; on classification system, 196–197; on hiring procedures, 124, 125, 128, 145, 154, 155; on personnel staff, 92, 94, 95; and problem employees, 161, 164, 168, 182, 183
U.S. Office of Personnel Management (OPM), 8, 66–67, 120, 129, 149, 270–271; and classification system, 195–196; hiring activities of, 125–128, 145, 152, 153; on Navy demonstration project, 218, 220, 221; and personnel staff, 91, 92; recruiting activities of, 128–129

V

Values: of federal managers, 22–23. See also Competing values model
Van Riper, P., 3
Veterans preference, 48, 54, 126, 147–148, 249, 283n2
Veterinary Services (VS), 48, 54
Volcker Commission. See National Commission on the Public Service
Volcker, P., 8
Von Glinow, M. A., 276

W

Wages. See Pay levels
Warman, J. S., 195, 196
Waterman, R. H., Jr., 10
Weber, M., 23, 29–30
Wheeler, H., 170
White House Personnel Office, 6
Wildavsky, A., 4
Wilkins, A. L., 276
Wilson, J. Q., 5, 10, 13, 269, 278
Winter, W., 9
Winter Commission. See National Commission on the State and Local Public Service
Wolf, J. F., 272
Wolohojian, G., 246
Women, in personnel, 94–95
Worker-managers, 63–65, 68–69, 224–225; and problem employees, 163–164. See also Managers
Workforce: cutbacks of, 85–86, 260–262. See also Reductions in force (RIF)

Y

Yin, R. K., 15
Yukl, G. A., 68